Praise for

PLAYING
WITH
PURPOSE

INSIDE THE LIVES AND FAITH
OF THE MAJOR LEAGUES' BIGGEST STARS

"This book reminds me why I love the game of baseball so much: It is a sport rich in history—our nation's pastime through times of war and times of peace. I am encouraged to see baseball players today using their platform to make a difference. This book brings to life the testimonies of ballplayers who are living life and playing the game with a greater purpose and an eternal perspective. *Playing with Purpose: Baseball* will inspire readers to find a specific platform and make a difference right where the Lord has placed them."
—Clayton Kershaw, 2011 Cy Young winner and author of *Arise*

"*Playing with Purpose: Baseball* shares the testimonies of today's stars, like Albert Pujols, Josh Hamilton, Mark Teixeira, and Mariano Rivera. Great to read about Christian athletes who love Christ."
—Bobby Richardson, eight-time All-Star and 1960 World Series MVP

"*Playing with Purpose* is a worthwhile read for everyone, but especially young men and women who aspire to make a mark in athletics. In sports, faith is an asset on many levels. One's faith provides the strength to absorb failure and loss, even deal with injuries. Faith is the basis for a strong presence in the locker room, and leadership on and off the field. One's faith can be displayed on the field and absorbed by the fans as something to desire and work for. *Playing with Purpose: Baseball* describes how many of today's Christian athletes carry these assets of faith in their careers."
—Mike Schmidt, Baseball Hall-of-Famer

PLAYING
WITH
PURPOSE

INSIDE THE LIVES AND FAITH OF
ALBERT PUJOLS, MARIANO RIVERA,
JOSH HAMILTON,
AND TODAY'S TOP MLB STARS

MIKE YORKEY
WITH JESSE FLOREA AND JOSHUA COOLEY

BARBOUR
PUBLISHING

© 2012 by Mike Yorkey, Jesse Florea, and Joshua Cooley

Print ISBN 978-1-62029-814-5

eBook Editions:
Adobe Digital Edition (.epub) 978-1-60742-822-0
Kindle and MobiPocket Edition (.prc) 978-1-60742-823-7

Cover images (L to R): AP Photo/Reed Saxon; AP Photo/Bill Kostroun; AP Photo/Tony Gutierrez

The author is represented by WordServe Literary Group, Ltd., Greg Johnson, Literary Agent, 10152 S. Knoll Circle, Highlands Ranch, CO 80130

Published by Barbour Publishing, Inc., P.O. Box 719, Uhrichsville, Ohio 44683
www.barbourbooks.com

Our mission is to publish and distribute inspirational products offering exceptional value and biblical encouragement to the masses.

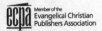

Member of the
Evangelical Christian
Publishers Association

Printed in the United States of America.

CONTENTS

INTRODUCTION

Baseball has been called, among many other things, timeless—which is an interesting statement when you consider that this great game is the only major sport in America contested without a time clock.

Beginning at the moment the umpire shouts, "Play ball!", baseball moves to its own distinct rhythms. The leadoff batter steps into the box, and the pitcher fidgets on the mound before hurling his first pitch—and then the game proceeds at its own pace. Throw the ball. Swing the bat. Three strikes and you're out. Four balls and take your base. Touch home plate and score a run. Nine innings make a game. The permutations of the game's outcome are seemingly as infinite as the stars in the heavens or the particles of sand on a seashore.

Baseball actually follows the patterns of nature. After a gloomy winter, baseball season begins in the spring with its promise of hope and sunnier times. The hot summer months are a proving ground, a time when greatness is forged in the crucible of the regular season. Fall is reserved for the final and decisive moments of baseball's playoffs, after which another dreary winter sets in.

Baseball may not be America's oldest sport—there's evidence that Native Americans played a game that resembled modern-day lacrosse in the seventeenth century—but nearly everyone agrees that baseball seeped into the national consciousness earlier than any other sport. The history of baseball dates back to the Revolutionary War, when George Washington's troops at Valley Forge batted balls and ran bases in a game that resembled cricket, a British pastime that played a role in the evolution of baseball. Lewis and Clark played catch during their exploration to the Pacific Ocean. Robin Carver's *Book of Sports*, first published in 1834, described how an American version of "rounders" rivaled cricket in popularity.

According to American folklore, Abner Doubleday invented baseball in 1839. But baseball historians, after reading Doubleday's diary, have discovered that he was never in Cooperstown, New York, when the first game was supposedly played . . . or any time after that. Instead, he was a cadet at West Point and never even mentioned baseball in numerous letters and papers found after he passed away in 1893.

Alexander Cartwright, a New York bookseller, is now generally credited with inventing the modern form of baseball. In 1845, he formed a committee that drew up rules for baseball—like limiting the number of outfielders to three and tagging the runner instead of throwing the ball at him. The new rules were widely adopted.

Cartwright founded the New York Knickerbockers Base Ball Club, and it wasn't long before other teams formed and new leagues banded together. By the turn of the twentieth century, "major league" baseball was played in the biggest cities in the Northeast, particularly New York City, as well as further west in Cincinnati and Chicago.

The game of bats and balls captured the hearts of the working class. Granted, there wasn't much competition in an era that predates radio, movies, and television. But it's irrefutable that baseball became woven tightly within the fabric of American culture, thanks in large part to the emergence of sports pages in daily newspapers and to the country's rapid industrialization and urbanization. Baseball provided an escape and a refuge from the pressures of daily life. The lush greenness of the baseball field in the middle of a gritty tenement-strewn city heralded a return to nature's simple and pure roots.

The first twenty years of the twentieth century saw an unprecedented rise in the popularity of baseball. Commodious new ballparks—New York's Ebbets Field and the Polo Grounds, Boston's Fenway Park, Chicago's Wrigley Field and Comiskey Park, and Tiger Stadium in Detroit—filled their box seats with prosperous businessmen and their bleachers with working-class Italian, Polish, and Jewish immigrants. *Philadelphia Inquirer* reporter Edgar F. Wolfe argued that the ballpark was a common meeting ground for Americans of *all* classes and backgrounds. The game suited the national temperament and enraptured presidents and paupers alike.

A decision in 1919 to strictly enforce new rules governing the size, shape, and construction of the baseball ushered in a golden era for the game. With the demise of the "dead ball" and the emergence of home run hitter Babe Ruth, baseball fever swept over the country. For the next fifty years, America's love affair with baseball was both singular and satisfying. Baseball even became a shibboleth during World War II—a cultural reference that only a true-blue American would know about. The question "Who won the 1943 World Series?" posed to Nazi spies was thought to reveal their true identity because every red-blooded GI knew that the New York Yankees beat the St. Louis Cardinals in the Fall Classic.

Just a generation later, though, the merger of the NFL and AFL pro football leagues in 1970 and the marketing of the Super Bowl into a quasi-religious festival along the lines of Rome's bread-and-circuses knocked baseball off its lofty perch. But the Grand Old Game refused to get off the field. In the past four decades, there have been dynamic changes in American society and culture, but one of the few constants has been baseball. Broadcaster Bob Costas had it right when he said, "So many things in our country have changed drastically, as they must, over the years and over the decades, and although baseball has changed, its essence remains the same. It's one of the enduring institutions in our country, and I think we take some comfort in that."

During today's uncertain times, with global upheaval, natural disasters, and terrorist mayhem in the forefront of people's minds, baseball's constancy is part of its allure, a sign of its strength. Sure, there's been a tweaking of rules over the years, like the shrinking of the strike zone and lowering of the pitcher's mound in 1969 as well as limited instant replay on home run calls starting in 2008. But, by and large, modern-day baseball is the same game Rogers Hornsby, Babe Ruth, Lou Gehrig, Mickey Mantle, and Willie Mays played.

Baseball is a team sport—and an individual sport—that harkens back to a simpler time when life was more manageable, understandable, and fair. It's the only major professional sport (NFL football, NBA basketball, and NHL hockey being the others) where the winning team can't run out the clock. The pitcher has to throw the ball over the plate and give his opponent a chance. Until the team that's ahead records twenty-seven outs in the scorebook, anything can happen.

There's no doubt that the passion for baseball is passed down from generation to generation. This is a strength but also a weakness of the sport because many fear that today's young fathers—many who grew up playing video games or taking part in action sports like skateboarding, paintballing, snow-boarding, BMX biking, and rock climbing—won't bother to introduce their sons and daughters to a fuddy-duddy game like baseball.

That wasn't the case when I (Mike Yorkey) was growing up in La Jolla, California, a beach community a few miles north of San Diego. My father *and* my mother loved baseball. Mom was a diehard Willie Mays fan who, if she tilted her Philco wooden radio just right and rapped her knuckles against the left side, could manage to pull in KSFO's staticky signal from five hundred miles away to listen in as Russ Hodges and Lon Simmons regaled listeners with the play-by-play of Willie's latest exploits.

After the San Diego Padres joined the National League in 1969 as an expansion team, Mom and Dad took me to the first major league game ever played in America's Finest City. (I even remember the score without going to Google—a 2–1 home team victory over the Houston Astros.) The following season, my folks became season ticket holders who shared four seats in the second row behind home plate at San Diego Stadium (today known as Qualcomm Stadium).

Mom and Dad remain season ticket holders to this day

at Petco Park, the Padres' handsome downtown ballpark that opened during the 2004 season. My wife, Nicole, and I attend a few games each year with my parents or our adult children and their spouses. And yes, we've kept the same second-row-behind-home-plate vantage point. I will admit that I'm a spoiled baseball fan.

My father was also my Little League coach, which is why the 1989 baseball movie *Field of Dreams* resonated with me. I wasn't so much taken with the way farmer Ray Kinsella plowed under part of his corn crop to build a baseball diamond in the middle of an Iowa farm field, thus fulfilling the voice in his head telling him, "If you build it, he will come." What caused a lump in my throat was a moment during the film's denouement, when a catcher on the field removed his mask. Ray recognized that the catcher was his father as a young man. He gathered enough courage to ask his father a simple question: "Hey, Dad. You wanna have a catch?"

If you've ever played catch with your father—or your son—the emotions connected with the simple tossing of a baseball back and forth are timeless and never forgotten. I can still remember asking my father if he would play catch with me after dinner back in my elementary school years. Even though he was pretty well spent after a day of hand-sawing two-by-fours and pounding nails at the construction site, he'd get into a catcher's crouch and let me pitch to him. When I outgrew our small backyard, he brought in dirt and built a mound in the front yard so I could continue practicing my curveball during my Little League days. (I was known as a "junk ball" pitcher back then.)

I continued that father-and-son tradition as soon as my son

Patrick could hold a mitt. We started with a soft, light ball and graduated to hardballs in our games of backyard catch. Then I coached his Little League team—just like my father did for me. Except this time we weren't living in sunny San Diego but in weather-volatile Colorado Springs, Colorado, where the start of Little League season—March—happened to be the snowiest month on the calendar. I can remember pitching batting practice while huge, wet snowflakes danced in the air before evaporating when they hit the no-longer-frozen ground. I wasn't happy pitching with fingers numb from the sleet, but no one would get me off that mound while my son was on the team.

Now, in 2012, Patrick is a young father with a son, Joshua, celebrating his first season of life. Since the passion for baseball seems to be passed from parent to child, I expect Joshua to be our family's next big fan. There's a real and tangible emotional element in baseball—a tie that is often directly connected to the game's history in our own lives.

It will be interesting to see what the game of baseball is like when Joshua grows up. Nineteenth-century poet Walt Whitman once deemed baseball as the "hurrah game of the republic" because of its "snap, go, and fling of the American atmosphere." But baseball has since relinquished its crown as the national pastime to football. Baseball attendance has steadily dropped the past four years, and though the hurting economy may be the culprit, few can deny that baseball has lost some of its appeal, especially with the younger generation gravitating to other pastimes or used to texting, watching TV, and surfing the web—all at the same time.

Today's younger audiences demand entertainment that asks them to do little more than sit back and be amazed.

Baseball, however, is a strategic and cerebral game. Full enjoyment of baseball requires more than surface-level observation. Once you begin to understand the nuances—the batting order, the pitcher's count, the timing of the bunt, the positioning of the infielders, the hit-and-run, the pitchout, the intentional walk, the pinch hitter, and playing for the double play—the game becomes fascinating. The variables reset between batters, supplying the mind with many more contingencies to consider. Because of this, baseball demands considerable attention while offering a unique capacity for numerical analysis, thanks to a treasure trove of statistics that would fill the Library of Congress.

Baseball is probably the only game in which statistics are discussed, dissected, debated, and treasured. Batters are remembered—and paid accordingly—for their batting average, number of hits, doubles, triples, home runs, bases on balls, intentional walks, stolen bases, and runs batted in. Pitchers are judged by their win-loss records, earned run averages, strikeouts, walks, and innings pitched, to name a few measurements.

Some of those numbers have a way of sticking with you. Anyone with a modicum of sports knowledge knows that Babe Ruth hit 714 home runs before Hank Aaron passed him up as baseball's all-time leader with 755 round-trippers. Even casual fans are aware that Joe DiMaggio once hit safely in 56 straight games, that Roger Maris smacked 61 homers in 1961, and that Ty Cobb stole 96 bases back in 1915.

Even players' contracts are memorable. Alex Rodriguez's ten-year, $252 million contract, signed before the 2001 season, was the most lucrative contract in sports history at the time and was worth $63 million more than the second-richest baseball deal. A-Rod was heralded everywhere as the "252 million-dollar man."

When Rodriguez signed a new ten-year, $275 million contract with the New York Yankees on December 13, 2007—the newest "biggest contract ever"—baseball fans barely noticed for two reasons. One, because such mega-deals were becoming more commonplace and seemed beyond the scope of reality to the average fan, and two, because the explosive Mitchell Report was released the *very same day*. The 311-page report—an independent investigation into the illegal use of steroids and other performance-enhancing substances by major league ballplayers—blew the lid off a scandal that had been brewing for nearly a decade.

It all started innocently enough during the 1998 season when St. Louis Cardinals slugger Mark McGwire was running neck and neck with the Chicago Cubs' Sammy Sosa in a chase to break Roger Maris' single-season record of 61 home runs. Their home run derby treated the nation to a summer of stroke and counterstroke, of packed houses and adoring media attention.

Then, during a game at Shea Stadium in New York, baseball writer Steve Wilstein noticed a small brown bottle sitting on the top shelf of Mark McGwire's locker. The bottle's label said, "Androstenedione."

Wilstein did some checking around and learned that "andro" was an anabolic steroid precursor that converted to strength-building testosterone in the body. At first, McGwire denied using the drug but later admitted that he'd been taking "andro" for a year. "Everybody I know in the game of baseball is using the same stuff I use," McGwire said.

Baseball fans shrugged their collective shoulders. Andro-stenedione was legal at the time, and baseball didn't have a drug-testing policy in force. Besides, who wanted to rain on McGwire's home-run parade during that magic summer of 1998?

Then Barry Bonds—jealous of the attention heaped upon McGwire and Sosa—transformed his body seemingly over-night into the Incredible Hulk. He obliterated McGwire's home run record with another number that has earned mile-stone status: 73 home runs during the 2001 season.

The cracks started forming in the baseball's facade in 2003, however, when a San Francisco grand jury investigated the machinations of the Bay Area Laboratory Co-operative (BALCO), owned and operated by Victor Conte, who had discovered a way to distribute then-undetectable steroids. And Conte knew Bonds through his trainer, Greg Anderson, which led to *a lot* of speculation that Bonds' swollen head and bloated physique was the result of pharmacology.

Two influential books built the case that there was trouble in River City. *Game of Shadows* by Lance Williams and Mark Fainaru-Wada, a pair of *San Francisco Chronicle* reporters privy to BALCO transcripts and court documents, outlined the entire BALCO scandal and led readers to a path that de-posited them at Bonds' front door. Then former big-leaguer Jose Canseco's "tell all" book, *Juiced: Wild Times, Rampant 'Roids, Smash Hits, and How Baseball Got Big*, unabashedly championed steroids as a means to greater home run produc-tion as well as a fountain of youth. Canseco matter-of-factly described his steroid use and how he injected teammates Mark McGwire, Jason Giambi, Rafael Palmeiro, and Juan Gonzalez.

Pressure was mounting to do something about steroid use in baseball, and in the spring of 2005, several players were subpoenaed to appear before a U.S. congressional committee. By all accounts, McGwire's appearance was disastrous to his credibility and likely wrecked his chances of ever being elected to the Baseball Hall of Fame. Under the hot glare of scrutiny and pointed questioning about steroid use, he repeatedly told several U.S. congressmen that he was "not here to talk about the past."

But the past had caught up with McGwire—and with the rest of baseball. The final nail in the coffin representing baseball's steroid era occurred just before the start of the 2009 season when *Sports Illustrated* reported that Alex Rodriguez had tested positive for two anabolic steroids during the 2003 season. The test results were supposed to remain anonymous, but a coded master list of 104 names was leaked to the press.

Citing an "enormous pressure to perform" after signing his whopper $252 million contract, Rodriguez admitted to using anabolic steroids and other performance-enhancing drugs from 2001 to 2003. Mark McGwire fessed up as well, finally admitting before the 2010 season that he had been taking steroids all along. "Looking back, I wish I had never played during the steroid era," he said.

Say it ain't so, Joe.

But it was so. Even though baseball's dalliance with performance-enhancing drugs (PEDs) will leave a lingering smell on the game for a long time to come, there is some good news to report. Today, it's harder to cheat—*a lot* harder— thanks to random and more sophisticated tests. And there are players who have chosen to fashion careers without performance-enhancing drugs, choosing instead to place their faith in their God-given abilities to play this great game straight up, the way it was meant to be played.

Exhibit One is Albert Pujols, who understands that people are watching his every move. "At the end of the day, as long as I glorify God and those forty-five thousand people know who I represent out there every time I step out on the field, that's what it's all about," he said. "It's about representing God."

I believe Albert hasn't taken PEDs. I believe that because I know he's a mature Christian who's playing with purpose. He understands how much damage there would be to the Kingdom if he *were* juicing. That's why I don't think we'll see a young kid, ball cap on his head, approaching the Los Angeles Angels star on the street and saying, "Say it ain't so, Mr. Pujols."

But we still need to pray for Christian ballplayers like Albert Pujols and Josh Hamilton—who *did* take steroids during his prodigal years—to stay strong in the face of the temptation to gain an edge on the ball field. They are truly playing with purpose, and it's their stories, as well as those of Adrian Gonzalez, Mark Teixeira, Ben Zobrist, Brian Roberts, Carlos Beltran, and pitchers Matt Capps, Clayton Kershaw, and Mariano Rivera, that you will read about in *Playing with Purpose: Baseball.*

So my co-authors, Jesse Florea and Joshua Cooley, and I invite you to sit back, grab a box of Cracker Jack, and enjoy our baseball version of *Playing with Purpose.* As you'll learn in the following chapters, these players are something special, and it's for reasons that go far beyond balls and strikes.

1

CLAYTON KERSHAW:
STANDING ON THE PRECIPICE
OF GREATNESS

"You are God's field."
1 CORINTHIANS 3:9

In the gloaming, the curious children came.

Their little heads bobbed up and down in the tall, weed-infested field like inquisitive prairie dogs. They came from their hillside village—a shantytown, really—where ramshackle homes populate the landscape and hope remains a street urchin.

In the distance, the sun was setting over this forgotten corner of the world, casting long shadows over the village. Shadows are nothing new in Zambia. Moral decay, poverty, and deadly disease have veiled this small, south-central African nation in spiritual darkness for many years. The bleakness, visitors say, is palpable.

Past the field, the children gathered on both sides of a

skinny dirt road. Their clothes were tattered and their feet were dusty, but their smiles were radiant.

They came to marvel at the stranger.

"*Musungu!*" some of them exclaimed. Others didn't know what to say. They had never seen a white man before.

Standing 6 feet, 3 inches tall and weighing 215 pounds, the Texan towered over the children as he and another foreigner threw an odd, white spheroid with red stitches back and forth. Soon, the *musungu* handed a glove to one of the boys, backed up a few feet, and played underhanded catch. He did the same for every child. The youngsters giggled with delight. No language barrier could conceal the fact that everyone was having the time of their lives.

But the *musungu* hadn't traveled across ten time zones to promote baseball. He had come to pierce the oppressive shadows with the light of Jesus Christ.

Five months later, on a beautiful Southern California morning, the screaming children came.

Their energetic legs churned as they sprinted across the manicured fields of Pasadena Memorial Park like excited puppies. Here, in the prosperous shadows of the City of Angels, hope and opportunity soar upward like the lush mountain peak of Mount Wilson to the north and the skyscrapers of Los Angeles to the south.

The children came to marvel at their sports hero.

"It's Clayton Kershaw!" they cried incredulously.

The children surrounded—accosted, really—Clayton, his wife, Ellen, and two of the Kershaws' childhood friends as the adults were coming back from breakfast. In a region known for its celebrity sightings, the kids had hit the jackpot. Lacking paper or baseball cards, several boys thrust out their arms for Clayton to autograph their flesh. One boy lifted his shirt.

"Whoa, whoa, whoa!" Clayton said, smiling as he stymied the impromptu tattoo session. Ellen got some paper from their car nearby, and he obliged every child.

Somewhere, between these two disparate fields of dreams, you can find Clayton Kershaw. The Los Angeles Dodgers' budding young superstar lives at the intersection of Christianity and Growing Fame. It's a tricky junction, with plenty of distracting, and often dangerous, traffic coming at him from all directions. Some terrible wrecks have happened there.

But Clayton seems different. He has a strong faith, a great support network of friends and loved ones, and a humility that is as striking as his vast career potential, which portends multiple Cy Young Awards.

Consider this: At the callow age of twenty-two, he became the staff ace on one of baseball's most historic franchises in America's second-most populous city, just a long fly ball away from the glitter of Hollywood. Yet when his sublime abilities are the subject of conversation, he squirms—seems even a bit repulsed.

How many professional athletes do you know like *that*?

"It's never about him," said longtime friend John Dickenson. "It's humility at its best."

THE NATURAL
Clayton didn't always live at this complicated intersection. Life used to be much different.

Born on March 19, 1988, Clayton grew up as an only child on Shenandoah Drive in Highland Park, a posh northern suburb of Dallas known as "The Bubble" for its insular qualities. Highland Park is a white-collar town of forty-something professionals with a median household income hovering around $150,000—more than three times the national average. Houses are huge, crime is low, schools are great, and people are nice. It's Pleasantville.

The Kershaws were typical suburbanites. Clayton's dad wrote TV commercial jingles, and his mom was a graphic designer. The only reason they stuck out in Highland Park is because they didn't live in one of the town's ubiquitous mansions.

Fame? That was a foreign concept. Well, Clayton *was* the great-nephew of Clyde Tombaugh, the man who discovered Pluto. But Great-Uncle Clyde died before Clayton was born and, heck, poor Pluto's not even considered a planet anymore. So that probably doesn't count.

Young Clayton was always on the move. As a child, his favorite toy was a life-sized Flintstones car with a hole for his feet to touch the floor, so he could scoot around just like Fred and Barney.

That *yabba-dabba-doo* energy was quickly parlayed into athletic prowess. Clayton learned to walk at seven months, and his first word was "ball." Before he lost all his baby teeth, he earned the nickname "The Brick Wall" for his soccer goaltending skills in a local select league.

Losing his baby fat was another matter. When he was in high school, Clayton stood about 5 feet, 10 inches tall, but his waistline housed a few too many burritos from Qdoba's, a local Mexican restaurant where he loved hanging out with his buddies.

"Growing up," Dickenson said, "he was always a chubby puffball." It's nice to have pals, eh?

It also must be nice to have natural athleticism oozing from your pores. Clayton excelled at virtually any sport he played—basketball, football, tennis . . . you name it. Even Ping-Pong. His long arms and great hand-eye coordination meant his childhood buddies were no match for him. In fact, they still aren't.

"He's an amazing Ping-Pong player," Dickenson said. "If he could, he'd give up baseball to do that."

About the only sport Clayton isn't good at is golf. "We played golf the day before his wedding," said Josh Meredith, Clayton's best friend. "He hit one [drive] from the tee box that ricocheted off a tree and landed fifty yards from where he hit it. I laughed pretty hard at that."

By ninth grade, Clayton's athleticism had landed him on the varsity football and baseball teams at Highland Park High School, a rarity for a freshman. During the fall, he played center, snapping to a quarterback whose name you might recognize: Matthew Stafford, the Detroit Lions' number one overall draft pick of 2009.

But Clayton's true love was baseball. That spring, he earned the number two spot in the varsity rotation and soon became one of the most ballyhooed prep pitching prospects ever in Texas, which has produced its fair share of future stars (see "Ryan, Nolan," "Clemens, Roger," "Pettitte, Andy," et al.). With colleges banging down his door, Clayton signed with Texas A&M University, largely because that's where Ellen Melson, his girlfriend and future wife, was going.

Clayton's sublime senior season in high school had the whiff of legend, like a real-life pitching version of *The Natural*.

Highland Park, like most of Texas, is batty for high school football, but on days Clayton pitched, the Scots' modestly sized baseball stadium became a hub of interest. Folks wanted to witness the tall, powerful lefty with the mid-90s fastball and sweeping curve do something amazing—which happened often.

Scouts, too, came out in droves. Like a conductor's baton cueing orchestral instruments, dozens of radar guns would pop into position behind home plate whenever Clayton started his windup.

The whole scene was surreal, especially for those who remembered Clayton's freshman physique.

"Early on, he was baby-faced, almost roly-poly," said Lew Kennedy, his former Highland Park coach. "Pretty soon, he lost all that baby fat and turned into a monster. At times, he was virtually untouchable. Batters were happy just to foul one off."

That's not hyperbole. Clayton's statistics as a senior prompt a double-take: In 64 innings, he posted a 13–0 record, 0.77 ERA, and 139 strikeouts. No typo there.

Clayton appeared mortal in the Scots' regular-season finale after a strained oblique muscle sidelined him for several weeks. But when he returned to action against Justin Northwest High in the regional playoffs, he one-upped himself with the rarest of gems—a perfect game in which he struck out *all fifteen batters* in a five-inning, mercy-rule-shortened contest.

True to form, as his teammates celebrated around him, he calmly walked off the field with a satisfied smile. To each teammate who showered him with praise, he simply replied, "Thanks, man." Nothing more.

"He was so soft-spoken," Kennedy said. "Very humble.

He was one of the guys. He didn't lord it over anybody. Everybody looked up to him."

After the season, the accolades came rolling in, none more prestigious than the Gatorade high school national baseball player of the year award. He entered the 2006 draft ranked as *Baseball America's* top prep pitching prospect and the sixth-best prospect overall.

The fun was just about to begin.

FAITH IN THE HEART OF TEXAS

On America's extra-large Bible Belt, Dallas is the big ol' shiny brass buckle. On any given Sunday, you can find a church as easily as a Cowboys jersey. Same for the Highland Park bubble. Everywhere you went, people called themselves Christians.

So Clayton did, too.

He grew up in a Bible-believing home, got confirmed at Highland Park United Methodist in sixth grade, and, because of the company he kept, thought his ticket to heaven was punched. Badda-bing.

But life in a fallen world isn't that easy, as Clayton quickly learned. When he was ten, his parents divorced and his dad moved out. It was an emotional hand grenade in his young life. To this day, he prefers not to discuss it publicly.

Clayton's mom, Marianne, sacrificed much for her son. Their house was a two-bedroom shoebox compared to some of the old-money mansions in Highland Park, but Clayton was never in want. Marianne began working from home so she could be there when Clayton returned from school, and they continued attending church.

Spiritually speaking, though, Clayton was on autopilot.

Presented with a Bible trivia game, he could've fared well, but his faith was, well, trivial. Then the Holy Spirit began prodding him. He started considering deep spiritual questions that shook him out of cruise control: *Is the Bible really the inspired, inerrant Word of God? Was Jesus Christ really who He said He was? How can Christianity be true and all other religions false?*

By his senior year, Clayton understood his desperate need for a Savior. The deep, life-altering words of Ephesians 2:8–9 became truth to him: Salvation is by grace and faith alone, not by works. None of his upbringing, church attendance, or good deeds merited God's eternal favor. Only Jesus Christ could provide that.

"When you grow up in [Christianity], you assume it's the only way—'Oh, everybody is this,' " he said. "But when you get a little older and a little smarter, you hear about other religions and beliefs, and you start thinking, 'Why do I believe this?' That's when you make your faith personal."

Clayton already had a solid group of friends, so the transition to his new faith wasn't hard. Around age sixteen, he and seven other Christian buddies made an agreement: They didn't need alcohol to have a good time.

While other kids were sleeping off weekend benders on Sunday mornings, Clayton's crew was worshipping. One of his buddies, Robert Shannon, would drive through the neighborhoods and fill up his big Chevy Suburban with half a dozen guys. With Third Eye Blind cranking on the sound system, they'd all head to Park Cities Presbyterian Church in Dallas and then head out for lunch together. Holy rollers indeed.

"We all got very lucky with our group of friends," Meredith said. "It made it easy for us to live the right way at such a young age. A lot of people at our high school were doing their partying on weekends. All of us, we were doing our partying without the alcohol or whatever else was there."

PRINCESS ELLEN

Clayton spent plenty of time with the fellas in high school. But he always made time for someone else.

Life, it seems, has never been without Ellen, even though they didn't meet until their freshman year. Theirs is a true high school sweetheart story, with all the cute, funny, and awkward moments that usually accompany that sort of thing.

At the beginning, it was heavy on the awkward. In the Courtroom of Clumsy Teenage Love, Clayton was guilty as charged:

• **Exhibit A: The first meeting**

Before they started dating, Clayton and Ellen had never spoken to each other. Ellen, a short, pretty girl on the school's dance team, had no clue that Clayton played baseball. She just knew him as a "goofy kid" with "a ton of friends." One day, between school periods during their freshman year, Clayton stopped her in the hallway and mumbled something about going steady. She said yes.

And after that?

"We didn't speak for the first year of our relationship except at our locker and in large groups at lunch," Ellen said.

• **Exhibit B: The first hangout away from school**

"We played basketball at a park," Clayton recalled, laughing. "I tried to teach her how, and she wasn't too interested." It was the start of a good-natured yet unsuccessful attempt to turn Ellen into an athlete. Clayton hasn't given up yet.

"It still doesn't work out so well," Ellen admitted. "I've always been a dancer, and he's always wanted me to be more athletic. One year, he bought me a pink baseball glove just to give me an incentive to help him throw over the summer." But aren't dancers athletic in their own right? "I don't know if he buys that," Ellen said with a chuckle. "I don't think he thinks it's a sport."

• **Exhibit C: The first time he met his future in-laws**

Imagine you are the loving parent of four children. You are trying to raise them well and instill proper values. Your second youngest, a girl, has an infectious smile and soft heart. Then, at the impressionable age of fourteen, she brings home a football player who has "55," his jersey number, shaved into the back of his head, thanks to a hazing ritual by his upperclassmen teammates. Now, ask yourself: What would *you* do?

"My parents were like, 'Who are you dating?' " Ellen said.

• **Exhibit D: The first kiss**

The epic moment happened at Caruth Park, a popular local hangout just north of Highland Park. Who better than Clayton's best buddy to provide the scoop? "The first time they kissed," Meredith said, "Ellen had some trouble breathing."

Ellen doesn't deny it, but she provides a bit of context: "Clayton and I were each other's first kiss," she said, laughing. "We were fourteen years old. Neither of us had experience." Fair enough.

Clayton and Ellen just seemed *right* together, despite the fact that they are polar opposites. She is 5 feet, 5 inches tall; he stands 6 feet, 3 inches. She likes watching girly TV shows; he likes video games and anything involving competition. She eats like a bird; he consumes like a hyena.

"Their No. 1 date spot was a Chili's [restaurant]," Dickenson recalled. "Ellen, she doesn't eat that much. She's tiny. She'd always get mac and cheese, and he'd get a huge platter. She'd eat two bites, and he'd finish it. Even with his buddies, he'd wait for us to finish, and then he's eyeing everybody's meals. The guy can eat."

The couple's memorable dating stories are as plentiful as young Clayton's food intake. Once, early in the relationship, Ellen and some girlfriends were watching *The O.C.*, one of their favorite TV shows, at her house. Suddenly, Clayton and his buddies barged in, screaming and throwing a football around. They were wearing nothing but shorts and football shoulder pads. For whatever reason, Mr. and Mrs. Melson didn't install perimeter fencing that night.

Another time, the guys invaded the girls' *Friends*-watching party, turned off the TV, and pillaged their cake. Annoyed, the girls hatched a plan to lure the guys out of Shannon's house, where they often played "Halo" for entire days, to steal their Xbox.

On the day of the Great Video Game Heist, the girls drove into the neighborhood, parked the car down the street from Shannon's house, and turned off the car. Ellen called Clayton's cell phone. "Clayton," she said, feigning excitement, "Jennifer Aniston is in Highland Park giving autographs!" Seconds later, the door flew open. Scientists are still investigating claims that this group of teenage boys broke the cheetah's land-speed record.

At the car, the guys practically dove feet-first through the windows, à la *Dukes of Hazzard*, fired the engine, and raced down the street, past Ellen and her giggling friends. The girls' plan seemed to be working perfectly . . . until they saw brake lights. Down the road, the guys' car was turning around. The jig was up.

The girls had made one crucial error: They didn't factor

in one of Clayton's strangest abilities. As the boys were whizzing past, Clayton had recognized the plates on the girls' car. Somehow, he can remember the license plate numbers of friends' cars after only one glance.

"It's one of the weirdest things," Ellen said.

All things considered, Ellen didn't mind the failed plan. It was another chance to see "my Clayton," as she's fond of calling him.

The affection is a two-way street. Clayton has always been smitten with Ellen, too. Take, for instance, the alert on his cell phone. Whenever she calls, the screen reads: "Princess Ellen."

"When he wakes up every day, he just treats her like that—like his little Princess Ellen," Meredith said. "That's just the way it's always been."

In 2006, the Dodgers drafted Clayton out of high school and quickly shipped him to their Gulf Coast League rookie affiliate in Vero Beach, Florida. Ellen enrolled at Texas A&M. The distance was tough on the couple, but the time was "some of best years of our lives," Ellen said.

By 2009, Ellen was ready to tie the knot—but to stay sane, she convinced herself it might not happen soon. Clayton, meanwhile, was planning and scheming. He knew Christmastime was Ellen's favorite part of the year, not only for the holidays but also because it was one of the few months when the couple was back together in Highland Park.

Clayton went all-out for the proposal. This is a man who gets ragged on by richly garbed teammates for rolling into the Dodgers' clubhouse every day in cargo shorts and a T-shirt. But he showed up to Ellen's house in a new suit—and a white limo. The couple ate in downtown Dallas at Wolfgang Puck's Five Sixty, a skyscraper restaurant that offers a stunning vista of the city from the fiftieth floor. He even shaved for the first time in years.

"That," Ellen said, "was a point of contention for years—his dadgum chinstrap [beard]."

After dinner, Clayton took Ellen to his new townhouse, which he had decked out as a winter wonderland, complete with music playing and rose petals strewn about the living room. There, he gave Ellen a box with a little Santa figurine holding a green velvet ring box before dropping to his knee and proposing.

After their heartbeats leveled off, they went to Ellen's parents' house for a prearranged engagement party. Not bad for the once-awkward freshman.

Clayton and Ellen were married on December 4, 2010, at Highland Park Presbyterian Church. At the reception, they picked a humdinger of a first dance. No slow jam for this couple. Instead, they performed a choreographed dance to Usher's hit, "DJ's Got Us Falling in Love Again." Ellen, it should be noted, achieved lieutenant status on the high school drill team. Clayton . . . well, he tried hard.

In front of five hundred people, Clayton sauntered onto the dance floor wearing shades and neon Nikes along with his tuxedo and tried to keep up with his bride. Those who witnessed their first dance will never forget it.

Someone uploaded the dance video to YouTube, and the Kershaws initially left it there so loved ones who weren't at the wedding could see it. By the time they removed the video a month later, however, it had attracted twelve thousand hits.

"Ellen was a dancer in high school, so she nailed it," Meredith said. "Clayton was lost."

"MIGHT AS WELL GO BY ZEUS"

It's not that Clayton is some sort of attention-allergic hermit. Clearly, the wedding dance antics prove otherwise. But he's never felt entirely comfortable with all the acclaim his bestowed-by-heaven talents have invited. Hullabaloo has always been the obnoxious kid brother he can't shake.

When Los Angeles drafted Clayton seventh overall, the hype machine revved into action. Dodgers scouting director Logan White compared Clayton to Dave Righetti, a sixteen-year big leaguer who won the 1981 American League Rookie of the Year award, played in two All-Star games, and was once the best closer in baseball. Clayton had just turned eighteen.

Two weeks later, Clayton officially signed with the Dodgers for $2.3 million (no need to scavenge other people's mac and cheese anymore) and headed to Vero Beach, where he dazzled coaches and players. Still, he needed some seasoning. In 2007, he started with the Dodgers' Class A affiliate in Midland, Michigan—the Great Lakes Loons. Welcome to baseball's boondocks.

Clayton lived in a duplex—four players on one side and four on the other. The furniture in Clayton's unit consisted of two beanbags, a TV resting on a folding chair, and a card table with a few other chairs for dining. All the guys slept on air mattresses. Road trips consisted of twelve-hour bus rides and sharing hotel rooms with a half-dozen other guys.

"He loved it," Ellen said. "He had no other responsibility but to show up at the field and play baseball."

The décor was lacking those years, but Clayton's burgeoning legend wasn't. After another strong season, he entered 2008 with high hopes—he and every Dodgers fan on planet Earth.

During a spring training game against Boston, he struck

Los Angeles starter Clayton Kershaw, twenty-five, is one of the brightest young pitchers in the major leagues. In his first five seasons, he has won 61 games with a 2.79 ERA. (AP Photo/Alex Gallardo)

out three-time All-Star Sean Casey on an 0–2 curveball so nasty that Hall of Fame broadcaster Vin Scully proclaimed it "Public Enemy No. 1." Two days later, Dodgers legend Sandy Koufax, whom some would call the greatest left-handed pitcher of all time, watched Clayton throw a bullpen session and predicted that he'd be called up to L.A. soon. As endorsements go, those are hard to beat.

After thirteen games at Double-A Jacksonville (Florida) to start the season, he had a 1.91 ERA. The hype machine's RPMs were redlining. A *Yahoo! Sports* article trumpeted his curveball as "probably the best in the world." The Dodgers could no longer justify keeping him in the minors.

On May 25, 2008, after only 48 minor league games, Clayton made his big league debut. Chavez Ravine was electric. The Dodgers beat St. Louis, 4–3, but Clayton got a no-decision despite a stellar effort: two earned runs on five hits and one walk with seven strikeouts in six innings.

The reviews were overwhelmingly positive. The following day, a *Yahoo! Sports* story said Clayton "might as well go by Zeus for all the mythology that accompanies him."

The dam of self-restraint had officially been breached. Praise flooded in from every direction.

"These guys don't come along often," Dodgers pitching coach Rick Honeycutt gushed in the same article. "There's been other guys—Doc Gooden comes to mind—who get it at this early an age."

Amidst towering expectations, the rest of the season didn't go as smoothly. Clayton finished 2008 with a pedestrian 5–5 record and 4.26 ERA in 22 games. The following year, he was even-steven again with an 8–8 record, although he pitched appreciably better, sporting a 2.79 ERA and 185 strikeouts.

Those who had been around baseball a long time saw nothing but upside. By 2010, the hype machine was running full-throttle again, spewing out hyperbole at a rapid-fire rate. "Ceiling? There is no ceiling," Honeycutt said of his then-twenty-one-year-old protégé in spring training.

No pressure, Clayton. Honest . . .

If he felt any pressure, he sure didn't show it—not with a 2.91 ERA and 212 strikeouts in his second full big league season. His 13–10 record would have been more impressive if the Dodgers, who finished a middling 80–82, would have scored more than 17 total runs in his 10 losses.

Clayton's standout year, at age twenty-two, elevated him into rarified air within one of baseball's most venerable franchises. For perspective, consider how some of the all-time Dodgers greats fared at the same tender age:

- Among the Dodgers' Hall of Famers, Dazzy Vance went 11–14 for the Superior Brickmakers in the old Nebraska State League (1913). In his second year with the Dodgers, Don Sutton had a losing record (11–15) and finished with an ERA barely under 4.00 (1967). And even Koufax was mortal at age twenty-two, finishing his fourth year with the Dodgers with a .500 record and a 4.48 ERA (1958).
- Orel Hershiser was still three years away from cracking the Dodgers' rotation with a lackluster 4.68 ERA at Double-A San Antonio (1981).
- Future 27-game-winner Don Newcombe was still trying to make it out of Triple-A Montreal (1948).

Did we mention that Koufax didn't have a sub-3.00 ERA

until his eighth season, at age twenty-six? Clayton has had *three* such seasons by age twenty-three.

No pressure, Clayton. We're just sayin' . . . .

Before the 2011 season, Honeycutt went so far as to compare the excitement buildup around Clayton to "Fernandomania," the hysteria that surrounded Fernando Valenzuela, the pudgy, look-to-the-sky Mexican sensation who won the National League Cy Young and Rookie of the Year awards and led the Dodgers to a World Series title in 1981—at age twenty.

"I was there when Fernando [played in L.A.]," said Honeycutt, a Valenzuela teammate from 1983 to 1987. "It's getting to be kind of like that hype. The fans are putting their hopes and dreams on this guy [Clayton] leading the team back to greatness and the World Series."

In February 2011, Dodgers manager Don Mattingly officially named Clayton the team's Opening Day starter. The move made Clayton, at twenty-three, the Dodgers' youngest such pitcher since, well, Valenzuela in 1983.

Clayton opened the season by throwing seven shutout innings in a 2–1 win over San Francisco, the defending World Series champion. The pitcher he outdueled? None other than Tim Lincecum, the two-time Cy Young Award winner.

If only the rest of the season had been so rosy. Clayton's season-opening gem was barely in the books when at least two men attacked and severely beat a Giants fan, Bryan Stow, in the Dodger Stadium parking lot, sending him into a coma.

The vicious assault only underscored the chaos plaguing the franchise in recent years under Dodgers owner Frank McCourt. Among the tabloid fodder:

- A bitter divorce court battle between McCourt and

his ex-wife, Jamie, over control of the team dragged through the 2011 season.

- The revelation from court documents that the Mc-Courts had borrowed more than $100 million from Dodgers-related business to fund a profligate lifestyle.
- Major League Baseball's assumption of team control in April 2011 and its ensuing rejection of a new, multi-billion-dollar TV deal between FOX and the Dodgers, forcing the troubled franchise to file for bankruptcy protection in August.
- McCourt's agreement on November 1, 2011, to sell the team, Dodger Stadium, and the surrounding parking lots in cooperation with Major League Baseball through a court-supervised process.

In the midst of the mayhem, Clayton was magnificent. He won the National League's "Triple Crown" of pitching with a 21–5 record, a major league-best 2.28 ERA, and league-leading 248 strikeouts to earn his first All-Star appearance and win the NL Cy Young Award. He even claimed his first Gold Glove Award for good measure.

(Note to the curator of the sizeable Dodgers pitching pantheon: Time to create another wing. Clayton became the franchise's first Cy Young recipient since closer Eric Gagne in 2003 and the first Dodgers starter to win the award since Hershiser in 1988.)

Clayton's twentieth win, which came in a dominant 2–1 victory over the rival Giants in his penultimate start of 2011, made him the first Dodgers pitcher to go 5–0 against the Giants in a season since Vic Lombardi in 1946. And four of those victories came against none other than Lincecum.

Dodger fans love a Giant slayer.

Then there's this telling nugget: Only one lefty in Dodgers history has recorded more strikeouts in a season: Koufax.

"There's no reason to really set limits on him as far as how much better he's going to get," Mattingly said, "because he's still young and he works awful hard."

No pressure, Clayton . . . aww, who are we kidding?

"FOR HIS GLORY"

How do you respond when fans, media, former All-Stars, and front-office cognoscenti are all tripping over themselves to adequately describe your abilities? Clayton simply shrugs it off.

"I've got a really, really, really long way to go," he said.

This is not false modesty. This is Spirit-led Clayton modesty. And it sticks out like a sore thumb in Tinseltown, where the twin gods of fame and riches are worshipped religiously.

Clayton is so *un*-Hollywood. The red carpets, velvet ropes, glittering marquees, screaming fans, and insatiable paparazzi of his six-month home are foreign to him. He's one of the best pitchers in the world, yet he and Ellen still get a touristy kick out of the area's palm-tree-lined roads, the Hollywood Walk of Fame, and the mansions of Beverly Hills.

"I have my own version of celebrity stars tour," Ellen said. "I could be a certified stalker if I took people over there anymore."

Clayton has shot the breeze with Koufax, learned to bunt from Maury Wills, and achieved rapid renown in starry-eyed L.A. Yet you'd never know his day job if you saw him strolling hand-in-hand with Ellen in Malibu. At heart, he is just a big kid from Texas with a Lone Star lilt and a wide, toothy smile.

He honestly doesn't understand what all the fuss is about.

Like the crush of autograph seekers leaning over the railing after games. Or the trash bags filled with fan mail that started piling up in 2010.

"He couldn't even get his head around it," Ellen said.

Those closest to him say he's the most humble person they know. C.S. Lewis once said, "Humility is not thinking less of yourself, but thinking of yourself less." It's a vertical-relationship thing, and Clayton seems to get it.

"Clayton doesn't lie about his abilities," Dodgers chaplain Brandon Cash explained. "He knows how good he is. But he realizes that no matter how good of a baseball player he is, it doesn't mean anything when he'll stand before God."

Said Clayton, "You have to understand what this platform is for."

Never was Clayton's humility more on display than during the 2010–2011 offseason. Less than a month after getting married, as their loved ones were clinking glasses and singing *Auld Lang Syne* in the States, Clayton and Ellen were half a world away, toiling in a bleak, oppressed land. With sweat-soaked shirts clinging to their backs, they rang in the new year in Zambia.

The trip marked Ellen's fifth visit, and Clayton's first, to the small, south-central African nation. Ellen had tried to prepare Clayton for what to expect, but no prior warning can fully assuage the culture shock.

Disease, destitution, hunger, moral neglect, and religious syncretism are like gloomy shrouds veiling the country in darkness. Zambia is one of the poorest nations in the world. Many people live on a dollar a day. Homes are often plastic tarps or tents with earthen floors. Affluence means your one-room home is made of cinder blocks or concrete and features an outdoor stovetop to cook on. Dishes and babies are washed in the same tub. A child's wardrobe is what he's wearing. Trash and raw sewage are everywhere.

So, too, are the orphans. Thanks to a widespread HIV/AIDS epidemic, nearly 47 percent of Zambia's population is zero-to-fourteen years old, and the median age is 16.5 years, according to 2011 U.S. government figures. It's a place where kids are raising kids—where unmarried mothers abandon their children, like an endangered ship purging jetsam, to seek a different life in another province.

"It's an overwhelming task because you can't get to every kid," Clayton said. "It's hard. Some people don't go because you think, 'It's just one person.' But one kid you do help is one life affected."

The Kershaws affected plenty. During a nine-day missions trip with a non-profit organization called Arise Africa, Clayton, Ellen, and other Christians visited various "compounds," or slums, on the outskirts of Lusaka, the capital city.

The group delivered two thousand pounds of supplies to two schools that double as orphanages, constructed a four-room building for one of them, hosted a Bible camp for two hundred children, and cared for impoverished families. Clayton also got to meet twenty young orphan girls Ellen has spiritually invested in over the years.

To stay in baseball shape, Clayton ran and threw each day. The local children flocked to him, and he played catch with them every night. Using his God-given talents, he reached across a broad cultural chasm to shine the light of Christ. It was Matthew 19:14 in action.

"He has a heart of gold," said Alissa Hollimon, a college friend of Ellen's who started Arise Africa. "He jumped right in to whatever we were doing. I think he liked seeing Ellen in her element."

The trip said much about Clayton's priorities. Pitchers of his caliber don't just happen. It takes an extraordinary amount of work, especially in the offseason. Winters are also crucial downtime for athletes consumed by their profession from February through September.

Clayton could have just supported Ellen's passion project from a distance, by cutting a check and keeping his golden arm comfortably within American borders. Instead, he chose to travel to an ignored back alley of the world and open compassionate arms to those enslaved in darkness. For such a quiet man, this spoke volumes.

"He's characterized by humility," Cash said.

It's a humility that seeks to serve others wherever he is. Despite being one of the youngest players on the roster, he is the Dodgers' Baseball Chapel representative—the guy Cash looks to for getting guys in Sunday morning chapels and midweek Bible studies. He does charity work in greater L.A. through the team, and he speaks to the Fellowship of Christian Athletes group at his old high school each offseason.

Most of all, he and Ellen are looking forward to continuing their work in Zambia each offseason. Inspired by their trip, the couple started Kershaw's Challenge, an effort to raise $70,000 to build an orphanage outside Lusaka called Hope's Home, named after an eleven-year-old, HIV-positive orphan they'd met. Before the 2011 season, Clayton pledged to donate a hundred dollars for every strikeout he threw, which resulted in a $24,800 donation based upon his career-high 248 punch-outs.

Think God was at work there?

THE PARABLE OF THE TALENTS

Yes, the children will continue to come. They will travel across fields of indigence and affluence, through the forsaken slums of Africa and the shiny turnstiles of Chavez Ravine, all to see the meek wunderkind. Heck, plenty of adults will come, too. People are always attracted to greatness, and that's the precipice upon which Clayton stands.

This, of course, creates a lot of racket. The quiet, lanky Texan is still getting used to all the attention. His immense gifts, for some, might be the object of regular worship on *SportsCenter*, but he sees them through the lens of Jesus' parable in Matthew 25.

"I think it's for His glory, to make people aware that it's not something where I was lucky to throw baseball," Clayton said. "In Matthew, it says God gives everyone at least one talent. One guy hides his talent and gives it back, and God says, 'Cursed are you.' He doesn't want us to hide our talents; He wants us to put them in the spotlight and glorify Him.

"That's a pretty cool thing."

2012 season update: Los Angeles starter Clayton Kershaw followed his National League Cy Young Award-winning season of 2011 with another standout performance when he led the NL with a 2.53 ERA, earned his second straight All-Star Game appearance, and finished second to New York Mets knuckleballer R. A. Dickey in Cy Young voting.

2

BEN ZOBRIST:
THE PK WHO'S A ZORILLA ON THE FIELD

It's called "entrance music"—a snippet of a song that's played loudly over the stadium speakers whenever the hometown hitter walks from the on-deck circle to home plate. Relief pitchers also get their own "walk-up" song when they jog in from the bullpen to save the day for the local nine.

The choice of music provides players with a rare opportunity to inject their personality into the game or reveal their musical tastes, which vary from hip-hop tunes and unvarnished rock 'n' roll to, well, Justin Bieber. (Colorado Rockies shortstop Troy Tulowitzki stepped into the batter's box during the 2011 season with the sound of J-Bieb's "Baby" swooning the teen-girl set.)

Most of the time, though, the entrance music makes a strong and raucous statement. When slugger Mark McGwire stepped up to home plate in St. Louis, "Welcome to the Jungle" by Guns N' Roses pumped up the crowd for a home run hitter who was already pumped up with something else. Trevor

Hoffman, the great San Diego Padres closer, intimidated visiting teams with the ominous gong of his entrance anthem, "Hell's Bells" by the heavy metal band AC/DC. Mariano Rivera, one of the players featured in this book, has said that he's tired of the Metallica dirge "Enter Sandman," which plays whenever he takes the mound in a save situation, but Yankee fans would give him the Bronx cheer if he tried to change tunes now.

If you go to Major League Baseball's website (mlb.com), you'll find a list of the walk-up or entrance songs for every player on every team, but only one batter strides to the plate hearing a song sung by his *wife*—and that's Tampa Bay Rays second baseman Ben Zobrist.

During the 2011 season, Ben's walk-up track was "Only You," sung by Julianna Zobrist, who's cut a CD of Christian-themed electronic pop/rock songs. Saying she was influenced by Plumb and Imogen Heap as well as childhood favorites like the Beach Boys and Gloria Estefan, Julianna sings an emotional *I want You and only You and no one else will ever do* as Ben digs in for his at-bat. " 'Only You' is about desiring God above anything else in your life," Ben said.

Ben first attracted notice for playing his wife's music during the 2009 and 2010 seasons when he chose Julianna's "The Tree," as his walk-up song. Julianna says "The Tree" speaks to the fact that "we are deserving of the wrath of the Almighty God, and He, out of His mere good pleasure, delivered us from the way of thinking that our own 'goodness' could justify us before Him."

Isn't that great? Julianna Zobrist uses her God-given gift for music to impact others, while her husband, Ben, uses his God-given athletic skills on the baseball diamond. Together, they make a pretty good team each time he steps to the plate at Tropicana Field. (Julianna also sang the National Anthem at one of Ben's playoff games in 2010.)

The big stage they find themselves on today is light years away from the humble beginnings of this pair of PKs—pastor's kids— from the nation's heartland. She's from Iowa City, Iowa, and Ben hails from the checkerboard farmlands of central Illinois, having grown up in Eureka, a small town of five thousand people once known as the "pumpkin capital of the world" back in the 1950s. Eureka is also the home of Eureka College, whose most illustrious alumnus is President Ronald Reagan, a 1932 graduate.

Zobrist—pronounced Zoh-brist—is a Swiss name. Ben's great-great-grandfather—Jakob Zobrist—immigrated from Switzerland's Alpine meadows in 1867 as a nine-year-old boy. His family settled in Illinois' verdant flatlands to farm and milk cows in the Morton area. Jakob begat a son named Noah, who begat a son named Alpha, who begat Tom, who begat Ben in 1981. Ben is the second of five children, with an older sister, a younger sister, and two younger brothers.

Tom, Ben's father, is a pastor with a love for baseball inherited from his father, Alpha, who was a St. Louis Cardinals fan. The Gateway City is just three hours away from Eureka, so every summer the Zobrist clan—aunts, uncles, and cousins—would travel to St. Louis to take in a major league baseball game.

"That was our big treat for the year, our big vacation," Ben said. "We didn't really travel much except to one baseball game a year in St. Louis."

Tom has been ministering at Liberty Bible Church, which has a congregation of two hundred, since 1988. He and his wife, Cindi, raised their five children in a farming community with two stoplights, a courthouse, a small downtown, a private college, and abundant parks. It was Tom who put a slender yellow plastic bat into Ben's hands when he was a three-year-old tyke and underhanded a perforated plastic Wiffle ball to him in the living room. It wasn't long before Tom and Ben had to move batting practice to the backyard.

Wiffle ball was a big deal in the Zobrist family. There were Sunday-afternoon tournaments with the extended family in their backyard, and little Ben was always begging to take his cuts. By the time he was in elementary school, he was playing baseball in organized leagues and neighborhood pickup games.

"I played a lot of sandlot ball growing up," Ben said. "There was a lot across the street from one of my friend's houses, and a bunch of us kids would play with a metal bat and a tennis ball. We liked playing with a tennis ball because it would fly a lot farther and make us feel like we were hitting long home runs. During the school year, Sunday afternoons were the big times because we'd play after church. We'd just go to the sandlot and play."

This was *unorganized* baseball—just Ben and his buddies choosing up sides and inventing different games. No umpires, no coaches, just kids going out and having fun swinging a bat and hitting a ball. He and the neighborhood kids would play for countless hours during the summer.

It was playing sandlot ball that got Ben—a natural righty—learning to switch-hit. Since there were usually just enough players to play one side of the field, if Ben announced that he was batting left-handed, then all the players would move to the right side of the field. "I liked batting left-handed because the fence was closer. I liked hitting a line drive into the backyard and getting a home run."

There was another benefit to playing with a tennis ball—no broken windows.

Ben played other sports growing up—youth football, AYSO soccer, and junior basketball—and he even ran track when he was in middle school, posting a 5:01 mile in the seventh grade that remained a school record seventeen years later.

But Ben came from a baseball family, and he wanted baseball to be his sport when he got to high school. He had designs on playing varsity ball at Eureka High during his freshman year, but there was a problem—Ben was a small kid. "I was about 5 feet, 5 inches tall and 112 pounds, but somehow I played varsity my freshman year," he said. "I added about two inches and fifteen pounds my sophomore year, but then I hit my growth spurt in my junior year. I shot up to 6 feet, 1 inch, but I only weighed 150 pounds or so. I was eating frozen pizza and applesauce since we were always on the run with different extracurricular activities. We had school stuff, church activities, and sports. It was a busy time."

One summer before his junior year of high school, Ben built his own "Field of Dreams"—a Wiffle ball diamond in his backyard. He used white spray paint for the foul lines, lined the outfield with two-foot-high rabbit fencing, dug holes in the grass for each base and home plate, and planted a flag beyond the center-field fence.

"Alpha Memorial Field"—named after Ben's grandfather—was the home of the Ben Zobrist Wiffle Ball League. There were four teams with five guys on a team, and they even played night games. His dad helped him illuminate the field by going to Home Depot and finding a pair of twenty-foot poles that they topped with bright lights. All they had to do was run an extension cord from the house, and they had the only night Wiffle ball field in Illinois . . . maybe in the entire country.

Sometimes Ben and one of his best friends, Jason Miller, would pitch batting practice to each other using a sponge ball that traveled a little farther than a Wiffle ball, but most of the time, the Ben Zobrist Wiffle Ball League adhered to its regularly scheduled games. Some Wiffle ball games lasted past midnight before Dad said, "It's time to go home, boys."

As any parent of energetic teens will tell you, when you put ten testosterone-laden teen boys into a small backyard and set out the plastic bats and Wiffle ball, you can expect the fur to fly. One evening, Ben was pitching—one of the rules of Wiffle Ball League was that pitches had to be tossed "friendly" toward home plate, not "burned" in there—to a friend named Ryan. The pitch sailed over the plate. Ryan flicked his wrists and homered over the leftfield rabbit fencing.

As Ryan rounded the bases, he chortled and gave Ben the business. Ben was wearing a cheap plastic helmet—the type that he had received at the Cardinals' "Helmet Day"—when Ryan veered toward Ben and whacked him on the back of the head, striking his plastic helmet with his hand. The action stung a bit, so Ben unfurled a few choice comments at his friend.

Just as Ryan was crossing home plate, Ben yelled out, "I dare you to step over this line."

Challenged before their mutual friends, Ryan couldn't back down. He charged the mound, and the next thing Ben knew, he was in the midst of an old-fashioned, bench-clearing baseball brawl. Ryan tackled him to the ground, but in typical baseball brawl fashion, no punches were thrown. They wrestled with each other in the grass as the other players dove in. It was one big dog pile!

"Ryan and I were the guys running the league," Ben said. "It didn't bother our friendship, but when Ryan said, 'I don't want to play Wiffle ball anymore,' things kind of disbanded after that."

BASEBALL AFTER HIGH SCHOOL

When spring came around, Ben set his sights on hardball again. He says he was maybe a better-than-average high school ballplayer—a solid pitcher and sure-handed infielder who could hit for average—but he didn't win any All-Conference awards until his senior year. Despite playing well, and despite being thought of as one of the top high school players in his region, Ben wasn't on any college coaches' radar throughout his last season of high school baseball.

Ben saw a spiritual component to what was happening. Sure, he was apprehensive about the future—where he'd go to college and if he'd get to play ball—but he felt like the Lord wanted him to trust Him for his future, so that's what he did. Ben got on his knees and said, "Lord, my life is yours, and I'm not going to be in charge. As for baseball, You can have that, too."

And that's how it went—God was in control. If baseball wasn't in his future, that was okay. If that's the way it turned out, Ben knew it was God's will for his life.

Still not sure where he wanted to go or what he wanted to study, he settled on Calvary Bible College in Kansas City, Missouri, the school his dad attended when Ben was a pre-schooler. His older sister Jessica was attending Calvary Bible at the time, so the family's thinking was that his big sister could ease Ben's transition into college life.

Calvary Bible College didn't have a baseball team, but

they did have a basketball team, so Ben figured he could play hoops in college. Again, this would be fine with him. In many ways, Ben was a seasonal athlete whose favorite sport was the one he was playing at the time. As high school graduation loomed, he assumed he had played his last game of organized baseball and would be done with the sport forever.

Then the high school coach at Brimfield—thirty-five miles west of Eureka—called not long after graduation. He said a dozen college coaches were holding an open tryout at Brimfield High because they were looking to fill holes on their rosters. He thought Ben had a good chance of playing college baseball somewhere. "You never know what might happen," said the Brimfield coach.

Ben thought about the request for a moment. "Are they going to have guns there?" he asked, referring to radar guns that measure how fast a pitcher throws the ball. He had never thrown for a radar gun.

Told yes, Ben said he wanted to come. In his mind, this was a chance to learn how fast he threw. But there was just one minor detail—the Brimfield coach said the open tryout cost fifty dollars.

When Ben talked to his father about the tryout, Tom said, "I'm not paying the fifty dollars. If you want to go, you'll have to pay for it."

Tom wasn't being obstinate—just realistic. For the pastor of a small church with five children to care for and two in college, fifty bucks wasn't small pumpkins, er, make that small potatoes.

"You think about it and pray about it," he told his son.

Ben was a teenage kid just out of high school, without much money. The next day, after giving the matter some prayer, Ben said he wanted to take his birthday present money from his grandparents and go to the tryout.

This one decision changed his life. Because Ben paid the fifty dollars his grandparents had given him and then showed up at that ball field in Brimfield, he is playing major league baseball today.

On Friday, the morning of the tryout, however, rain poured from the skies. The tryout was postponed until Monday.

That complicated matters. There was another open tryout—this was being held by the Atlanta Braves—on Monday as well. This tryout was in Normal, Illinois, about twenty-five miles southeast of Eureka. Even though the tryout was free, the odds of signing with the Braves organization were astronomically low.

There was also another moving part—the start of a weeklong Bible conference that Ben's youth group was participating in. It began Monday night and was being held a little farther east than Normal.

When Ben's Friday tryout at Brimfield High was washed out, Tom said, "Son, you're going to have to blow off Brimfield. I don't see how you can do it."

Tom said this because Brimfield was a good forty minutes *west* of Eureka, and the youth Bible conference was eastward a couple of hours away.

Tom and Ben called the Brimfield coach and explained the situation—and asked if the fifty dollars was refundable. It wasn't.

"Mr. Zobrist, I don't want to tell you what to do," the coach said, "but I guarantee you that Ben will get some money for college if he comes."

Tom turned to his son.

"I sorta would like to go," Ben said.

Tom relented, even though that meant a lot of extra driving for Ben.

Ben arrived to find dozens of players yearning for a chance to make a good impression before the watchful eyes of a dozen college coaches. After running the 60–yard dash, each player took six ground balls at shortstop, which they were to field and throw hard to first base. Next was the batting portion—twelve swings per player. Ben was a switch-hitter, so that meant six hacks on each side of the dish. Ben didn't go yard or put on a Josh Hamilton-like home run jag, but he lined several ropes into the outfield.

Then Ben finished with six pitches from the mound, which were timed by the radar gun. He topped out at 84 miles per hour, which Ben was happy with. Now he knew how fast he threw.

And that was it. Ben was gathering up his stuff and getting ready to head out when one of the coaches caught up with him.

"Hey, my name is Elliot Johnson, and I'm from Olivet Nazarene University," he said, sticking out his hand to shake Ben's.

"Pleased to meet you," Ben replied.

"I heard that you are a Christian," he continued. "I'm a Christian, too, and I heard that you might be going to Calvary Bible."

"That's the plan," Ben said.

"Well, we're a Christian school near Chicago with a good baseball program, and I'm just letting you know that I might give you a call to come take a visit up in Olivet some time. But believe me, I don't want to take you away from God's will for your life."

And that's how Coach Johnson left it.

Ben thought their interaction was interesting, but he didn't give their conversation any more thought because he had to get on the road and drive several hours to the youth Bible conference. That night, he learned that the theme of the week was to be open to what God wants to do in your life. "I was like, *I'm cool with that idea,*" Ben said.

Meanwhile, the phone was ringing off the hook back home. By Tuesday night, Jessica, the Zobrists' oldest daughter, had taken five calls from five different college coaches, all of whom wanted Ben to come play for their school.

Tom and Cindi came home a day or two later to do some things while Ben stayed with his youth group at the conference. The sudden interest in Ben's ball-playing abilities surprised them. When they spoke on the phone with Coach Johnson, he explained that he was looking for one more pitcher to round out his staff, and he thought Ben would be perfect for the Olivet Nazarene team. Everyone agreed that the next step was for Ben to come look at the campus.

The following week, Ben drove with his high school coach, Bob Gold, to Olivet Nazarene University in Bourbonnais, Illinois, two hours away. Tom and Cindi had a commitment that day and couldn't accompany their son. Coach Gold, who was the FCA Huddle leader for Eureka High School, had always encouraged Ben to follow God's will through sports.

Upon their arrival, Ben heard Coach Johnson explain that his goal for the team was to bring in Christian players who would have a positive influence on the non-Christian team members and represent the school *and* Christ well. (About half the players were not believers.)

"That's why I would like to offer you a full-ride scholarship to play baseball at Olivet Nazarene," the coach said, adding that he saw Ben as the type of player who would pitch and play some shortstop for the team. But he was recruiting Ben primarily to be a pitcher.

Ben was stunned to hear the out-of-left-field offer, which came as a result of fielding six ground balls, taking twelve swings, and throwing a half-dozen pitches. But he was pleased as well. The only thing that concerned him was that he thought he was a better hitter and position player than a pitcher . . . but at least he would be playing baseball again.

When Ben got home and talked with his parents about the scholarship offer, Tom and Cindi were pleasantly surprised. They had figured Ben's baseball-playing days were over. But here was a Christian coach offering their son a college athletic scholarship—which would certainly help the tight Zobrist family budget—to play baseball at a Christian college. Olivet Nazarene was a nice school with nice facilities, a nice coach, and a nice offer of free tuition and room and board. Other than the pitching situation, what was there not to like?

But Tom and Cindi weren't immediately sold on the scholarship offer. They told Ben they wanted to pray about where God was leading him and then meet with the coach to discuss the situation. An appointment with Coach Johnson in Bourbonnais was quickly made.

After sitting down and exchanging pleasantries, Cindi asked a pointed question: "Coach Johnson, you've never seen Ben pitch or play in a game. How do you know he's worth this much money?"

"Ma'am, I've coached baseball for many years," Coach Johnson replied. "I've seen Ben's curve ball, and I know he can get college players out with it. I also see your son's desire to glorify God with whatever he does."

Tom asked if the family could have an hour to discuss the situation. Told yes, they drove over to a Cracker Barrel restaurant near campus to get something to eat. Remember, all this was transpiring in late June, a month after high school graduation.

Cindi was upset by this sudden turn of events. She felt like Ben was supposed to go to Calvary Bible College—and now this. Through tears, she said the opportunity to play baseball at Olivet Nazarene was happening too fast for her.

Tom listened and turned to his son. "Ben, you've been praying about this. You're a young man now, and you need to decide what you believe God wants you to do. I can't make this decision for you."

"I'll do anything you want me to do, Dad," Ben replied. "If you believe it's right for me to go to Calvary, then I'll go to Calvary. I trust your judgment."

Hearing Ben say that—and seeing how he was willing to submit to his authority—told Tom that his son was mature enough to make this decision on his own. "Ben, this needs to be your decision," he said.

Ben took in a deep breath. "I believe I'm not done playing baseball. I want to see what God has in store for me."

Tom looked at Cindi, who nodded her assent. "Okay, let's do it," his father said. "You'll be only two hours from home, so that means we could come watch you play."

The family returned to the Olivet Nazarene campus, where a smiling Ben informed Coach Johnson that he wanted to play ball for him.

Olivet Nazarene was not an NCAA division school, however. The Olivet Nazarene athletic teams played in the NAIA, which had different eligibility requirements. When Ben turned out for fall ball his freshman year, Dan Heefner—a senior who was the team's leading home run hitter and had a batting average of .402—took Ben under his wing. "He was kind of *the* guy," Ben said. "He was the big MVP and team leader who led

Bible studies. Dan discipled me and put me on the right path."

Ben needed some steadying because when the season started, Coach Johnson—as promised—had him work on pitcher-conditioning drills and not take infield or batting practice. When the team took its annual spring break to Daytona Beach, Florida, to open the season, Ben was part of the five-man pitching staff. He was a curve ball artist who wasn't afraid to throw the yakker on a full count.

When the season opened, the Olivet Nazarene shortstop booted a few ground balls that cost them a couple of games. He was replaced by another shortstop who also struggled in the field. Needing to plug a gaping hole in the infield, Coach Johnson turned to one of his pitchers—Ben Zobrist.

Once in the lineup, Ben played like a younger Derek Jeter, vacuuming up every ground ball hit his way and making the throws. He also got his fair share of hits (he batted .330 his freshman year) even though he was still called upon to pitch every fourth or fifth game.

"By the end of the season, my arm was about to fall off, but doing both—pitching and playing shortstop—turned out to be a very successful year for me," Ben said.

So why did he perform so well, especially early on when he didn't take infield or batting practice?

"Guys like Dan Heefner told me that I had to take extra batting practice *after* practice if I wanted to get better," Ben said. "So whenever I had free time, I would go to the batting cage and set up the hitting tee and hit the ball into the back of the net. I worked on trying to control my swing because I wanted to be ready if I got the opportunity." He also asked teammates to hit him ground balls after practice so he could get in some glove work. He was always the last one to leave the ball field and the locker room.

There was something else that Ben learned from watching guys like Dan Heefner—take your walks. "When I was in high school, I would hack at the ball and didn't walk much. Then when I got to college, I saw that the better hitters were walking more. Before they got two strikes, they were looking for one pitch in a specific zone, and if the pitch wasn't there, they weren't going to swing. That's when I started to learn 'plate discipline' and the importance of looking for that one pitch."

After his freshman year was over, Ben wanted to play summer ball, but the college leagues around the country didn't have any room on their rosters for freshman players. When no offer came, Ben heard about an opportunity from Coach Johnson to play on a baseball "missions trip" with Athletes in Action, a ministry of Campus Crusade for Christ International (known today as Cru). During a six-week tour, the Athletes in Action team would travel to Mexico and Nicaragua, playing local teams and sharing the gospel after the final out was made.

Just one problem—Ben had to raise his own support, which was a couple of thousand dollars. But with the backing of his dad's church and all the Zobrist next-of-kin chipping in, Ben got enough money to pay for the missions trip.

This was the first time Ben had been out of the country, and taking buses around the Mexican and Nicaraguan countryside was an experience he wouldn't soon forget. Sometimes they pulled into tiny villages where a ragtag team of gray-hairs and grandkids were waiting for them. Other times they competed in small cities against local All-Star teams who could play some serious ball.

Whether they had to take their foot off the gas or play

hard, each game ended with one of the AIA players sharing his testimony—through an interpreter who followed the team—of how he came to know Jesus Christ as his personal Lord and Savior. Then a second speaker would share the Four Spiritual Laws—the Christian message of salvation contained in the Bible. "It was definitely more a ministry summer baseball experience than a pure baseball experience, but that was fine with me," Ben said. "I had an awesome time."

Playing in Mexico and Nicaragua raised Ben's game more than he thought. He had a sensational sophomore year at Olivet Nazarene, and Coach Johnson lightened his pitching load, just bringing him in to throw in relief situations.

When his sophomore season was over, Ben didn't have a summer league team to play on, so he took a job at the Christian Center, a multi-use recreational center with ball fields in Peoria, Illinois, about twenty miles west of Eureka. His uncle, Matt Zobrist, hired Ben to mow the grass, rake the infield dirt, and line the fields.

An old youth baseball coach named Dave Rodgers ran the sandlot program that encouraged kids to show up and play pickup games with no parents, coaches, or umpires involved. He asked Ben to give him a hand with the sandlot program as well.

Coach Rodgers had been around the horn and even coached New York Yankee catching great Joe Girardi (who's presently the Yankees skipper) back when he was a Little Leaguer growing up in East Peoria. The longtime coach had seen Ben play, knew all about him, and was concerned that Ben wasn't playing that summer.

Coach Rodgers took it upon himself to call the manager of the Twin City Stars, part of the Central Illinois Collegiate

League, and tell him that he needed to have Ben on his team. "This boy is too good," said the old coach. "He needs to be playing somewhere."

The Twin City Stars played in Bloomington, Illinois, less than thirty miles from Eureka. Their coach was reluctant, saying he had enough guys, but Coach Rodgers pressed his case.

"Okay, I'll give him a one-week tryout," the Twin City Stars coach said.

Ben's tryout lasted one night. He went 5 for 5—3 for 3 batting left-handed and 2 for 2 batting right-handed. "You're on the team," the coach said after the game.

That summer, Ben joined a Christian Center bus trip to go see a Cardinals game in St. Louis with dozens of kids in the sandlot program. His father and Uncle Matt came along as chaperones. The large group sat in Busch Stadium's upper deck—the "Bob Uecker" seats. During the middle innings, Ben snuck down behind home plate to get a closer look at big league pitching.

When he returned, his father asked him where he had been.

"Checking out the pitchers," he said. "Dad, I think I can hit these guys. I think I can play in the major leagues."

Tom didn't see how that was possible, but he didn't want to discourage his son. "We'll see where it goes from here," he said. "Maybe you'll end up playing in the majors some day."

At the start of Ben's junior season, Coach Johnson moved him over to second base, saying he wanted to save Ben's arm from the long throws from deep in the hole.

The move felt like a demotion, however. Friends and family members said moving him to second base didn't make sense, but Ben's attitude was that it was the coach's decision to make. "I just went with it," he said. (His flexibility at the time has served him well because today he's one of the best utility players in the majors.)

That attitude was typical of Ben, who was exhibiting spiritual growth off the field, as well. He was the leader of the campus Fellowship of Christian Athlete's Huddles, the weekly Bible studies for sports-minded students. Teammates and friends were impressed at how Ben invested in their spiritual lives and helped make everyone around him spiritually stronger—as "iron sharpens iron."

Ben also showed leadership on the field, where he hit .409, made nine appearances on the mound, going 3–0 with two saves, and was named Player of the Year in the Chicagoland Collegiate Athletic Conference, an NAIA All-American, and an NAIA Scholar-Athlete.

Ben had become a skilled baseball player in a few short years. And now that he had filled out to 6 feet, 3 inches and 185 pounds, he was on the scouts' radar screen.

Ben had seen other NAIA All-Americans drafted, and scouts told him that he could find himself signing with a major league team. But nothing happened in the 2003 June draft, held shortly after the end of his junior season.

God was in control, right?

Time for summer ball, and this time Ben chose to play in the Northwoods League, a sixteen-team association that plays in small towns and cities in Wisconsin, Minnesota, and Iowa. Ben joined the Wisconsin Woodchucks of Wausau, Wisconsin.

His manager was Steve Foster, who played for the Cincinnati Reds and scouted for the Florida Marlins. He told Ben, "I have no idea why you're here. You should have been drafted and be in pro ball now."

Coach Foster set Ben up for a meeting with a scout that summer, but the middle infielder never received an offer good enough to leave school, where he had a full scholarship. Still, the episode boosted Ben's confidence that he could play professional baseball at a high level. "I know what these guys are like, and you can play," Coach Foster said.

Playing in the Northwoods League turned out to be a great experience for Ben. "Learning how to play almost every night in front of decent crowds of two or three thousand people was a big deal for college players," Ben said, "and good for my baseball abilities."

The team randomly assigned roommates, and Ben was thrown together with Jeff Gilmore. Here's where Ben's story gets even more interesting: Jeff Gilmore was a fine ballplayer at Dallas Baptist University who knew Dan Heefner well—very well.

Why?

Because Jeff's older sister Liz had married Dan Heefner back when Dan was leading the team at Olivet Nazarene.

With that in common, Ben and Jeff hit it off. They swapped stories about their college ball experiences, with Jeff telling him that Dallas Baptist was moving up to play NCAA Division I baseball the next season. That meant the team would be playing a lot of Big 12 schools like the University of Texas and Oklahoma State.

"Oh, and there's one more thing," Jeff said. "We need a shortstop."

Shortstop? My old position?

The wheels started turning in Ben's mind. The higher level of competition in Division I would bolster his chances to play pro ball. He had one year left, so if he was going to make a move, it was now or never.

Ben talked to Coach Johnson about the idea, but his coach wasn't thrilled with the prospect of losing one of his star players. Nonetheless, Olivet Nazarene released Ben from his scholarship so he could transfer. At Dallas Baptist, Ben moved right into the starting shortstop role. His days as a pitcher were over.

A QUICK TRIP TO THE BIG LEAGUES

Ben had a great senior season at Dallas Baptist, which earned him a closer look from major league scouts. This time around, the Houston Astros made him a sixth-round pick in the 2004 draft.

"I was obviously very excited to go play," he said. "To me, coming from Eureka, where no other athlete had played anything in professional sports, was definitely huge. It was like God was saying, *Look what I can do if you commit your work to Me and you just follow Me where I want you to go. I can do some things that you don't think are even possible."*

Ben was assigned to the bottom rung of the ladder—the Class A Tri-City ValleyCats in the New York-Pennsylvania League (NYPL). The night before Ben left for his assignment in New York, his parents threw him a going-away party filled with family, friends, and old coaches. After everyone left, Ben and his father found themselves alone in Ben's bedroom.

"Dad, this is more important to others than it is to me," he said. "The way I look at it, I'm a missionary but I don't have to raise support. Instead, I'm going to reach people for Christ, whether it's my teammates, fans, or whatever."

His father looked at him. "Here's what is important to me. I don't care what you do for a living as long as you live for God."

Ben led the NYPL with a .339 batting average, which

earned him a promotion to the South Atlantic League. His All-Star play and .333 batting average got him selected to Team USA, which played in the World Cup, held in the Netherlands. The international experience was invaluable.

It's amazing that Ben played so well because he was head over baseball cleats for a young woman named Julianna. She was studying music at Belmont University in Nashville, Tennessee, and she'd set her sights on a career in Christian music.

"She was just this awesome, godly woman who I put on a pedestal," Ben said. "I just decided to put myself out there and see if she had any interest."

Julianna said she had been praying intentionally about the person God wanted her to marry. "When Ben had felt this urgency to know if I felt anything for him, I was like, *Okay, Lord, I get it.* We started dating that night."

After more than two years of courtship, the Zobrists were married on December 17, 2005—the same anniversary date as Ben's parents. (Ben and Julianna asked if that would be okay, and of course Tom and Cindi were thrilled.) Ben's old roommate and teammate at Dallas Baptist, Jeff Gilmore, was there at the wedding as well, which seemed only right to Ben.

You see, Jeff was Julianna's brother. And Liz Heefner was Julianna's older sister.

Meanwhile, Ben continued his meteoric rise from the minors to the majors. Houston assigned him to their Double-A team in Corpus Christi, Texas. During a road trip to play the Springfield Cardinals in Springfield, Missouri, Ben's parents took a week off to see him play in the southern Missouri city.

At 8:30 in the morning, Ben received a phone call from the Astros organization informing him that he had been traded to the Tampa Bay Rays. His new club would be assigning him to their Triple-A club in North Carolina—the Durham Bulls. If possible, his new team wanted him in Durham that night.

Ben was shocked at the trade because he was playing really well for Corpus Christi. He had yet to learn that in the baseball world, sometimes you get traded because you're good, not because you're bad.

The trade set off some momentary pandemonium. The decision was made that Ben would fly immediately to Corpus Christi, where he and Julianna would pack up their belongings and drive nearly four hours to Houston. Julianna would drop Ben off at Houston Bush International Airport so he could catch a flight to the East Coast and wait for her father-in-law to fly in from Springfield. Upon Tom's arrival, they would drive together to Durham—a twenty-hour one-way trip.

"When you hear about guys getting traded, you don't think about all the things these guys have to go through with their wives and their families and their cars," Tom said. "They don't make a lot of money yet, so they can't hire people and companies to help them move or take their cars somewhere."

Ben wasn't in Durham long, though, because the parent club called him up on July 31, 2006. This time, the move to Tampa Bay was a lot easier, and the family back home in Eureka was ecstatic. His father had always said, "Ben, if you make it to the big leagues, I'll be there."

The next day, August 1, was the twelfth birthday of Ben's youngest brother, Noah. What a way to celebrate. Noah, brother Peter, and Tom and Cindi bought plane tickets that morning to Tampa Bay and arrived in time to see Ben take the field against the Detroit Tigers. He went hitless that night, but they were in the stands a couple of days later when Ben notched his first major league hit—off Boston Red Sox ace Curt Schilling. Ben finished the 2006 season playing 52 games and batting .224.

Ben's 2007 and 2008 seasons were *interesting*, to say the least. He slumped early in the 2007 season, which resulted in a demotion back to Durham. He bounced back and forth between Tampa Bay and Durham but stuck with the team during the Rays' magical run to the 2008 World Series. Even though Tampa Bay lost to the Philadelphia Phillies, Ben got to start two games—and his parents were there in person to watch their son play on baseball's biggest stage.

It was during Ben's breakout season in 2009 that he became known as "Zorilla" for his monster home runs and ability to play anywhere at any time. Ben played seven positions during the 2009 season—all three outfield positions and all four infield positions. He batted everywhere in the lineup except ninth, and his approach to batting—swing mechanic Jaime Cevallos and old teammate and now brother-in-law Dan Heefner had helped him overhaul his stroke during the offseason—changed from being an OBP-oriented gap hitter to a major league slugger. His 27 home runs, .297 batting average (he was over .300 for much of the season before tailing off near the end), 91 RBIs, and .543 slugging average raised eyebrows around the league and earned him a handsome long-term contract.

How handsome? Try going from $438,100 a year to $4,500,000 in a single season. And Tampa Bay has a $7 million option for 2014 and 2015, if Ben keeps producing. Fortunately, the 2011 season was a good one: a solid .269 batting average, a third-best 46 doubles, and 20 home runs.

Ben was also part of a special team that won the AL wild card

Tampa Bay Rays infielder Ben Zobrist is one of the most versatile players in baseball today, capable of playing outfield or any number of infield positions. He overcame a slow start in 2012 to fashion a solid .270 year with 20 home runs. (AP Photo/Tony Gutierrez)

spot on the season's final day, coming back from a late-inning seven-run deficit to beat the New York Yankees 8–7 and pass the Boston Red Sox, who blew a nine-game wild card lead in September. The Rays then lost in the ALCS to the Texas Rangers.

Sure, being part of a Cinderella team and winning big games in dramatic fashion was a lot of fun, but when I (Mike Yorkey) interviewed Ben, he told me that his mind-set was, *How can I be a better player today than I was yesterday?* He was quick to add that he took the same approach with his spiritual walk.

How can I grow closer to the Lord?

How can I not become complacent?

How can I join up with people who are really loving God and seeking after God?

It's not the easiest situation when you're a major league baseball player living away from home and playing six games a week. He takes advantage of Baseball Chapel, an organization that provides a weekly church service on Sundays before games as well as Bible studies during the week that players can tap into. Today's technology makes it easy for Ben to listen to podcast sermons from his pastor, Byron Yawn of Community Bible Church in Nashville, Tennessee.

Ben and Julianna make their home in Music City so she can pursue her singing career while being a mom to their son, Zion, who came into their lives on February 1, 2009, and their daughter, Kruse, born September 19, 2011. (Kruse is the maiden name of one of Ben's grandmothers.) Ben has received permission from the Tampa Bay organization to fly home on his off days, so he tries to get home every chance he can during the regular season.

Each time Ben steps into the front door of his home, he hears a different type of "walk-up music"—the sound of home life.

3

ALBERT PUJOLS:
A HOME RUN HITTER WITH
A HEART FOR OTHERS

Every time All-Star first baseman Albert Pujols steps into the batter's box, the crowd buzzes in anticipation. They know something amazing *might* happen.

Albert has lifetime batting average over .325, so the odds are pretty good that something remarkable *will* happen. No player in the history of baseball has amassed the kind of statistics Albert has put together during his first eleven years in the sport.

Not Babe Ruth.

Not Joe DiMaggio.

Not Ted Williams.

Not Barry Bonds.

Nobody.

And on this fall afternoon in 2010, Albert was about to give the crowd a treat.

The slugger walked confidently into the box and took

his iconic stance. Feet wide apart. Hands held high. Legs crouched like a linebacker ready to explode into a tackle. When the ball left the pitcher's hand, one thing was certain—that piece of cowhide was about to get whacked.

That's because Albert doesn't hit a ball; he punishes it.

As the ball neared the plate, Albert's powerful swing was already in motion. His hands ripped through the hitting zone and sent a towering home run well over the left field fence.

The crowd leapt to its feet cheering. Albert's teammates emptied out of their dugout. Even the opposing players spilled onto the field to embrace Albert at home plate.

After all, this wasn't a major league contest before a full house. This was an exhibition softball game at a baseball field the Pujols Family Foundation helped build in Albert's hometown of Santo Domingo in the Dominican Republic.

Everybody was excited to be there and to see Albert do what he does better than anyone else: swing a bat. They also knew they had nearly missed the opportunity of watching their hometown hero in action. That's because a hurricane had skirted the country the previous day, leaving the field a muddy mess. A grounds crew had worked feverishly to get the field ready, even using gasoline to burn off the puddles. With the water semi-evaporated, the game went on as planned, and Albert provided the memorable moment.

Every year, Albert returns to his home country to help the people in his old *batey*, what the shantytown neighborhoods are called in the Dominican Republic. The Pujols Foundation works year-round to provide the people there with medical care, food, clothing, and other necessities. It has even given new mattresses to families whose kids had doubled or tripled up on worn, lumpy beds.

Conditions in the *batey* aren't great, but some things are much better than when Albert was growing up in the D.R. in the 1980s. For one thing, he didn't have a nice baseball field to play on back then.

Albert developed his love of the sport using a stick for a bat, a milk carton for a glove, and a lime as a ball.

Today, though, children in Batey Aleman can play on a field where Albert's and several other players' pictures are painted on the outfield wall. The kids practice on Tuesdays and Thursdays and play games against each other on Saturdays all day long.

"That was me twenty-five years ago. I was one of those little boys with no hope and just a dream," Albert said in a *60 Minutes* interview in 2011 as he watched some kids he had been helping in his old neighborhood. "This is not so I can be looked at as 'Mr. Nice Guy.' I don't care less about that."

Albert helps out in the D.R. for one reason: He feels God has called him to give back. And Albert wants to honor God in every area of his life.

"Believe it or not, baseball is not the chief ambition of my life," Albert writes on his foundation's website. "Becoming a great baseball player is important to me, but it is not my primary focus because I know the Hall of Fame is not my ultimate, final destination. My life's goal is to bring glory to Jesus."

That's saying a lot, considering those words are coming from the best player in baseball during the first decade of the twenty-first century.

From the time Albert broke into the majors with the St. Louis Cardinals in 2001, he's put up monster numbers and been recognized for his talent. He won the National League Rookie

From 2001 through 2011, Albert Pujols played in St. Louis, where he helped the Cardinals win two World Series championships and put up Hall of Fame statistics. (AP Photo/Charlie Riedel)

of the Year his first season. From 2001 to 2010, he won three Most Valuable Player awards, six Silver Sluggers (given to the best offensive player at each position in both leagues), two Gold Gloves, and was named to nine All-Star games.

Between the 2001 and 2010 seasons, he became the only player in major league history to hit better than .300, hammer more than 30 home runs, and drive in at least 100 RBIs every season during his first ten years in the big leagues. No player had posted similar numbers in his first *two* years in the league, let alone ten. Unfortunately, that streak ended in 2011 when he came within a whisker—a hit with a player in scoring position—of doing it for an eleventh season in a row when he batted .299 and had 99 RBIs to go along with his 37 home runs.

No matter. Albert's body of work would be phenomenal for any player, but it's especially impressive for someone who was selected 402nd in the Major League Baseball draft.

401 MOTIVATIONS

Coming out of high school, Albert wasn't on many professional scouts' radars. He'd lived in the United States for just a few years after his family emigrated from the Dominican Republic in 1996.

He ended up settling in Independence, Missouri, because his uncle already lived there. Not many Spanish speakers lived in Independence, but the town did have baseball. And on the diamond, there was no language barrier for Albert to overcome.

Baseball had always been a constant for Albert, even when nothing much else remained the same.

He was born José Alberto Pujols Alcántara on January 16, 1980. His mom and dad divorced three months later. His father, Bienvenido, had played baseball and was known as a good pitcher. Despite the divorce, Bienvenido stayed involved in Albert's life and was there for him and his mother.

But nobody was a bigger part of his life than his grandmother, America. (Yes, that's her real name.) She took on a lot of the duties raising Albert. His ten aunts and uncles were also around to provide guidance and a helping hand.

By United States standards, Albert grew up dirt poor. But he never saw it that way. He says he didn't feel poor because he ate breakfast, lunch, and dinner every day. Many of the kids around him were fortunate if they got just *one* meal. In his mind, *those* were the poor kids.

Living in the *batey*, Albert spent most of his time playing baseball. Before he was a teenager, he realized that his skills were ahead of those of his peers and that he might have the ability to make it to the big leagues.

"Growing up in the Dominican Republic, that's pretty much all I did is play baseball," Albert said. "That's pretty much everybody's dream, to play professional baseball."

When Albert moved to Missouri at age sixteen, one of the first things he did was walk into Fort Osage High School and say through an interpreter that he wanted to play baseball.

In his first season, Albert played shortstop and helped the Indians win the Class 4A state championship. His hitting totals were especially impressive: a .471 batting average with 11 home runs and 32 RBIs. *USA Today* recognized him as "honorable mention" in its All-USA baseball rankings.

Albert stayed hot in summer ball. Playing 60 games for an American Legion team, he blasted 29 home runs and had 119 RBIs.

The seventeen-year-old returned to Fort Osage in the fall and asked if he could repeat his junior year. Although he had cousins at the school who could translate for him, he struggled to pick up English. Albert really wanted to master the language and earn his high school diploma. The school and the Missouri State High School Activities Association agreed, giving Albert an extra year of high school eligibility.

During the 1998 season, Albert was a force for the Indians, hitting .660. The problem was, he couldn't sneak up on teams anymore. Everybody knew who he was and didn't want to give him a good pitch to hit. Albert drew a record-setting 26 walks that season, 18 of them intentional.

In the summer Albert's stature grew even more as he broke his own home run record by bashing 35 round-trippers, including one that caught the attention of *Independence Examiner* writer Dick Puhr, who described one of Albert's grand slams as a "blast down the left-field line [that] was higher than the light standards and sailed, not only over the fence, but the railroad tracks and landed in a mulberry bush."

His summer coach, Gary Stone, said, "It's the farthest and hardest I've seen a baseball hit."

Of course, Stone was already a big fan of Albert's. During a tournament the previous summer in which all the players had to use wooden bats instead of aluminum, Stone noted that Albert would "have power even if he used a toothpick."

While Albert's talents on a baseball field were obvious to everybody who saw him play, he didn't attract the praise of many scouts. They didn't like Albert's footwork at shortstop and said that he lacked control on his throws.

Albert came back for his senior year in 1998 but earned

enough credits to graduate early. He enrolled at Maple Woods Community College in Kansas City in January and started playing for the college team that spring.

Immediately, Albert proved he had the ability to play at the next level.

In his first game for the Monarchs, Albert turned an un-assisted triple play at shortstop and hit a grand slam off Mark Buehrle (now a four-time major league All-Star who's thrown a no-hitter and a perfect game).

For the season, Albert hit .461 with 22 home runs and 80 RBIs.

When baseball's 1999 draft rolled around on June 2, Albert watched in anticipation. He knew his dream of making it to the pros was about to come true.

The Tampa Bay Devil Rays (now just the "Rays") selected Josh Hamilton first overall. Josh Beckett went second to the Florida Marlins. Nearly everybody close to baseball believed those two players would go right away. Albert figured he'd probably go in the first few rounds. The *Examiner* agreed, writing that he'd be drafted in the top three rounds. Other experts had him pegged to go anywhere from the fifth to eighth round. Scouts still didn't like Albert's throwing motion and worried because he'd gained a little weight in junior college.

After the first day of the draft was over, Albert's name was still on the board.

He had to wait until the morning of June 3 to hear that St. Louis had drafted him in the *thirteenth* round with the 402nd pick.

Albert was devastated. His girlfriend at the time, Deidre

Corona, said he cried like a baby. He even talked about quitting baseball.

Deidre persuaded him not to give up on his dream.

When St. Louis offered Albert a $10,000 signing bonus (Hamilton had been given $3.96 million), he turned it down because he felt like he was worth more.

To prove his worth, Albert went to the Jayhawk League, where college-aged players showcased their talent over the summer. In 55 games, Albert led the team in home runs and batting average. St. Louis came back and offered him $60,000. He took the deal and joined the team.

But the sting of being drafted in the thirteenth round didn't go away. Albert knew he had the talent and work ethic to make it in the pros, and he wanted to show his detractors they were wrong about him.

Albert had lived with doubters. But when coaches worked with him and saw his daily dedication, they often became his biggest fans.

"He's the best hitter I've coached or seen," said Marty Kilgore, Albert's coach at Maple Woods Community College. "But what impresses me most about Albert is his work ethic. A lot of coaches in the area told me he didn't have good work habits and that he was moody. I've seen just the opposite. He's the first player at practice, the last to leave, and when practice is over, he's heading over to the batting cage to take some more swings."

Albert developed his swing during his younger years and continued to hone it with countless repetitions. These days, he estimates that he takes between fifteen and twenty thousand practice swings a year in the batting cage. He works so hard to get his mechanics exactly right that it's no wonder he's earned the nickname "The Machine."

As it turns out, it was the scouts who didn't get a whole lot right in the 1999 draft. Only twenty-three of the fifty-one players drafted in the first round ever made it to the big leagues. Carl Crawford and Justin Morneau went in the second round. Shane Victorino was selected with the 194th pick, and amazingly, Jake Peavy, a future Cy Young winner, was picked *after* Albert at the 472nd spot.

Being slighted in the draft has been a driving force for Albert—even to this day.

"I'll never, never get over it," he said.

With 401 reasons fueling his drive to succeed, Albert played just one year in the minor leagues. During that same time, he worked more on his physique, turning his body into a muscular 6-foot, 3-inch, 230-pound baseball-bashing machine.

Albert started the 2000 season with the Class A Peoria Chiefs in Illinois. After playing third base and being named the league's most valuable player, Albert had a brief stay at Double-A before jumping up to the Triple-A Memphis Redbirds.

The Redbirds were preparing to enter the Pacific Coast League playoffs. In Albert's first seven games, he hit .367 with two home runs. Then he helped lead Memphis past the Albuquerque Dukes and into the championship series against Salt Lake City. On September 15, 2000, the twenty-year-old showed no signs of nerves as he hit a walk-off home run in the thirteenth inning of Game 4 to give the Redbirds their first-ever PCL championship. For his efforts, Albert earned the league's Most Valuable Player award in the postseason.

In 2001, Albert entered spring training with the hopes of gaining a spot on the Cardinals' twenty-five-man roster.

Most people close to the team figured Albert would spend another year with the Redbirds before he'd be ready for the majors. Albert wanted to prove them wrong. He took extra fielding practice to learn how to play first base and outfield, and he always looked strong at third.

When the Opening Day lineup was announced, Albert found himself playing left field against the Colorado Rockies.

FIRM FOUNDATION

While Albert's baseball career was taking off, his personal life was doing the same.

In the summer of 1998, the teen went salsa dancing at a club in Kansas City, where he met a young woman named Deidre. It wasn't love at first sight, but the two became dancing buddies.

After several weeks, Albert worked up the courage to ask Deidre on a date. When they were out together, he admitted to lying to her about his age. He had told her that he was twenty-one when he was really only eighteen years old. Deidre also had a confession to make: she had just given birth to a baby girl with Down syndrome.

Instead of running away from the relationship, Albert wanted to meet Deidre's daughter. When Albert met Isabella for the first time, he didn't see her as child with Down syndrome. Instead, he just looked at her as a beautiful little girl.

Albert continued to date Deidre and to act as Isabella's occasional babysitter. Deidre had recently rededicated her life to Jesus Christ and encouraged Albert to attend church with her. She also explained the existence of heaven and hell to him and said the only way to heaven was through a personal relationship with Jesus Christ.

"I went to church every once in a while growing up," Albert said. "At that time, I didn't realize how important it was to go to church and have a relationship with Christ."

His grandmother had raised Albert to have good morals and to be a good person. He didn't drink, smoke, or have any tattoos. But he also didn't know God or have a relationship with His Son.

Albert began attending church every week and learning more about Jesus. Once Albert understood the truth of the gospel, he walked down the aisle and prayed to give his life to Christ on November 13, 1998.

"I wouldn't say it was easy and that the Lord started turning things around [right away]," Albert said. "There were still challenges and still some tough times in my life, but the Lord was preparing me for the big things."

That included getting married and being successful in baseball.

Albert and Deidre were married on New Year's Day—January 1, 2000. When Albert was assigned to play in Peoria, Deidre and Isabella accompanied him.

Albert made around $125 a week playing baseball in the spring of 2000 (these days, his on-the-field salary is more than $280,000 a week, which doesn't include endorsement income). This wasn't enough money for a young family with a special-needs child. The couple barely had enough money to pay rent or buy furniture. Albert remembers going to Walmart and purchasing a cheap card table and folding chairs so they could have a seating area.

When Albert made the jump to the majors in 2001, that all changed. His salary shot up to $200,000 for the year. And after Albert won NL Rookie of the Year honors by batting .329 with 37 home runs and 130 RBIs, his salary tripled to $600,000 the following year.

As Albert's statistics grew and his consistency became obvious—he was no one-season wonder!—the Cardinals kept rewarding him with larger contracts.

In 2005, his annual salary reached eight digits . . . $11 million to be exact. That was also the year that he and Deidre started the Pujols Family Foundation.

"I had been praying for God to be able to use Albert to share Jesus and wanted it to be bigger," Deidre said. "Todd Perry had been calling and presenting us with an idea [for the foundation]. It took about a year to get everybody in the same place. Our mission is faith, family, and others."

The Pujols Family Foundation helps families and children who live with Down syndrome and also works in the Dominican Republic to improve the quality of life of needy children. Perry has worked as the executive director from the beginning. Albert and Deidre don't just write a check and help raise money; they get physically involved with the people their organization touches.

One of the highlights of Albert's year is hosting a formal dance for teenagers with Down syndrome. The kids show up at this gala event in fancy dresses and tuxedoes, walk the red carpet, and enjoy the prom-like atmosphere. And, of course, all the girls want to dance with Albert.

At the end of the 2010 celebration, Albert dripped with sweat but had a huge smile on his face.

"It must've been the highlight of the year for them," the *60 Minutes* reporter said to Albert during his interview.

"And for me, too," Albert quickly responded. "Every time I'm around them, I enjoy it and have a great time."

As the Pujols Family Foundation got going, Albert's own family was growing. Isabella got a little brother when Albert Jr. (known as A.J.) was born a couple of years after Albert and Deidre married. In 2005, Sophia came along, and more recently, Ezra was born.

"One thing I have learned is that it's not about me; it's about serving the Lord Jesus Christ," Albert said. "His plan was bigger than what I ever thought. I have a beautiful family and four beautiful kids."

Albert doesn't only want to be a role model to his own children; he hopes to positively influence other kids. During a recent season, the slugger had the opportunity to meet two young men who made an especially big impact on him.

One of them was Jacob Trammell, a fifteen-year-old who had been diagnosed with a cancerous tumor and had gone through chemotherapy and radiation. Through the Make-A-Wish Foundation, Jacob got to hang out with his idol. Albert showed Jacob around the Cardinals' clubhouse and took batting practice with him at Busch Stadium. ESPN recorded the events for its show "My Wish."

"He's like the best baseball player in baseball now," Jacob said about Albert. "He's a good Christian man. He's my role model because my dad had left."

The teenager, a good baseball player in his own right, dreamed of playing in the majors and got some hitting tips from Albert. With a few tweaks of his swing—such as keeping his hands high and swinging in one fluid motion—Jacob was smacking line drives all over the indoor hitting facility at Busch Stadium.

"That's the stroke I've been looking for all year," Albert quipped after Jacob stroked a streak of solid hits.

According to Jacob's mom, Debbie, it was the high point of Jacob's year.

"Albert is such a great player," she said. "Jacob likes his morals and the way he uses his Christian background, giving all the glory to God. Jacob is kind of like that, too."

A few weeks later, during the 2010 season, Albert lashed his 400th major league home run, making him the third-youngest player to accomplish that feat. Only Alex Rodriguez and Ken Griffey Jr. reached that benchmark at a younger age.

Four days after reaching that milestone, Albert took the bat that hammered the historic home run and gave it to Brandon Johnson, a thirteen-year-old battling a malignant brain tumor at Texas Children's Hospital. Albert didn't go with a lot of fanfare or television cameras. He just quietly slipped away after the game with the Houston Astros, went to the hospital, prayed with Brandon, and stayed for about an hour.

Faith, family, and others. It's not just the mission of Albert's foundation—it's the foundation of his life.

MAKING HISTORY

While many of the best athletes in the world make head-lines with little indiscretions or poor decisions, Albert makes headlines with the good he does—on and off the field. With a bat in his hands, he's put up numbers that are unparalleled in the long, storied history of baseball.

In his first eleven years in the big leagues, he hit more than 40 home runs and drove in better than 120 RBIs six times. He's won the National League's Most Valuable Player award three times (2005, 2008, and 2009). He led St. Louis to the World Series three times. The Cardinals lost to Boston in 2004, but the Redbirds came back two years later to beat Detroit. And during the recent 2011 campaign, Albert was at the front of the charge as St. Louis won its National League–leading eleventh World Series title.

The seven-game victory over Texas will be remembered as one of the most unlikely championships in baseball history. St. Louis was 10½ games back in the NL wild card race at the end of August when the Redbirds went on a tear in September. Albert hit .355 that month with five homers and 20 RBIs as St. Louis clinched the wild card spot on the final day of the regular season.

The underdog Cardinals defeated mighty Philadelphia in five games in the National League Divisional Series. Then they got past Milwaukee to set up the finale against the Rangers.

Albert had a slow start in the World Series but then erupted for one of the best games ever by hitting three home runs and knocking in six RBIs in a 16–7 victory in Game 4. Albert's 14 total bases stand as a World Series record, and it marked the first time since 1977 that a player had hit three dingers in the Fall Classic. Only Reggie Jackson and Babe Ruth had accomplished the feat before.

"I'm glad it was him," the Hall of Famer Jackson said of Albert tying his record. "He's a fabulous representative of the game. . . . I told him I admire the way he went about his business. I know he has a charity; I know he's a good, Christian man, a good team guy. He's got great focus."

Albert displayed that laser-like focus in the 2011 post-season by batting over .350 with five home runs and 16 RBIs.

After signing a ten-year, $254 million deal with the Los Angeles Angels, Albert struggled early in the 2012 season but rebounded to hit 30 or more home runs for the twelfth straight year. (Larry Goren/Four Seam Images)

"I think the last month of the season, that's where it started," Albert said. "Different guys were coming huge, getting big hits, and we carried that into the postseason and here we are, world champions."

Fans, sportswriters, opponents—even his manager—marvel at what Albert accomplishes on the diamond.

"Enjoy it. Respect it. Appreciate it," said long-time Cardinals manager Tony La Russa, who retired following the 2011 World Series victory. "I'm left with just watching him. And if you watch him, he'll do something to show you how great he is."

Now American League fans will get a chance to witness that greatness. In December 2011, Albert signed a ten-year, $254 million contract with the Los Angeles Angels that broke the hearts of Redbird fans.

Albert was one of the most highly prized free agents ever. After ten years in the sport, he'd won six Silver Slugger awards at three different positions—third base, outfield, and first base. He was also a two-time Gold Glove winner (2006 and 2010) at first base, proving that his fielding, throwing, and catching were also among the league's best.

But perhaps nothing showed Albert's ability better than an illustration that Fox Sports put on TV screens during one of Albert's World Series games. When a batter came to the plate, a graphic would flash on the screen to show where pitchers could throw the ball to get him out. When Albert's graphic came up, there were no spots that pitchers could pitch to. He was capable of hitting any pitch at any count and making his opponents pay.

"Albert has no glaring weaknesses, and he doesn't chase many bad pitches," Hall of Famer Tony Gwynn said.

It's not just the hundreds of thousands of practice swings that have made Albert a great hitter. He has studied the game and worked on his weaknesses. He's spent hours talking with Cardinal pitchers about how they work certain batters and vary their pitches. This helps Albert get into the mind of a pitcher, so that he'll know what to expect in different situations.

All of his efforts have paid off. Albert hits for average, hits for power, and is known for coming through in the clutch. No Cardinal has hit more grand slams than No. 5.

As of the end of the 2012 season, Albert had tallied 12 grand slams. He's nearly automatic with the bases loaded; in 2009 alone, he came to the plate with the bases full about ten times and hit a home run on five occasions.

And his bat doesn't disappear during the postseason, when the pitching is better and the pressure ratchets up. Through the 2011 season, he's hit .330 in the playoffs with 18 home runs and 52 RBIs.

"He's the face of baseball," said ESPN baseball analyst Peter Gammons. "When we're looking at history, he's an icon. And we should appreciate him because he's never done anything that's stained his reputation."

During an era where baseball's best power hitters have been embroiled in steroid rumors, Albert has stayed above the fray. Despite his prolific numbers and prodigious physique, he's never failed a drug test and never been accused of using any kind of performance-enhancing drug. It gets his dander up, though, when people voice suspicions about his Hall-of-Fame-worthy statistics.

"I would never do any of that," Albert said about taking performance-enhancing drugs. "You think I'm going to ruin my relationship with God just because I want to get better in this game? You think I'm going to ruin everything because of steroids? . . . I want to be the person who represents God, represents my family, and represents the Cardinals the right way."

On many occasions, Albert has invited baseball to test him every day. He has nothing to hide and wants people to know that he walks his talk.

In fact, Albert looks for ways to tell people about what God has done in his life. He's often said that God doesn't need him, but he needs God to live a successful life.

Since the early 1990s, the Cardinals have hosted a Christian Family Day when players share their testimonies with the fans at Busch Stadium after the conclusion of the game. From the time Albert joined the team, he and Deidre have become regulars at this event and others like it around the country.

The Christian Family Day organization also created a special testimony card for Albert and other members of the team. It looks like a baseball card, but instead of statistics on the back, it's packed with a player's personal story of accepting Jesus and a prayer that people can pray to invite Christ into their lives.

Albert signs the cards, and he and Deidre look for opportunities to pass them out to young fans.

Deidre has said that she sometimes feels like she's hitting a home run when she gives the card to people and sees the look on their faces. But when it comes to hitting balls out of major league parks, the former softball player leaves that up to her husband.

Even in 2011, when an early season slump and fractured forearm hurt Albert's statistics, he managed to hit more than 30 home runs for the eleventh consecutive year.

Not surprisingly, no player in Cardinals history has put

together more multiple home run games than Albert. During the 2011 season, he hit two or more home runs in 42 games—breaking Stan Musial's record of 37. Mark McGwire was third on the list at 28 games. Albert has five career three-homer games (the most of any active player), and some say his record-setting 465-foot blast in Busch Stadium during the 2011 season still hasn't come down to earth.

Albert's fans often can't decide what's their favorite thing about a Pujols home run. Is it gawking at a towering drive as it leaves the yard for some distant destination? Or is it seeing him glide around the bases until he approaches home plate, where he does his trademark shuffle step as he looks up and points to heaven?

Albert doesn't point to the sky to disrespect his opponents. He does it to show his respect to his Savior.

Many experts have tried to dissect Albert's swing and figure out the secret to his success. But Albert already knows the answer.

"I don't believe in all that science stuff," Albert said. "I believe in Jesus Christ, who gave me the strength and power and talent to honor Him. You can always try to figure it out and be scientific and look for success. Not me. It's dedication, hard work, practice, and God."

The All-Star's plan for moving forward is simple: He'll keep working hard, keep swinging the way God created him to, and keep pointing to heaven.

Because in playing for the Los Angeles Angels, Albert has even higher places to go.

2012 season update: Albert hit 30 home runs becoming the first player in major league history to hit 30 or more home runs during his first twelve seasons. He also led the Angels in RBIs with 105.

4

CARLOS BELTRAN:
PRAYING ALL THE WAY
TO THE BALLPARK

The choice wasn't momentous.

It wasn't like it would determine the fate of Carlos Beltran's eternal soul or anything like that. Still, what happened was significant because of what it said about his priorities.

Carlos was in his second or third year as the New York Mets' much-ballyhooed center fielder. Young, telegenic, ridiculously talented, and filthy rich, he was the type of five-tool star who graces the top of every major league team's wish list. In January 2005, he had signed a whopping seven-year, $119 million contract with the Mets. Gotham was his personal playground.

Carlos was also a faithful chapel attendee, so when he missed the pregame service one day at Shea Stadium, chaplain Cali Magallanes went looking for him. Carlos was finishing a clubhouse interview with a media outlet from his native Puerto Rico. He asked Magallanes if they could go pray together, so the two men searched for a private room.

Just then, Jay Horwitz, the Mets' media relations director, tapped Carlos on the shoulder. "The governor of Puerto Rico is here," Horwitz said. "He'd like to speak to you."

So much for prayer, Magallanes thought. When you make nearly $21,000 every time you step into the batter's box, as Carlos did at that time, everybody wants your time. Even high-ranking politicians.

But then, the unexpected happened. Without hesitation, Carlos told Horwitz, "Tell him I'll be right out. I have something more important to do."

Magallanes was pleasantly surprised.

"That really impacted me," Magallanes said, adding that he was impressed the Met outfielder didn't want to be distracted— even by the governor of Puerto Rico—until he had finished praying.

Prayer has been a vital part of Carlos' life ever since he placed his faith in Christ in 2001 during a postgame Bible study with former teammate Luis Alicea. He prays every morning and on his drive to the ballpark. During games, he often prays while patrolling the outfield.

"Some people might think I'm crazy, but I try to do that," he says.

No, Carlos isn't crazy. He's just healthily dependent on God. Prayer always comes in handy, even—and sometimes *especially*—for guys making a fortune.

Carlos' humble beginnings portended none of the life he now knows. He was born on April 24, 1977, in Manatí, Puerto Rico, a modest-sized town near the island's north-central shoreline. His father, Wilfredo, worked hard at a pharmaceutical warehouse so Carlos' mother could stay home with their four children.

By the time he could spell *plantain*, Carlos had fallen in love with baseball. It's easy to do in his home country. For every banana this U.S. territory exports, Puerto Rico seems to produce a baseball star, too.

In 1942, Hiram Bithorn became the first Puerto Rican major leaguer, and there have been more than two hundred since, including Hall of Famers like Roberto Alomar, Orlando Cepeda, and, of course, the great Roberto Clemente.

Wilfredo encouraged young Carlos to work hard at baseball, just like everything else. "Anything worth having is worth working for," Wilfredo would say. So Carlos worked hard at baseball, modeling his game after another Puerto Rican great, Bernie Williams, the New York Yankees' five-time All-Star center fielder.

In June 1995, the Kansas City Royals drafted eighteen-year-old Carlos in the second round out of Fernando Callejos High School, and by 1999, the franchise had anointed him as its starting center fielder and leadoff hitter. He responded by hitting .293 with 22 home runs, 108 RBIs, and 112 runs scored, marking the first time a rookie had totaled 100 RBIs and 100 runs in the same season since Fred Lynn performed that feat in 1975. That fall, Carlos got married and found out on his honeymoon that he had won the American League Rookie of the Year award. Not a bad year, eh?

At that moment, Vegas was probably giving good odds on Carlos reaching the Hall of Fame. He was a Puerto Rican Picasso, and baseball diamonds were his canvas.

But now, in the twilight of his career, what are we to make of Carlos' body of work? Much has happened in between that clouds the perspective. He became a star in Kansas City, a postseason legend in Houston, a hero/goat in New York (depending on whom you speak to), and a rent-a-bat acquisition for San Francisco at the 2011 trade deadline.

This much is obvious: Plenty of players would envy Carlos' career. Through 2011, he had earned six All-Star appearances, three Gold Gloves, and two Silver Slugger awards. He had reached the 100-RBI plateau eight times and eclipsed the 300-home-run mark for his career. He swiped 42 bases in 2004 and smashed 41 homers in 2006. But his career will always be dogged by that most haunting of sports questions: *What if?*

When the New York Mets signed Carlos before the 2005 season, he was the hottest free agent on the market, coming off one of the greatest postseasons in history. The previous fall, after a midseason trade from Kansas City to Houston, he had helped the Astros come within one win of reaching the World Series, hitting .435 with eight homers, 14 RBIs, 21 runs, and 6 stolen bases in 12 playoff games.

Carlos' mega-contract with the Mets made him only the tenth player in major league history at the time to land a $100 million deal. That's a ton of money . . . and a ton of expectations. Carlos took everything in a spiritual stride.

"It's good to have a big house and a nice car, but it's better when you have Jesus Christ in your heart," he said. "He's more important than anything."

New Yorkers, though, are a demanding bunch. Carlos' arrival, along with that of pitching ace Pedro Martinez, had

Carlos Beltran agreed to a two-year deal with St. Louis in late 2011. The next season, he helped the Cardinals knock out the 98-win Washington Nationals in the National League Division Series to reach the NL Championship Series against his former team, San Francisco. (AP Photo/Charlie Riedel)

plenty of Mets fans planning for the franchise's first World Series championship since 1986. But the team's grand visions of annual National League East dominance quickly morphed into maddening mediocrity. While the Mets finished above .500 in four of Carlos' six full seasons in New York, the team made just one playoff appearance (2006).

For his part, though, Carlos mostly dazzled when he played. In six-and-a-half years in New York, he amassed 149 home runs, 208 doubles, 100 stolen bases, and 559 RBIs.

But the trick was keeping him on the field. From 2003 to 2010—during the age span of twenty-six to thirty-three, the prime of his career—Carlos missed an average of 32 games per season. There were oblique strains in 2003 and 2007, a scary outfield collision with teammate Mike Cameron in 2005 (resulting in a facial fracture and a concussion), and a myriad of debilitating knee issues. Thanks to his arthritic joints, he played in just 81 games in 2009 and 64 in 2010.

Fair or not, perhaps the most indelible memory of the Carlos Beltran era for Mets fans came in Game 7 of the 2006 National League Championship Series against St. Louis. Facing a 3–1 deficit with two outs in the bottom of the ninth, Carlos came to the plate with the bases loaded. A single would tie the game. A home run would win it and send the Big Apple into juicy delirium and the Mets to the World Series. But Cardinals closer Adam Wainwright froze Carlos with an 0–2 curveball. Game over.

In 2011, during the final year of Carlos' contract, the struggling Mets shipped him to San Francisco at the trade deadline. After finishing the season with the Giants, Carlos was a free agent. He signed a two-year, $26 million deal with the St. Louis Cardinals, who had lost Albert Pujols to the Los Angeles Angels.

How does Carlos respond to life's big changes? He gets on his knees.

"I pray every day when I wake up and while I'm driving to the ballpark," he says. "Before I go out and play, I try to read the Bible and memorize it and think about it the whole game."

All things considered, the highs have far outnumbered the lows in Carlos' career. He will go down as one of the greatest all-around players in Mets history. And in 2011, healthy for the first time in three years, he played in 142 games between New York and San Francisco and hit an even .300 with 22 home runs.

Through everything, Carlos sees God's fingerprints all over his life . . . which, of course, is something he prays about.

"He's going to put you in different situations to see how you deal with it and what path you're going to take," Carlos says. "I pray for every decision in my life. I can see everything to a point, but God can see farther. I know every decision God makes is perfect. I'm not perfect, but He is."

2012 season update: At age thirty-five, with a history of knee problems, Carlos Beltran can still hit. That much was clear in 2012 when the Puerto Rican star recorded 32 home runs and 97 RBIs in his first season with St. Louis. Helping the Cardinals' offense transition from the Albert Pujols era, Beltran earned his seventh All-Star nomination and, in typical fashion, enjoyed a phenomenal postseason. In 42 playoff at-bats over three series, he collected 15 hits (a .357 average), including six doubles, three home runs, and six RBIs.

5

ADRIAN GONZALEZ:
GONZO FOR GOD

Excitedly, the boys scattered the baseball cards across their bedroom floor without regard for the merchandise's future value on the trading market.

Crease marks? Fuzzy corners? *Who cares!* This was no time to worry about a mint-condition collection. There were bedroom baseball lineups to be picked, for Pete's sake!

Speaking of Pete, he was available on the carpet. You could do a lot worse than Pete Rose, baseball's all-time hit king. But young Adrian Gonzalez always reached for someone else first: Tony Gwynn. As a San Diego area native and a left-hander, Adrian adored Gwynn, another lefty whose .338 lifetime batting average for the hometown Padres punched his ticket into both Cooperstown's and Adrian's hearts.

Usually, Will Clark was drafted next. My, oh my, Will the Thrill sure had a sweet stroke. Then, another lefty: Darryl Strawberry. With his pre-pitch bat waggle, exaggerated leg kick, and powerfully loopy swing, the Straw Man was always a favorite.

On and on it went until Adrian and his two older brothers, David Jr. and Edgar, finished their lineups. Each team had to reflect all nine defensive positions. (Stacking the lineup with Mike Schmidt *and* Wade Boggs—two third basemen—was strictly taboo.)

Out came the plastic bat. Next, the ball—usually a wad of tape or balled-up socks. Finally, the bases . . .

Uh, let's see. How about the bed, the closet door, and that pile of dirty clothes? What about home plate? Aw, heck, let's get started. Just throw something down on the floor.

And batter up!

Once bedroom baseball started, the boys tried to mimic each player's real-life swing. Every square inch of the room was demarcated for the type of hit it produced. The top of the far wall was a home run. There were plenty of those.

Adrian and Edgar's battles, in particular, were epic.

"When I got back from school, they were already playing," recalled David Jr., who is eight years older than Adrian and four years older than Edgar. "Whoever won, they were the champions of the world. When Adrian won, he'd be shouting it all over the house. Edgar would get mad and want to play again. Same thing the other way."

Adrian has come a long way from those halcyon childhood days, bathed as they were in baseball, simplicity, and the SoCal sun. He is now the Boston Red Sox' newly minted superstar, a $154 million slugger who is quickly etching his name into franchise history with his gorgeous swing. After the magnificent season he fashioned in 2011—a .338 batting average that was second best in the major leagues and 213 hits that tied him with Michael Young of Texas for the most in the majors—Adrian is generally acclaimed as one of this generation's greatest hitters.

Just don't expect any of this to faze him. All the hubbub in Hub City elicits little more than a shoulder shrug from this twenty-nine-year-old batsman who's in the prime of his career. Don't let his nonchalance fool you, though. Adrian's levelheaded outlook has as much to do with his deep Christian faith as it does with his mellow personality. He mixes his *SportsCenter*-highlight abilities with genuine Christlike humility as well as anyone in the game today. For Adrian, the dichotomy fits like a well-oiled mitt.

"I don't want to be remembered in baseball," he said. "I want to be remembered as a good witness for Christ."

At this point, Adrian is destined for both.

ALL IN THE FAMILY

Born on May 8, 1982, in San Diego, Adrian always dreamed big. If he wasn't imitating his favorite baseball hero's swing, he was imagining himself as a music star. In one classic family photo, he sported a heavily gelled Mohawk while using a tennis racquet like a Jimi Hendrix Stratocaster. (To this day, family members are still puzzled at what the ski gloves and boots were for.)

Alas, musical stardom never panned out for Adrian. But boy, the kid sure rocked it on the diamond.

Adrian's love for baseball comes from his father, David Sr., who grew up dirt-poor in Ciudad Obregón, a large city in Mexico's arid Sonoran Desert region, where he sold popsicles and ice cream sandwiches to anyone with a parched tongue and a few *pesos*. When he grew older and was asked to help support his family, David Sr. dropped out of high school and started working for an air conditioning company. He was always a good handyman.

But he could also play *béisbol*. He was a big, strong first baseman with huge wrists that required custom-made watches. Maybe that's what happens when you lug AC units up and down stairs all day long.

While those Popeye forearms produced plenty of pop, he was also stealthily fast on the base paths, enough to earn the nickname *El Correcamino*—"The Roadrunner."

David Sr.'s skills are part of Gonzalez family lore. In the days before the San Diego Padres' inaugural major league season in 1969, as the story goes, a Padres scout saw the Gonzalez clan playing baseball during a family reunion in the San Diego area and set up a scrimmage. After Team Gonzalez beat the pro squad, the Padres extended tryout offers to David Sr. and his cousin, Robert Guerra. David Sr. declined for financial reasons, but his passion for the game never waned.

He played for the Mexican national team in the late 1960s and early 1970s and attracted other professional offers. But by then, his business was making more money than Mexican baseball paid.

The family immigrated to Chula Vista, a San Diego suburb a few miles north of the border, prior to Adrian's birth and moved to Tijuana when Adrian was a year old. But the air conditioning business was doing so well that the Gonzalezes could afford to keep a home in both cities. Oftentimes, the family would spend their weekends in Tijuana—Adrian played in elite leagues in Mexico growing up—but would return to their Chula Vista home on Sunday nights since the boys had school in the morning. The consistent border crossings aided Adrian's baseball and bilingual abilities.

As each son came along, David Sr. baptized him into baseball. From his earliest memory, Adrian recalls throwing a tennis ball against the side of his house, glove in hand, eagerly awaiting his older brothers' return from school to play with him.

David Sr. would often take his sons to a nearby field for infield practice—David Jr. at shortstop, Edgar at second, and Adrian at first. Even as an ankle-biter, Adrian wouldn't stand for any patronizing lobs.

"I can catch it!" he'd squeal in protest.

"No you can't," his brothers retorted, laughing.

But sure enough, little Adrian showed a preternatural ability to catch bullets and dig out bouncers.

"He always wanted to be a part of us," David Jr. recalled. "He was always above his age group. We didn't baby him."

As David Sr.'s business took off, he was able to provide his sons with opportunities that he never had growing up. He built an enormous backyard batting cage at their Chula Vista home. That was really cool until one day . . . *crash!* The boys had used the cage so much that a hole had formed in the protective netting. The poor window in the neighbor's house never saw it coming.

For the good of all houses within range, the brothers took up Wiffle ball. But this wasn't just any ol' casual game. When it came to competition, the Gonzalez brothers didn't *do* casual. This was no-holds-barred Wiffle.

At first, Edgar seemed to have the upper hand. So Adrian bought a book on how to throw Wiffle pitches—yes, that's correct; he actually purchased a book specifically designed to improve one's Wiffle pitch arsenal—and developed a wicked curve that Edgar couldn't solve.

"He was always looking for an edge to win," Edgar said.

Baseball was like oxygen for the Gonzalez brothers. When they weren't swinging in the bedroom or the backyard cage, they were playing baseball games on Atari and Nintendo. On vacations, the family would bring bats, balls, and gloves so the boys could practice on the closest field or beach.

Even religion took a backseat to baseball. The Gonzalezes were practicing Catholics, but weekend tournaments often trumped Mass. "God will forgive us if we don't go to church," David Sr. told his boys, "as long as we're playing baseball." Dubious theology, yes, but you catch the drift.

Each brother became a star in his own right. David Jr. was good enough to spark college interest from the University of California Riverside and San Diego State. The Montreal Expos even offered to sign him as an undrafted free agent. He ended up at Point Loma Nazarene University, an NAIA program in San Diego, where he led the team in runs scored (38) as a junior in 1996, played every position during one game as a senior, and graduated with an engineering degree.

Edgar, meanwhile, starred at San Diego State before Tampa Bay drafted him in the thirtieth round in 2000. In 2011, he completed his twelfth professional season with the Fresno Grizzlies, the San Francisco Giants' Triple-A affiliate, where he hit .315 with career highs in home runs (14) and RBIs (82). Even if he never gets back to the majors, Edgar can always say that he played alongside Adrian at Petco Park, appearing in 193 games for the Padres between the 2008 and 2009 seasons.

The best of the Gonzalez bunch, though, was the baby brother. A power-hitting first baseman, Adrian destroyed opposing pitching as a prep star, batting .559 in his final two seasons at Eastlake High School in Chula Vista. As a senior, he hit .645 with 13 home runs and earned Player of the Year honors from the California Interscholastic Federation and the *San Diego Union-Tribune* newspaper.

Later that year, the Florida Marlins drafted him No. 1 overall, making him the first high school infielder since Alex Rodriguez in 1993 to be the top pick. Before Adrian, the only other first baseman selected first since the draft started in 1965 was Ron Blomberg (Yankees) in 1967.

One day after being drafted—only twenty-nine days after his eighteenth birthday—Adrian signed with Florida for $3 million. He splurged on a Cadillac Escalade, but, always the sensible kid, he invested most of his remaining bonus.

Stardom seemed inevitable. But it didn't come easily.

DESTINED FOR GREATNESS

Things started well enough. The Marlins quickly assigned Adrian to their Gulf Coast League rookie affiliate in Melbourne, Florida, where he hit .295 in 53 games and showed a deep hunger to improve.

At night, the Marlins' prized bonus baby would sneak into town to take extra batting practice at a local cage, feeding quarters into the machines like an eager Little Leaguer. When manager Kevin Boles found out, he quickly put the kibosh on it. No overexertion for this future star, thank you.

"I still have my reports on him from back then," Boles said. "I put down 'Franchise-type first baseman. Offensive force. Multiple Gold Glove winner.' "

Call Boles prescient. In 2001, Adrian exploded, hitting .312 with 17 home runs and 103 RBIs in 127 games for the Class A Kane County Cougars in Geneva, Illinois. He won the Midwest League's MVP honors and the Marlins' Organizational Player of the Year award. He continued his power surge in 2002 with 17 homers and 96 RBIs at Double-A Portland (Maine). But that August, he suffered a wrist injury that required offseason surgery and sapped most of his pop the following season, when he hit just .269 with five home runs and 51 RBIs at two different minor league levels.

Worried about Adrian's future power and desperate to make a second-half playoff push, the Marlins packaged him in a July 2003 trade to the Texas Rangers for reliever Ugueth Urbina, who eventually helped wild card Florida shock the mighty 101-win New York Yankees in the World Series that fall.

Suddenly, Adrian had become expendable trade bait—a still-valuable commodity bubble-wrapped in question marks. It was a terribly frustrating year for the twenty-one-year-old.

"There were a lot of times of doubt and wondering what was going to happen," he said.

Ironically, as Adrian's career suddenly entered a stage of whitewater rapids, his love life was enjoying smooth sailing. In January 2003, he married Betsy Perez, his teenage sweetheart. Adrian and Betsy had met at Bonita Vista Middle School in Chula Vista, but it certainly wasn't love at first sight.

"At the beginning, Adrian was always trying to go out with her," Edgar Gonzalez recalled. "She had a boyfriend and was always standoffish."

Eventually, the Gonzalez charm won out. Adrian and Betsy became an item, even though they attended separate high schools. For Betsy's graduation ceremony, Adrian spent some of his signing bonus on a plane that flew overhead towing the message: "I love you, Betsy. . . . Congratulations."

"He was pretty romantic," Edgar said.

Early in the 2003 season, newly married and facing a professional crisis as he struggled at Triple-A Albuquerque, Adrian felt an uneasy emptiness in his heart. He had been attending Baseball Chapel services for a while, but faith in Jesus Christ hadn't yet sprouted in his heart.

Betsy was a believer, though, and the couple's desire to build their marriage on a strong spiritual foundation spurred Adrian. They began attending Bible studies outside the ballpark. Baseball Chapel sermons started penetrating his soul. And in April 2003, he repented and turned to Christ.

"It's been a blessing since," he said.

Adrian's spiritual rebirth didn't immediately resolve his baseball struggles. He made his major league debut with the Rangers on April 18, 2004, but with Mark Teixeira firmly entrenched at first base, Adrian shuttled back and forth between the parent club and the minors three times before Texas shipped him to his beloved Padres in a six-player deal in January 2006.

Adrian finally caught his big break later that year when Ryan Klesko, San Diego's incumbent first baseman, suffered an early season shoulder injury. Adrian grabbed opportunity by the throat, hitting .304 with 24 home runs and 82 RBIs in his first full regular season. The Padres made the playoffs in 2006, and Adrian's slashing swings flummoxed St. Louis pitching at a .357 clip during a four-game National League Division Series loss. Just like that, the Padres had a hometown hero.

"Now, looking back, I'm grateful for everything that happened because it made me a stronger person and made me understand you have to leave it all up to Christ and His path for you," Adrian explained. "If everything would've been gravy and you breeze right through the minor leagues and make it to the big leagues, you don't see the need for God. It really allowed me to see that, no matter what, my focus has to be on God."

In hindsight, the trade that sent Adrian from Texas to San Diego goes down as one of the best in Padres history. With 161 home runs, 501 RBIs, three All-Star selections, and two Gold Gloves in five seasons, he became arguably one of the three greatest position players in franchise history, alongside Hall of Famers Tony Gwynn and Dave Winfield.

Aside from his baseball prowess, Adrian was marketing gold—a well-respected Latino playing in a diverse metropolis just across the Mexican border.

"He was very popular," longtime Padres chaplain Doug Sutherland remembered. "Being Hispanic and [the team being] close to the border, he was a great influence among the people who are Latin. Everybody had a Gonzalez jersey. He was highly thought of in the community."

One of the greatest thrills of Gonzalez's career was playing on the same team as Edgar. "That was a lot of fun," Adrian said of competing with his brother. "It was a dream come true playing in San Diego."

Inevitably, the dream had to end. Baseball economics aren't sympathetic to small-market teams like San Diego, which often can't afford to retain their young stars once they become eligible for free agency. So rather than watch him walk away after the 2011 season and get nothing in return, the Padres traded him to Boston for a trio of highly regarded prospects.

"You don't make a trade like that without knowing pretty much what you're going to get," former Boston manager Terry Francona said. "We gave up a lot of good players for one really good player, but it is nice to see it in person. You read all the scouting reports and certainly you know about him, but when you see him every day, it's pretty exciting."

Welcome to Beantown, Adrian.

FAME, FORTUNE, AND THE FISH BOWL

The proud, old building at 4 Yawkey Way in downtown Boston is not exactly holy ground. But for baseball nuts, it might as well be. This is where the pilgrims sojourn.

Awash in green paint and vivid memories, Fenway Park opened its doors on April 20, 1912—five days after the *Titanic* sank. The revered baseball shrine drips with history like a brimming bowl of clam *chowdah*. Here is where the Sultan of Swat—Babe Ruth—launched his first moon shots, where Lefty Grove added to his trove of pitching victories, and where the double-play combination of Joe Cronin and Bobby Doerr was magic up the middle. It's where the Splendid Splinter—Ted Williams—hit .406 in 1941, where Carl Yastrzemski was Triple Crowned in 1967, and where Carlton Fisk waved it fair in 1975.

The stories this creaky New England cathedral has generated have tiptoed between reality and mythology for generations. From Bridgeport to Bangor, young and old alike tell its tales each year at bars, on fishing piers, and in living rooms. Venerable Fenway, the oldest stadium in the majors, is the nerve center of Red Sox Nation.

And now it's Adrian's personal playground.

Playing in Boston is a far cry from anything Adrian was used to before. Despite his sublime stretch in San Diego, he never achieved top billing on Major League Baseball's marquee. Not even the great Tony Gwynn, his childhood idol, could do that. A mediocre franchise history, small-market budget, near-perfect weather, and too much surf and sand all conspire to keep the Padres in baseball's roadside motel.

Boston, meanwhile, enjoys the penthouse suite. Thanks to the New England Sports Network, a regional cable company that is partially owned by the Red Sox and reaches four million homes in the six-state New England area, the team is flush with cash. Consider: In 2011, the Padres' payroll was a skosh below $46 million. Boston's was $161 million.

On April 15, 2011, Adrian officially tapped into those riches, signing a massive seven-year contract extension that will pay him $21 million a year starting in 2012. That's a lot of beans, even for Beantown.

"Remember," Edgar told his little brother after the deal was completed, "that the money is not yours. It's God's. He gave it to you. It's a bigger stage for you to glorify Him."

"Yeah, I know," Adrian said. His tone wasn't haughty. It simply reflected a heart that was already prepared for such bounty.

Adrian Gonzalez, a sweet-swinging left-hander and a four-time All-Star, was the premier piece in the blockbuster trade between the Red Sox and the Dodgers in August 2012. (AP Photo/Lenny Ignelzi)

"At the end of the day, you're not taking any of that with you," Adrian acknowledged. "When you pass away, God's not going to say, *Oh, that's a great contract you acquired.* He's going to say, *Because of Me, you had that contract, so what did you do with it?* There's nothing I've obtained or done that hasn't been because of Christ."

Still, all that money brings expectations by the truckload. In breezy San Diego, baseball is often an afterthought. In Boston, Red Sox fanaticism borders on clinical. This, after all, is a place that blamed eighty-six years of playoff futility on the fabled curse of a barrel-chested slugger with pipestem legs nicknamed "the Bambino."

When Red Sox Nation pays a superstar that much coinage, it expects results. Everything about Boston's amiable "Next Big Thing" will be scrutinized like never before. Fair or not, Adrian was expected to slay the Yankees single-handedly and ensure Boston's third ticker-tape parade since 2004. But hey, no pressure, right?

"There is *no* pressure," Adrian said straight-faced. "I've said all along, people talk about pressure, but who are you trying to satisfy? If you're trying to make the writers or the front office or certain people happy, then you can put pressure on yourself. But for me, it's being good for Christ, so my statistics don't matter."

Fair enough. But they matter to everyone else in Boston.

Entering the 2011 season, the city was abuzz with talk of what Adrian could do with Fenway's cozy corners: *If he posted great numbers in cavernous Petco Park, just think what he could do to the Green Monster!*

Can you blame them? Adrian is a 6-foot, 2-inch,

225-pound hitting marvel who uses his lovely-as-a-Monet stroke to spray the ball to all fields.

Adrian's new teammates got caught up in wide-eyed curiosity, too. Early in the season, they would often stop and stare at the novelty and beauty of his pregame batting-practice swings.

"He's so fun to watch," Red Sox catcher Jarrod Saltalamacchia exclaimed. "He's so smooth. It's just a beautiful swing. Number one is obviously still Griffey," he said, referring to Ken Griffey Jr. "Griffey's swing was the most beautiful swing ever made, but Gonzo's is right there, man."

Still, considering the fact that Adrian underwent right shoulder surgery in October 2010, only extreme optimists would have predicted what actually transpired in 2011. By the All-Star break, he was unquestionably the best hitter in baseball, leading the majors with a .354 batting average, 77 RBIs, 29 doubles, and 214 total bases. His 128 hits at that point were the most by any player in Red Sox history—more than Jimmie Foxx, Nomar Garciaparra, Manny Ramirez, Jim Rice, Carl Yastrzemski, and, yes, even the great Ted Williams.

"He can ruin your day really quick," said San Francisco reliever Jeremy Affeldt, who faced Adrian when the latter played for San Diego.

While Gonzalez has always possessed power, it was his first-half batting average that induced awe. At the break, it was a whopping 70 points higher than his career average and 50 points higher than his single-season best of .304 in 2006.

You can attribute that to "smaller ballparks" like Fenway, as Adrian modestly does. Or you can say he benefitted from hitting in a lineup that featured names like Ellsbury, Ortiz,

Pedroia, and Youkilis. But the fact is, Adrian is maturing as a hitter, too, and the great ones perform on the game's biggest stages. They don't call him A-Gone for nothing.

"He uses the whole field," Francona said. "A lot of power hitters, like David Ortiz [Boston's designated hitter], they're going to take some of the field away from him. That's okay because that's the way [David] hits. Gonzo can manipulate the bat. You don't see that with power hitters that much. He can loft the ball to left field. Sometimes, it looks like a right-handed hitter, which is impressive."

The fireworks continued at the All-Star Game in Phoenix, Adrian's fourth straight Midsummer Classic. In the Home Run Derby, he launched 30 bombs and finished second to the Yankees' Robinson Cano. In the All-Star Game itself, his blast to right-center off Phillies star Cliff Lee accounted for the American League's lone run in a 5–1 loss.

Adrian tailed off a bit in the second half of the season, losing the batting title in the last week of the season to Miguel Cabrera. He finished 2011 batting .338, despite being one of the few lefties in the game today who warrant a defensive shift from opposing teams. Even though the Red Sox swooned in September and lost a nine-game lead in the AL wild card race to Tampa Bay, Adrian's long-term deal gives BoSox fans hope for another run at the Yankees.

"Everybody was just going crazy over him in Boston," said Dennis Eckersley, the Hall of Fame closer turned Red Sox TV analyst on the New England Sports Network.

While fame and fortune have kicked down Adrian's front door, his Christian faith has steadied him. He challenges himself by reading C.S. Lewis and fights pride by studying

C.J. Mahaney's book, *Humility: True Greatness*.

"He's really unimpressed with fame," said Doug Sutherland, the Padres' chaplain. "He shies away from it. He doesn't like to talk about it. If you try to talk about something, he'll change the subject. He knows where it belongs."

Adrian knows scripture and even injects biblical reminders into his at-bats. Every so often, he steps out of the batter's box and eyes his bat, a 35-inch, 32.5-ounce piece of lumber from the Trinity Bat Company. It's more than a between-pitches habit. His bat is inscribed with "PS27:1," a reference to his favorite Bible verse, Psalm 27:1: *The LORD is my light and my salvation—whom shall I fear? The LORD is the stronghold of my life—of whom shall I be afraid?*

Adrian is the antithesis of the stereotypical, modern-day superstar. He is quiet and unassuming. He looks you in the eye when speaking to you. And he's a bit of a homebody. Nightlife isn't his thing. He and Betsy "just like to hang out at home, hang out with our dogs, and maybe cook up a meal," he said.

"He's very easygoing, almost a little bit of a disarming figure," Red Sox chaplain Bland Mason commented. "You expect to have this giant personality with his skills, but he's pretty laid-back."

Fishbowl, schmishbowl.

A LIGHT IN BOSTON

"Watch this."

Adrian's eyes dance with mischievousness. It's July 2011, and Boston is in Baltimore for a three-game weekend series against its AL East foe. Game time is still three hours away, and Adrian wants to display a fun little clubhouse ritual he has.

"Jacoby!" he yells.

His teammate, All-Star center fielder Jacoby Ellsbury, doesn't respond. He's talking to a team public relations assistant.

Adrian tries again: "Jake!"

Ellsbury looks over.

"Say it loud and proud," Adrian says noisily. "Who's the man?"

"Je-*SUS*!" Jacoby bellows.

Adrian grins, satisfied. He explains that Miles McPherson, his pastor at San Diego's Rock Church, near his offseason home in La Jolla, does the same thing with the congregation during sermons.

"So I had Jacoby listen to it, and he loves it," Adrian says. "So now he'll yell it at me, and I'll yell it at him."

Baseball clubhouses aren't exactly church choir lofts. Foul language, raunchy humor, and lewd music are often the soundtrack *du jour* of locker rooms. In this dark environment, Adrian winsomely shines the light of Jesus.

His teammates, by all accounts, have responded at every stop. In San Diego, he once used his bilingual abilities to encourage a Spanish-speaking teammate to attend chapel ("If Adrian hadn't brought him, I don't think he'd be coming," Sutherland said), and he also helped save another teammate's marriage by pointing him to Sutherland for counseling.

"From that, this couple became Christians and have a great walk with the Lord," Sutherland said. "That's the kind of influence Adrian has. He's watching. He'll get guys to come to chapel and get counsel and encourage them. He's an influencer in that way. He's not aggressive in the sense of making people uncomfortable with Christianity. With his success, people listen, but they also listen because of his character."

After Adrian met Mason during his first Red Sox spring training in 2011, he immediately asked the Boston chaplain what his spiritual vision for the team was and offered to lead Bible studies on road trips. During the first half of the season, he led his new Christian teammates in a book study of Mahaney's *Sex, Romance, and the Glory of God*. (The previous year in San Diego, he led a book study of Jerry Bridges' *The Pursuit of Holiness*.)

During the 2011 season, he also helped organize Boston's first Faith Night in at least thirty years. Adrian, Saltalamacchia, outfielder J.D. Drew, and reliever Daniel Bard all shared their testimonies with the crowd after a game.

Adrian's presence has been "a big uplift," Saltalamacchia said. "That's kind of where we struggled as a team [before]. We've had some guys who have been in the faith, but Bible studies have been four guys or three guys. When he came in, we talked about it, and . . . he's delivered every bit of it. He's getting Bible studies on the road, he's getting Bible studies at home, and he's getting Faith Night in Boston. He's different, man—he's different than anybody else."

"He's done more than any other player that I've been around," Mason added. "He's earned instant credibility, and he's just a consistent guy. He doesn't shove Christ down people's throats, but he wants to share with all his teammates. He's a leader in the clubhouse, both as a player and a Christian."

Adrian is active in the community, too. In August 2008,

he launched the Adrian & Betsy Gonzalez Foundation, which helps underprivileged youth. And in 2011, he donated a thousand dollars to Habitat for Humanity for every home run he hit. He has been involved with several other San Diego area charities, and he's planning to expand his generosity into New England.

AN EXAMPLE TO FOLLOW

Who knows . . . right now, somewhere in Boston, a trio of fun-loving brothers could be playing bedroom baseball with Adrian Gonzalez trading cards. If so, here's a tip, kids: Don't worry about bending those card corners. Just mimic this man—both his swing and his faith. He is greatly blessed by God and greatly blessing others.

"God has put me in a situation where I have a big platform to profess Christ to people, so I've got to take advantage," Adrian said. "He's given me abilities to play this game, and I'm grateful for that. I do the best I can with them, and in return, try to be the best disciple I can for Him."

2012 season update: Adrian Gonzalez is hoping to rebound after a year that, by his lofty standards, was disappointing. Gonzalez, who started the year in Boston after signing a huge seven-year, $154 million contract in April 2011, hit .299 and drove in 108 runs. But his power numbers suffered (18 home runs, .463 slugging percentage overall) after the mega-trade in August that sent him to the Los Angeles Dodgers. Gonzalez also missed the All-Star Game roster for the first time since 2007. But he is considered one of baseball's elite first basemen and should thrive with a full season in the Dodgers' vaunted lineup.

6

JOSH HAMILTON:
BASEBALL'S BAT MAN COMES
BACK FROM THE BRINK

Yankee Stadium in New York City has witnessed its share of historic events.

Babe Ruth hit the first home run in the ballpark on Opening Day in 1923. Lou Gehrig, after playing 2,130 consecutive games and being diagnosed with a deadly illness, delivered his "Luckiest Man on the Face of the Earth" speech in 1939. Pitcher Don Larsen threw a perfect game during the 1956 World Series. Roger Maris hit his sixty-first home run to break Ruth's record for most dingers in a season. One-handed pitcher Jim Abbott tossed a no-hitter in these fabled confines in 1993.

But perhaps no performance was more awe-producing than when Texas Rangers slugger Josh Hamilton stepped into the batter's box for the 2008 Home Run Derby. On baseball's biggest stage, the first-year All-Star came up big. No, make that huge.

From his first swing, the people packed into the stadium knew they were witnessing something special.

"Are you getting this?" a fan asked his buddy, who was videotaping the action on his cell phone.

"I am," his friend shouted back. "This is big time."

The rules for the Home Run Derby are simple. A player doesn't have to swing at every pitch. But if he does swing, the ball had better leave the yard. Any swing that doesn't produce a home run counts as an out. Ten outs and the round is over.

Some of baseball's most powerful hitters have left the batter's box with a goose egg. That wasn't the case for Josh.

Bending his knees a couple of times and breathing deep to relax, Josh sent ball after ball into the dark New York sky.

One, two.

Teammate Ian Kinsler ran over to wipe Josh's face with a towel after he crushed his second home run at 502 feet. The two shared a laugh before Josh got back to work.

Three, four, five, six, seven, eight.

Almost immediately, New York's fickle-yet-intelligent fans started chanting his name.

"Ham-il-ton, Ham-il-ton, Ham-il-ton!"

The bat became a blur in his hands. *Nine, ten, eleven.*

With every swing of his arms and snap of his wrists, Josh hammered another ball into the stratosphere. Low pitch. *Smack.* A towering home run into the second deck of right field. *Number twelve.* High pitch. *Crack.* A line drive home run that zoomed over the fence into a fan's glove. *Number thirteen.*

Josh smiled at his pitcher. Being an All-Star and hitting in Yankee Stadium may have been new to him, but seventy-one-year-old Clay Council was a familiar face. Council often threw batting practice for Josh during summer baseball when he was a teen in North Carolina. Now Council was watching Josh live up to all the promise he saw in the youngster years before.

Fourteen, fifteen, sixteen. Pretty soon Josh's opponents turned into cheerleaders. David "Big Papi" Ortiz laughed and pointed as yet another ball jetted over the fence. *Seventeen, eighteen, nineteen.*

Ridiculous. Like guided missiles, every ball found its target in the right field bleachers. Pretty soon Josh started laughing. Nobody had ever hit like this before. *Twenty, twenty-one, twenty-two.*

"What's the record?" a fan said.

"I have no idea," his friend answered.

The answer was 24. Bobby Abreu set that mark in the first round of 2005's Home Run Derby in Detroit's Comerica Park.

But it wasn't just Josh's total that amazed. It was the magnitude of his drives. Three of his home runs sailed over 500 feet—the longest estimated at a massive 518 feet.

Yankee Stadium started feeling like a party. Fans sensed history was taking place. Competitors shook their heads and smiled. Would it ever end? At one point, Josh hit thirteen home runs in a row. *Twenty-three, twenty-four, twenty-five!*

Rangers teammate Milton Bradley ran up and gave the slugger a little back massage. Josh was hot. Incredibly hot. Fans began bowing down to Josh in mock worship.

He still had two outs left. *Twenty-six, twenty-seven, twenty-eight.* Finally, his last two hits fell short of the fence. Fellow All-Star Michael Young gave Josh a hug. Sportswriters started saying fans had just witnessed twenty of the most exciting minutes in the history of baseball.

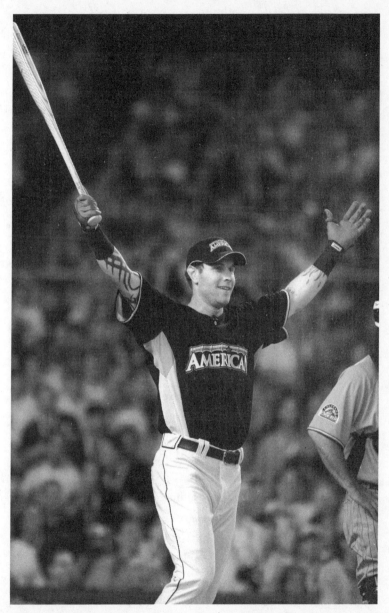

Josh Hamilton's 28 home runs in the first round of the All-Star Home Run Derby still stands as a Major League record. (AP Photo/Kathy Willens)

Before walking into Yankee Stadium on July 14, 2008, Josh was a relatively unknown center fielder for the Rangers playing in his first full major league season. Stepping out of the batter's box, Josh effectively introduced himself to the baseball world. Actually, maybe it's better to say he *reintroduced* himself to baseball.

A long battle with drug and alcohol addiction had nearly erased Josh from baseball's memory. With twenty-eight swings, Josh announced he was back.

But more important to Josh than the media attention was the opportunity to talk about the difference Jesus Christ had made in his life. Before, his life had been all about baseball. Now it focused on Jesus.

ONE GOAL

Just nine years before this historic night, baseball was abuzz with talk about Josh. As a 6-foot, 4-inch, 205-pound senior at Athens Drive High School in North Carolina, Josh was a can't-miss prospect. A five-tool player.

He could play outfield, first base, or pitch. He hit for power and still had a stunning batting average. And his arm in the outfield made opposing coaches think twice before trying to score a runner from second base.

During his senior year, Josh hit .529 with 13 home runs and 35 RBIs in 25 games. He struck out just seven times all year, while drawing 26 walks. His speed in the outfield allowed him to track down would-be base hits in the gap. He also stole 20 bases.

And pitching? His 95-mph fastball baffled hitters and amazed professional scouts. Josh tallied a 7–1 record his senior year with 91 strikeouts in just 56 innings.

At some games, more than fifty scouts would crowd together to watch the two-time North Carolina Player of the Year show off his talents on the diamond.

Not that Josh was a showoff. Sure, he knew he was the best player on the field every time his size-19 cleats stepped onto the turf. But he stayed humble and didn't mock the opposing team.

It was Josh's humility that most impressed Dan Jennings, the Tampa Bay Devil Rays' director of scouting in 1999. That spring, Jennings traveled to Raleigh to watch Josh play in a home game for Athens Drive. Nearly sixty scouts watched wide-eyed as Josh crushed a home run well over four hundred feet.

"But that wasn't the amazing thing," Jennings said. "After [Hamilton] returns to the dugout, he comes back out and serves as the batboy for his teammates. And there was this mentally challenged kid [on the team], and Josh was treating him like his best friend."

Josh and Ashley Pittman were friends. Pittman had Down syndrome. At first, a high school baseball star and special education student might have seemed an unlikely pair. But both shared a love for baseball. Pittman worked as the team batboy, and Josh was impressed with his dedication to the game. Pittman rarely missed a practice, never missed a game, and always came looking professional in his team uniform.

The two often ate lunch together. Pittman called Josh by his nickname, "Hambone," and Josh referred to his friend as "Big Ash."

Big Ash was devastated when Athens Drive lost in the state semifinals during Josh's senior year, but the Jaguars'

coach had a surprise at the year-end banquet. He was starting a special award to honor the player who best showed
what the qualities of compassion and sportsmanship were all
about.

The first winner of the Ashley Pittman Award was . . . of
course, Josh Hamilton.

"I've gotten a lot of trophies over the years, but the Ashley
Pittman Memorial Award is special to me," Josh wrote in his
autobiography, *Beyond Belief.* "It's still prominently displayed
in a case at my parents' house. More than any other trophy
or newspaper clipping, it reminds me of who I was and how
I lived at that point in my life."

Talent. Statistics. Size. Character. It was no surprise that
Tampa Bay chose Josh with the first overall pick in the 1999
draft.

More than fifty family members, friends, and reporters
were gathered at the Hamiltons' home on June 2 when Josh
got the call from Jennings. With his selection, Josh became
the first high school player to go number one since Alex Rodriguez went first in 1993.

"We've watched him for a long time," Tampa Bay general
manager Chuck LaMar said. "Josh Hamilton withstood every
test that we gave him, whether it be his performance on the
field or questions we asked. . . . We feel like he's the number-
one player in this draft."

Josh felt like he was the top player, too. It wasn't pride.
Josh had worked hard to get the most of his God-given abilities, and he was ready to make his mark on the major leagues.

After learning he was the first selection, he hugged his
mom and dad. His father, Tony, had coached him from

before he could attend school. His parents had rarely missed a game, often driving hundreds of miles to make it for the first pitch.

Then the giddy eighteen-year-old walked into his front yard for his first press conference. When asked how he envisioned his career, Josh replied: "I'm thinking three years in the minors, then fifteen years in the big leagues." Josh paused for a moment before adding, "Then I'll have to wait five years to get into the Hall of Fame."

Everyone laughed, but Josh really wasn't kidding. He'd always felt special on a baseball field. He'd always had one goal—being a baseball All-Star.

People recognized Josh's talent when he was very young. He was just six when a scout came to watch him for the first time. Okay, maybe the word *scout* isn't quite right.

Josh was practicing with his brother Jason's eleven- and twelve-year-old team. Despite being half their age, Josh kept up with and often surpassed the older players with his baseball skills. The president of the Tar Heel League needed to decide what to do with the precocious elementary student who played like a middle schooler.

Playing with kids his own age certainly wasn't a challenge. Josh could hit farther and throw faster than any of his teammates. His skills were so advanced that other parents asked if Josh could be moved up because they were worried their sons could be hurt by one of Josh's hits or throws.

"Their fears became real in our first game," Josh wrote in *Beyond Belief*. "I fielded a ball at shortstop and threw it across the infield as hard as I could to get the runner. There was a problem, though—the first baseman either never saw the ball or didn't react fast enough to catch it. He stood there with his glove turned the wrong way as the ball smacked into his chest. He went down like a sniper got him. . . . I felt terrible."

Shortly after, Josh was promoted to his brother's team. He turned seven on May 21, 1988, making him five years younger than his opponents.

But his talent bridged the gap. Batting ninth, Josh made his presence felt on the Hamilton Machine Little League team by hitting his first real home run. Just two weeks after Josh turned seven, a twelve-year-old pitcher learned an important lesson: Don't throw Josh a fastball over the plate. The youngster cracked it over the left-center field fence.

It was the first of many home runs to come.

ON THE RIGHT PATH

When Josh hits a baseball, it just sounds different. The speed of his swing combined with the impact of the bat draws *oohs* and *ahs* from onlookers.

After Josh's post-draft celebration, he jumped into the car with Jason and went to the high school field to hit some baseballs.

A family with two young boys lived in a house beyond center field. They often watched Josh play games or take batting practice. On that evening, the father and his two boys walked up to the backstop.

"I didn't expect you'd be out here tonight," the dad said. "But I can always tell when you're hitting. It just sounds different inside my house when your bat hits the ball. From the first crack of the bat today, my boys said, 'Josh is hitting.' "

Josh's hitting impressed the Devil Rays as well. They signed

him to a contract that included a $3.96 million signing bonus—
a record at the time for a No. 1 pick. And despite the fact that
Josh had a fastball that nearly reached triple digits, Tampa Bay
wanted him to play outfield so he could hit every day.

With the major league season already underway, Josh
was assigned to Tampa Bay's Class A Rookie League team in
Princeton, West Virginia.

Josh had just turned eighteen, so he hopped in the car
with his parents and drove to Princeton. In his first game, on
June 19, 1999, Josh hit his first professional home run.

With his mom making sure her son had clean clothes and
remained well fed, and his dad talking through at-bats and
situations, Josh stayed fully focused on baseball.

Sure, the other rookies didn't have their parents traveling
with them. But the other players probably weren't as close to
their families and didn't have the means (i.e., nearly $4 mil-
lion) that allowed them to come along.

Josh lived up to his hype in Princeton. In 56 games, he hit
.347 with 10 home runs, 48 RBIs, and 49 runs scored.

Tampa Bay bumped Josh up to Class A Hudson Valley in
New York in August. Instead of playing against rookies, he
now faced second- and third-year professionals.

Hudson Valley was in the middle of a playoff race, and
Josh was placed in the middle of its lineup. After struggling at
first, he turned things around and helped the Renegades win
the New York-Penn League championship by hitting .429
with two home runs and eight RBIs in the playoffs.

His rookie year had been a success. But during the season and back at home, he felt something was missing in his
life. He had occasionally attended church with his aunt and

uncle growing up, so he knew something about God. When he returned to North Carolina, he visited his aunt and uncle's house to discuss some spiritual issues that he was wrestling with. He ended up praying to accept Jesus Christ into his life.

"I got saved when I was eighteen years old," Josh said. "I accepted Christ in my aunt and uncle's living room. But I didn't know how to grow spiritually. I didn't know how to get in the Word. I didn't know how to pray like I needed to. I didn't know how to fellowship with other people. I tell people that Satan comes after you a lot harder when you're a child of God."

Everything seemed to be going according to Josh's plan professionally when he reported to Tampa Bay for spring training in 2000. He had a strong spring and was assigned to the Class A Charleston RiverDogs in the South Atlantic League. Many of these players were more experienced, with three or four years of minor league baseball under their belts.

Again, Josh's parents came with him. They were at every home game, even showing up early to watch batting practice. They traveled with the team for road games, staying in the team's hotel. And Josh continued to flourish. Surrounded by people he loved and playing the game he loved, he was named co-MVP of the South Atlantic League. He was also honored as the Player of the Year in Class A baseball, and the Devil Rays named him their Minor League Player of the Year. Check out his stats: a .301 batting average, 13 home runs, 61 RBIs, and 62 runs scored.

Going into the 2001 campaign, Josh appeared to be ready to make the leap to the Big Show. If he wasn't going to be with the big league club to start the season, he certainly seemed destined to join the Devil Rays soon. But in a split second, everything changed.

ACCIDENTS AND BAD DECISIONS

On March 3, 2001, Josh and his parents were driving to their home in Bradenton, Florida, following an exhibition game. His mom, Linda, was behind the wheel of the family's Chevy Silverado, while Josh half-dozed in the front seat and his dad sat in the back. As the family drove through the intersection of Victory Road and U.S. 301, a dump truck ran a red light and barreled into the driver's side of the pickup.

Josh saw the whole thing about to happen and reached over to pull his mom to him. The impact sent the Hamiltons spinning in their truck for about a hundred feet.

The family was rushed to Memorial Hospital. Linda had neck pain. Tony was treated for a skull fracture. Josh had some pain in his back but was untreated and went back to spring training the next morning.

Over the next few days, however, the pain got worse. Doctors were baffled. They performed MRIs and CAT scans to diagnose the problem. Prescription painkillers didn't help much. Physically, everything looked fine, but Josh felt anything but okay.

With his parents recovering in North Carolina and playing baseball not an option, Josh started hanging out in a tattoo parlor.

He had shown up that spring with six tattoos. His first ink featured his nickname "Hambone" in all capital letters around his right bicep. Soon the word "Hammer" graced his other arm. He didn't have many friends in Florida, and without baseball, he didn't have anything to do, so pretty soon Kevin and Bill in the tattoo parlor became his "friends."

Josh would show up at the tattoo parlor and spend hours

in the chair—sometimes getting two or three tattoos in a day.

The nineteen-year-old had six tattoos when his parents went to North Carolina. When they returned a few weeks later, he had twenty-one.

With doctors not finding a cause for his pain, Josh felt pressure to play. He was sent to Double-A Orlando to start the season, but he struggled. In 23 games, his stats were the worst of his professional career. He hit just .180 with no home runs and only four RBIs.

To make things worse, Josh tore his hamstring muscle running to first base in the first month of the season and was sent down to Charleston for an injury-rehabilitation assignment.

Josh's leg healed, but his back never felt right, so Tampa had him see a specialist in California. After doing an MRI, the doctor pointed to a white spot near the spine. It was a pocket of fluid pushing against a nerve. The doctor gave Josh a cortisone shot on the exact spot.

"He plunged the needle into my spine till it felt like it was grinding on bone," Josh said. "But as soon as the needle was removed, the pain was gone. I've never thanked a man so many times in my life."

Sporting a healthy back and renewed optimism, Josh headed into the 2002 season with something to prove. According to his timeline, this was the year he was supposed to break into the majors. Shortly after Christmas, he went to Florida to start training. He knew he had to make up for a disappointing year in 2001.

But one afternoon, he injured his back while training. The next morning he could barely get out of bed. Spring training was less than two weeks away. Depressed and disappointed, Josh returned to the comfort of the tattoo parlor.

His collection of ink continued to grow. Soon, he had a total of twenty-six tattoos. After hanging at the parlor one afternoon, Kevin and Bill asked Josh if he wanted to go out when the shop closed. Without thinking, he immediately said yes.

They took him to a strip club and ordered Josh a beer. He was still too young to legally drink and had never consumed alcohol before, but he downed that beer and a few more. Later, the trio went to Kevin's house, where Josh was offered some cocaine.

A little drunk and not thinking straight, Josh inhaled the drug.

"I had a lot of 'firsts' that night," Josh said. "[The cocaine] gave the adrenaline rush that I wasn't getting by playing baseball."

At first, when Josh was playing baseball, he didn't do drugs. But like in so many cases, soon the drugs took over. For the next three-and-a-half years, drugs and alcohol ruled Josh's life.

Despite being plunged into a personal darkness, the light of his talent shined through from time to time.

Playing Class A ball for Bakersfield, California, during 2002, Josh produced a few highlights that have become things of legend. One evening, he hit an opposite-field home run in Sam Lynn Ballpark that smashed a digital display so hard that it stopped working—kind of like in the movie *The Natural*. Years later, the display still hadn't been fixed and was covered by a banner that promoted the team's website.

Josh also described a mammoth home run he hit that traveled 549 feet and landed in the Kern River. And another time, Josh showed his arm was still a weapon when he caught a fly ball on the warning track and threw to home plate, nailing a runner who had tagged up at third and tried to score.

But Bakersfield was also the first place Josh used drugs during the season. After 56 games, his numbers weren't bad—he hit .301 with nine home runs, 44 RBIs, and 23 runs scored. Elbow pain caused Josh's season to end early. Surgery in Alabama and rest in North Carolina cured the elbow pain, but not the drug problem.

Josh was using cocaine nearly every day while rehabilitating his injury with the Triple-A Durham Bulls. He knew there was a possibility of being randomly drug tested, but even when he was asked to do one, he remained in denial. The test came back positive, and Josh was suspended from baseball for the first time.

Subsequent failed tests led to even longer suspensions until on March 19, 2004, Josh was suspended from baseball for one year for failing to comply with the MLB drug policy. Another failed drug test in August led to additional penalties.

In all, Josh played no professional baseball from the end of the 2002 season through most of 2006. Instead, he fell deeper into the darkness of drug addiction.

Not that everything was bleak in his life. During streaks of sobriety, he struck up a relationship with former high school classmate Katie Chadwick.

"Everybody knew who Josh was in high school," Katie said. "Everybody had a lot of respect for him, because he never did anything wrong."

Three years after graduating from high school, Josh was doing plenty of things wrong, but he called her out of the blue. She agreed to let him come to her house, and they ended up dating for three months. They broke things off but got back together in July 2004. Five months later, they were married.

Josh was attending Alcoholics Anonymous meetings and had convinced himself and Katie that his addictions were behind him. He had a slipup in January, but then on his twenty-fourth birthday, Josh went on a bender that led to a series a relapses.

Josh pulled himself together when the couple's first daughter, Sierra, was born on August 22, 2005. (Katie had another daughter from a previous relationship.) But three days later, Josh went to Walgreens to pick up his wife's prescription and ended up at a bar instead.

Over the next six weeks, he spent more than $100,000 on drugs.

By this time, Josh had turned to crack cocaine to get the high he used to get from the powder form of the drug. But while the highs were higher, the lows were lower.

Numerous times, Josh felt as if he might die—like his heart might thump its way out of his chest. He was never violent with Katie, but his erratic behavior caused her to get a restraining order against him. Trips to the emergency room weren't uncommon. Almost all of his nearly $4 million signing bonus was gone.

His life spiraled down until one night Josh found himself high, out of gas, and walking down a two-lane road.

"I was a shell of a human, a soulless being," Josh said. "I had stripped myself of self-respect and lost my ability to feel love or hope or joy or even pain."

On October 1, 2005, Josh showed up at his grandmother Mary Holt's house . . . at around two in the morning. He weighed 180 pounds and was almost unrecognizable.

"I was a wreck—dirty, twitchy, and barely coherent," Josh said. Granny's house had always been a place of refuge for Josh growing up. He'd even kissed Granny, as Josh affectionately called her, on the cheek before playing every baseball game growing up. Now, when he had nowhere else to turn, he went to his grandmother's. She fed him and tucked him into bed.

Within a couple of days, Josh was using crack again—this time in Granny's house. After just five days under her roof, the seventy-two-year-old had seen enough. She confronted Josh in the hall.

Of course, Josh had seen and heard it all. He'd been in and out of eight rehabilitation centers, spent days on counselors' couches, and talked for hours with his father, mother, and wife. But there was something in the way that Granny looked at him with a mixture of sorrow and anger that pierced Josh's heart.

"I went back in the room where I'd just been using drugs, grabbed a Bible, and the first verse I read was James 4:7," Josh said, referring to the verse that says: "Humble yourselves before God. Resist the devil, and he will flee from you" (NLT).

At that moment, Josh recommitted his life to Christ. Unlike the first time he prayed to accept Christ, this time he followed through with action. His life began to change as he started reading his Bible, praying, and going to church with his aunt and uncle. Then a few weeks later, on the advice of her pastor, Katie called Josh and told him she forgave him.

BEING SECOND

After more than twenty-four years of putting himself first in his life, someone new was on the throne: Jesus Christ.

Josh started living and eating right. And God began restoring everything that Josh had nearly destroyed. He quickly gained back the fifty pounds of muscle he'd lost. His family rallied to his side. He reconciled with his wife. He started working—good, honest work with his brother's tree service.

Then on June 20, 2006, Josh got the call reinstating him to Major League Baseball.

Amazingly, after abusing his body for years, his skills hadn't diminished. He played 15 games for Hudson Valley that summer—the same Class A team he'd played for in 1999—with solid results. He hit .260 and scored seven runs.

One day that December, when he was trimming trees for his brother, Josh learned that the Cincinnati Reds had acquired him through the Rule 5 draft.

Instead of languishing in the minor leagues like he probably would've done with the Rays, guidelines in the Rule 5 draft required the Reds to give him the opportunity to make the big league club. And Josh wasn't about to ruin his second chance.

Josh became one of the Reds' best hitters in spring training. He batted .403 and made Cincinnati's roster as the fourth outfielder behind Adam Dunn, Ken Griffey Jr., and Ryan Freel.

On Opening Day, Josh received nearly as big an ovation as Griffey. The fans were immediately drawn to him and his story of overcoming addiction. Josh has said many times that standing on a major league field again—with his family, his parents, and his wife's family in the stands and everybody on their feet—nearly brought him to tears.

But he wanted to be a professional, so he fought back the lump in his throat. Like Tom Hanks said in the movie *A League of Their Own,* "There's no crying in baseball."

Josh Hamilton started his major league career in Cincinnati in 2007. After moving to Texas in 2008, he put up All-Star numbers—including hitting .285 with 43 home runs and 128 RBIs during the 2012 season. (AP Photo/Charles Rex Arbogast)

A week into the season, Josh got his first start and re-warded the Reds with his first major league hit—a home run. By the end of the month, Josh was named National League Rookie of the Month.

"Baseball is third in my life right now, behind my re-lationship with God and my family," Josh said at the time. "Without the first two, baseball isn't even in the picture. Be-lieve me, I know."

The twenty-six-year-old rookie hit nearly .300 in his first season. He did end up on the disabled list twice during the year, once for a stomach ailment and once for a sprained wrist. He played eleven games at Triple-A Louisville, but he stayed clean the whole time—much in part due to Cincinnati manager Jerry Narron's brother, Johnny.

Johnny had coached Josh when he was a teenager in North Carolina. The Reds hired the faithful man of God as their video coordinator and gave him the extra responsibility of keeping Josh accountable on the road.

Proving he could play at the big league level, Josh ended the 2007 season with a .290 batting average, 19 home runs, 47 RBIs, and 25 runs scored.

That offseason, though, Cincinnati traded Josh to Texas. The Rangers needed power in the outfield, and Cincinnati needed pitching. Johnny Narron came along, too, as an as-sistant hitting coach.

Texas fans and his new teammates immediately em-braced Josh. He responded with monster numbers. Batting third for the Rangers, just ahead of Milton Bradley, Josh had 95 RBIs by the 2008 All-Star break.

In his first full major league season, Josh was voted onto

the All-Star team and made history at the Home Run Derby.

Before the derby, Katie prayed that Josh would hit at least one home run. He did much better than that. A lot of people were praying that night, including Josh and Council, who knelt down and prayed for God to be with them before stepping on the field for the first round.

And God answered big-time. All people remember from that July night in Yankee Stadium were Josh's 28 bombs in the first round. They don't remember that Justin Morneau beat Josh 5–3 in the finals. But Josh didn't care about losing—he'd already won because his story was being told on TV screens around the world.

"God has given me such a platform to share what He's done in my life," Josh said. While he was in one of the darkest, most drug-riddled parts of his life, he said, "My wife was telling me that God was going to allow me to get back into baseball. But it wasn't going to be about baseball. It was going to be about sharing how He brought me through the storm."

Josh stayed healthy the entire season, notching some impressive statistics. He hit .304 with 32 home runs, 130 RBIs, and 98 runs scored.

In the offseason, Josh wanted to prepare for an even better season in 2009. He went to Arizona to work out a month before spring training. But on January 21, 2009, he fell into old habits. Josh went into a restaurant that had a bar and ordered a drink.

"I was out there for three weeks and stopped praying, stopped doing my devotions, stopped reading the Word, stopped fellowshipping with my accountability partner," Josh said. "Doing all those things that had got me to where I was.

I thought I could have one drink. And that thought doesn't work out too well with me. One leads to about twenty, and I don't remember half the stuff I do. . . . Immediately, it hit my heart why I'd done those things, and it's because I took God out of first position."

Josh woke up the next morning and immediately called his wife and told her what happened. He called the Texas Rangers. He called Major League Baseball.

News of Josh's escapade didn't surface for seven months, but when it did, the revelations included several rather risqué photos of him and three young women in the bar. Josh didn't shy away from the controversy of being an outspoken Christian who had just shown up in some compromising photos. He addressed it head-on.

"I'm embarrassed about it for my wife, Katie, for my kids, and for the organization," Josh wrote in a press release. "I'm not perfect. It's an ongoing struggle, and it's real. It's amazing how these things can creep back in. But I am human, and I have struggles."

Josh flew home right after the incident in January to get things right with his wife and with God. For her part, Katie knew things would be okay the moment Josh came in the house.

"When he walked in the door, and I [saw] how broken and repentant and remorseful he was, and how he was so upset at himself for the sin and for hurting me, I was just encouraged because I was looking at a transformed man," she said. "It just made it so easy to extend that grace to him again."

In the past when had Josh relapsed, his attitude was, *Oh well, I might as well keep doing it.* But now Josh was different. He was committed to God, to his family, and to staying clean.

He redoubled his efforts to keep Christ first in his life through a multilayered support system that was described by *The Dallas Morning News* as "rooted in his Christian beliefs and his rigorous daily devotions. Its primary components are his wife, his parents, and a host of 'accountability partners' that includes a Texas Rangers coach, pastors from three churches, his Christian sports agent, and his father-in-law."

Josh knew he was weak when he counted on his own strength, but he found power in the Holy Spirit to live according to God's commands.

The 2009 season proved to be forgettable for Josh, although the Rangers showed improvement by posting an 87–75 record. Injures limited him to just 89 games, and his statistics suffered accordingly. His batting average dropped to .260, and he hit just 10 home runs and drove in only 45 runs.

Despite his subpar year, Josh had an All-Star offseason. He and Katie made more than thirty appearances around the country, speaking about redemption and forgiveness through their foundation, Triple Play Ministries. Their ministry also hosted Christian sports camps, did community outreach, and helped support an orphanage in Uganda.

Early in the 2010 season, it was obvious that the Rangers and Josh were going to have a special year. In June, the team posted a 21–6 record—its best month in the franchise's fifty-year history.

By August, Josh had distinguished himself as the definitive choice for American League Most Valuable Player. He led the league in batting average at .362, slugging percentage (.634), and hits with 161. Tom Verducci pointed out on SI.com that the last three players to bat over .360 with a slugging percentage of more than .600 while playing center field were Mickey Mantle, Stan Musial, and Joe DiMaggio. That's not bad company.

Verducci went on to describe a mid-August performance by Josh: "Just another night in the life of the best player in baseball went something like this: smash four hits all over the park; a single to left, a 440-foot bomb to center, a single and double to right; score from third base on a pop fly to deep shortstop/short left; score from second base on a ground ball to second; make a diving catch on the warning track and a leaping catch against the center field wall; cause the third-base coach to halt a runner from scoring from second on an otherwise routine run-scoring single to center field."

Being called the "best player in baseball" certainly felt better than being labeled one of the most disappointing No. 1 draft picks of all time. Josh was finally living up to his potential.

Despite missing nearly all of the final month of the regular season with broken ribs, Josh helped Texas reach the playoffs with a 90–72 record. His gaudy 2010 statistics looked like this: a .359 batting average to go with 32 home runs and 100 RBIs.

Things were going great for Josh and the Rangers. But late in the season, on one of the best nights in team history, Josh was noticeably absent. It was September 25, 2010, and Texas had just clinched its first American League West title in more than a decade with a 4–3 win over Oakland. But instead of celebrating with his teammates, Josh chose to be alone.

It's a long-standing baseball tradition for teammates to spray each other with champagne after making it to the playoffs. Josh didn't want any part of the alcohol. He didn't even want it to touch his skin—it had caused that much pain in his life.

A few weeks later, on October 12, after Texas defeated

Tampa 5–1 to advance to the American League Championship Series, Josh's teammates made sure he was part of the festivities. They grabbed him, gave him some eye goggles, and walked him into the clubhouse.

"Everybody yelled 'Ginger ale!' and I just jumped in the middle of the pile and they doused me with it," Josh said. "It was the coolest thing for my teammates to understand why I can't be a part of the celebration, and for them to adapt it for me to be a part of it says a lot about my teammates."

The Rangers faced the Yankees in the next round for the right to play in the World Series. Right away, Josh showed the Yankees that things would be different this time. He hit a three-run home run to open up the series.

When Texas won the second game 7–2, it broke a ten-game losing streak against New York in the playoffs. The Rangers eventually defeated the Yankees in the series, four games to two, to advance to the World Series for the first time in team history.

In the Fall Classic, the Texas offense struggled against San Francisco pitching, and the Giants claimed the title in five games.

About a month later, Josh won the American League Most Valuable Player Award. His 22 first-place votes and 358 points easily outdistanced Detroit's Miguel Cabrera's 262 points.

In February 2011, Josh was rewarded with a two-year, $24 million contract that included a $3 million signing bonus. He backed it up by hitting .298, knocking 25 home runs, and driving home 94 runners during the 2011 season, when the Rangers advanced to the World Series for the second straight year.

Josh nearly proved to be the hero of the Fall Classic when his two-run, tenth-inning home run in Game 6 put Texas just three outs away from its first world championship. The

St. Louis Cardinals, however, rallied to tie the game in the tenth and win it in the eleventh on David Freese's dramatic walk-off home run. Even though the Redbirds went on to win the title in seven games, the Rangers proved they were among the game's elite teams.

In a similar fashion, Josh has made it to the top of the major leagues. His path hasn't been straight—like the Israelites wandering through the desert, it took him awhile to find the Promised Land. But Josh has said many times that he wouldn't change his past.

"Could I have reached people being that clean-cut kid coming out of high school?" Josh asked rhetorically during an interview. "Probably so. How many more people can I reach having tattoos, having an addiction problem? I've been through that. . . . And I've come back."

His comeback has inspired countless people who are fighting their own demons to give their lives to God. Josh's message to them is simple: *Put God first.*

"One thing I can't live without is, obviously, Jesus," Josh said. "When I don't put Him first, my decisions don't work out too well for me."

The Hall of Fame may still be well into the future, but with Jesus first and his priorities firmly in place, Josh Hamilton is finally on his way.

2012 season update: Josh enjoyed a great start: Through the middle of May, he was batting .402, even belting four home runs and a double on a May 8 game against Baltimore. Josh's batting average cooled off to .285—but he still smacked 43 home runs for the season. On December 13, 2012, Josh made headlines by signing a five-year, $125 million contract with the Los Angeles Angels, joining Albert Pujols.

7

STEPHEN DREW:
GOOD THINGS COME IN THREES

Countless boys across America dream of being major league stars one day. But not many actually feel *pressure* to become one.

Welcome to Stephen Drew's world.

When you're a prep star whose two older two brothers were both drafted in the first round, pressure to reach The Show is inevitable. Stephen, the Arizona Diamondbacks' shortstop, was fourteen years old when Cleveland selected his middle brother, Tim, out of high school with the twenty-eighth overall pick in 1997. One year later, St. Louis chose Stephen's older brother, J.D., out of Florida State at No. 5.

"I always got compared," Stephen said.

Stephen was born on March 16, 1983—four-and-a-half years behind Tim and seven-and-a-half years behind J.D.—in Hahira, Georgia, a nondescript nook off I-75 near the Florida border. Never heard of it? Well, scan the map for neighboring towns like Adel, Barney, and Cecil, and you can't miss it. Honest.

With a population of roughly sixteen hundred during Stephen's youth, Hahira had one stoplight, a Main Street, and an old-time city hall. It's the type of place where the town barber knows your name, honeybee festivals draw a big crowd, and the collective twang in conversations sounds like competing steel guitars.

"It's growing a little," Stephen said in his sleepy Southern drawl. "Now we've got some eating restaurants—you know, the kind of little hole-in-the-wall places."

Like most brotherly trios, the Drew boys were a rough-and-tumble bunch. Sports and skinned knees ruled the days. The boys enjoyed baseball, basketball, football, hunting, and fishing. As long as the activity was outdoors, it made the cut.

But baseball was king. J.D., the quiet brother, a 6-foot, 1-inch lefty, was a power-hitting monster who became a two-time consensus All-American and the national Player of the Year in 1997 at Florida State University. Tim, the outspoken one, was a 6-foot, 1-inch righty with a blazing fastball who landed a professional contract without stepping foot in college.

As baseball mentors go, Stephen couldn't have asked for much more.

"Tim could throw the fire out of a ball," said Stephen, whose personality is a mixture of his brothers. "He was always a pitcher. It helped us out. He always threw harder than what I could hit. [J.D.] is the one who taught me to hit left-handed."

Stephen followed J.D. to Florida State, where he starred for three years after turning down a $1 million offer from Pittsburgh out of high school. He earned *Baseball America*'s college Freshman of the Year award in 2002 and *Collegiate Baseball*'s second-team All-America honors in 2004. When Arizona took him fifteenth overall in 2004, the Drews became the first sibling trio in major league history to be drafted in the first round.

"[Stephen] saw all that with us and continued to work hard," Tim said. "For him, he was never awestruck by anything because he's like, 'All right, I belong.' That's a God thing. God prepared him for something special."

God had been preparing Stephen's heart for a long time. His parents, David and Libby, raised their sons at Bethany Baptist Church, a dirt-road mile from the Drews' five-acre property. The family was at church every Sunday morning and Wednesday night.

By age nine, Stephen started realizing that good morals and his family's faith weren't good enough to appease a holy God. One night in bed, as he lay awake staring at the ceiling, all those Sunday school lessons and meaning-of-life questions started really percolating:

Did God really create the universe?

Why am I here?

Are heaven and hell real?

Was Jesus really who He says He was?

That night, he submitted himself to Christ.

"God speaks in different ways," Stephen said, "and that's how He spoke to me."

His faith came in quite handy after he was drafted. With hard-line negotiator Scott Boras as his agent, Stephen sat idle through yearlong contract talks. By April 2005, eager to play ball somewhere—*anywhere*—Stephen signed with the Camden (New Jersey) Riversharks of the independent Atlantic League.

Six weeks later, just minutes before a signing deadline would have sent him into the next draft, he finally agreed to

Stephen Drew, a 2004 first-round pick from tiny Hahira, Georgia, is one of three brothers who have played in the major leagues. His older brothers, J.D. and Tim, were also drafted in the first round. (AP Photo/Matt York)

terms with Arizona. Boras hailed him as the next coming of Alex Rodriguez. Talk about pressure.

But if Stephen felt any, it didn't show. He spent the next year feasting on minor league pitching before an injury to Arizona's starting shortstop, Craig Counsell, prompted his big league call-up in July 2006. For the rest of the season, Stephen looked like a seasoned veteran, hitting .316 in 59 games. A star had been born.

"Talent-wise, he's the most talented [of the Drew brothers]," Tim said in 2006.

But baseball, like life in general, can be a bumpy ride. After undergoing LASIK surgery that November, Stephen suffered through a season-long sophomore slump in 2007 (.238 batting average in 150 games) before exploding in the playoffs (.387) as the Diamondbacks reached the National League Championship Series. He rebounded in 2008 to hit .291 with 21 home runs and 67 RBIs in 152 games, but he has struggled to reach that level since.

The 2011 season looked like it could finally be the year everyone had been expecting from the youngest Drew. By the end of April, he was hitting .321 and appeared to be on track for his first All-Star Game appearance. But he slumped miserably over the next two and a half months.

Then disaster struck.

In a game against Milwaukee on July 20, Stephen suffered a gruesome, season-ending ankle fracture. As he slid into Brewers catcher Jonathan Lucroy at home plate, Stephen's right foot appeared to catch underneath him and twist violently, contorting about 100 degrees from its normal position. The video replays were enough to make even Gumby cringe.

Stephen had surgery the next day. While he finished the year with a cool .252 average, Arizona caught fire and won the NL West crown. The unwanted midseason vacation, though, allowed him to be there for his wife, Laura, during the birth of their second son, Nolan.

"Stephen is disappointed that he can't be out there to be helping the team make the drive to the playoffs, but at the same time he understands that the Lord is the one who directs his steps, like it says in Proverbs 16:9," Diamondbacks chaplain Brian Hommel said following the injury. "Stephen doesn't know why he got hurt, but he is okay with that because it has put his faith to the test, and a faith untested cannot be trusted."

Overall, Stephen's career has been solid, if unspectacular. Judged against his brothers, he currently falls ahead of Tim and behind J.D. on the scale of major league success.

Tim played eleven pro seasons overall, including parts of five in the major leagues, compiling an unsightly 7.02 ERA in 35 games with Cleveland, Montreal, and Atlanta from 2000 to 2004. He underwent surgery for a torn labrum in his right shoulder in January 2006 and retired at age twenty-nine after a failed comeback attempt with two independent league teams during the 2007 and 2008 seasons.

J.D., meanwhile, has struggled to live up to the billing of a top-five draft pick. Yet the oft-injured outfielder has still enjoyed an enviable career. Through 2011, he had played in fourteen big league seasons with four teams, hitting 242 career homers. He finished sixth in NL MVP voting in 2004, made an All-Star appearance in 2008, and has been to the playoffs eight times. In 2007, his first-inning grand slam in Game 6 of the AL Championship Series against Cleveland was a pivotal moment in Boston's drive to its second World Series title in four years.

Stephen would love to experience playoff euphoria like that. But whatever happens in his career, he finds great comfort in his faith.

"Things don't always go your way," he said. "People sometimes get a wrong perspective of Christians—like it's always easy [for us]. It can be the total opposite. But with Jesus sitting there with you, He can hold your hand through things. He's there with you. You might not be able to see it now, but you can look back and see He's got His hand on you the whole time. He's with me every day."

2102 season update: Stephen Drew began the 2012 season where he finished 2011—watching the game from the sidelines. Drew, the Arizona Diamondbacks' shortstop at the time, suffered a season-ending ankle injury on July 20, 2011, during a slide into home plate against Milwaukee. He didn't return to the lineup until June 27, 2012. Over the next two months, he struggled mightily, hitting .193 before Arizona shipped the 2004 first-round draft pick to Oakland for a minor leaguer on August 20. The change of scenery seemed to help Drew, who posted a .250 average in 39 games and helped Oakland win their first American League West Division title since 2006. He hit .211 in a five-game AL Division Series loss to Detroit.

8

JEREMY AFFELDT:
SOLUS CHRISTUS—BY CHRIST ALONE

Sitting in his office, David Batstone stared at his computer screen in disbelief.

This is a hoax, he thought. *One of my staffers is pulling my leg. There's no way a major leaguer really sent me an unsolicited e-mail.*

Still . . . what if? Batstone, an avid San Francisco Giants fan, couldn't help the initial surge of excitement as he read the message. It was late November 2008, and twenty-one months had passed since he had cofounded Not For Sale (NFS), a San Francisco Bay Area nonprofit that aggressively fights worldwide human trafficking and slavery. Public awareness of his project was growing slowly, but its gritty subject matter didn't exactly attract your average, charity-minded major leaguer.

Then again, Jeremy Affeldt is not—in any way—your average major leaguer. So there it was, an e-mail from Jeremy—or whoever was posing as him—sitting in Batstone's inbox only days after the veteran reliever signed a two-year, $8 million contract with the Giants. The e-mail expressed interest in meeting with Batstone in person and learning more about NFS.

Being a business professor at the University of San Francisco and a man of reason, Batstone scanned the e-mail again, scrutinizing the typed message for any signs of trickery. Then he checked with his NFS staff: *Okay, who's the jokester?*

But it was no joke. The e-mail was real.

The two men met in San Francisco soon thereafter. Before leaving, Jeremy cut a $10,000 check for an NFS-created medical clinic/rescue center in Thailand that cares for former child slaves. He also pledged a hundred dollars to NFS for every strikeout he recorded during the 2009 season. (He finished with 55.)

Just like that, Batstone had a celebrity advocate that most charitable organizations only dream of.

"It shocked me that he had some sort of awareness about what we do," Batstone said.

In today's age of wealthy, prima donna professional athletes, Jeremy is indeed unique. At first glance, he appears to be just like any other modern star. He blogs and tweets. He sports body art, frosted surfer hair, sideburns down to his earlobes, and a long, vertical strip of hipster chin hair.

But there's plenty of substance with the style. If he had pitched seventy or eighty years ago, during the Depression era, one could envision young newsboys heralding his stark distinctiveness on busy street corners:

> *"Extra! Extra! Read all about it: Professional Athlete with a Soul Patch, Tattoo, and No College Education Is an Intelligent, Articulate, Well-Read, and Theologically*

Grounded Force for Worldwide Gospel Proclamation and Social Reform!"

The "dumb jock" label dies hard. But Jeremy breaks—no, pulverizes—stereotypes with a faith-in-action sledgehammer. He crosses the often-great divides between elite athleticism, strong theology, and Christlike activism with a rare combination of grace, knowledge, and vision.

His public ministries of choice are revealing, too. Lots of pro athletes do charity. But few wade into the filthiest depths of humanity to shine the light of Jesus Christ like Jeremy does.

Put it this way: How many other pro athletes zealously work to stop forced child labor in Peru? Or the child sex slave industry in Asia? Or the use of the mentally handicapped for pornography in Romania?

How many sports celebrities fund the construction of orphanages in Uganda? Or get emotional when they hear the sound of running water from an African well they helped construct? Or seek to ignite the humanitarian flames of an entire next generation? Jeremy is a walking, talking embodiment of James 1:27 and 2:26, which speak of the faith-empowered good works Christians are to embrace.

Oh, and by the way, he's a mighty good pitcher, too.

"God is showing me how justice is a big deal to Him," Jeremy said. "He's all about righteousness and justice. Jesus said, 'I came to set the captives free.' "

REBELLION AND TRANSFORMATION

So how exactly does one become a Jeremy Affeldt? Were there any "Road to Damascus" moments? Any angelic visions at night or heavenly voices in the wilderness?

Not really. There was just a bunch of spiritual confusion, a bad apocalyptic movie, and a discerning basketball coach.

Okay, so that's a bit of a sweeping generalization. Let's rewind a bit and fill in the gaps.

Jeremy was born on June 6, 1979, the younger of two kids in a military family. David Affeldt, Jeremy's father, was an Air Force captain whose job kept the family bouncing around to Arizona, Minnesota, various parts of California, and Guam before finally settling in Spokane, Washington, during Jeremy's high school years.

All that moving exposed the Affeldts to a lot of different types of churches—Baptist, Evangelical Free, and nondenominational, to name a few. Jeremy's mom, Charlotte, grew up Southern Baptist, and David grew up Lutheran. It was quite a religious stew for a young man to digest.

Jeremy uttered the Sinner's Prayer at age five but admits he didn't understand what he was doing. At age twelve, he "re-upped" after being spiritually rattled by a 1970s movie about the end times.

"It had a guillotine," Jeremy recalled. "It tried to scare you to death—[like religion was] a fire insurance policy deal." His theological waters were getting muddy.

By the time he was an upperclassman at Northwest Christian School in Colbert, Washington, Jeremy was a confused kid with a rebellious streak.

One day during his junior year, he started teasing a girl before English class. Another classmate, Larisa Walker, a particularly spunky gal with sandy blond hair, had grown tired of Jeremy's antics. In front of everyone, she stood up and shouted, "I'll never marry a guy like you!"

(Insert the sound of crickets chirping in an otherwise awkwardly silent room.)

Jeremy's bad attitude worsened. During basketball season, his head coach suspended him from a Christmas tournament after he drew a technical foul for mouthing off at a referee. One more tech, his coach said, and he'd be thrown off the team.

While Jeremy watched the next game in street clothes, an assistant coach, Jim Orr, took a seat beside him. "We need to talk," Coach Orr said.

Coach Orr gave Jeremy a few books and met with him frequently, helping him work through his anger and connect the spiritual dots.

Initially, Jeremy's motive for personal growth was simply to stay on the team. But God's Spirit was at work. Soon, Jeremy came to a true awareness of the gospel and his need for a Savior. He repented and placed his faith in Christ. His understanding of God and Christianity changed. So did his life.

Spiritual fruit immediately began to blossom. Jeremy apologized to girls at school whom he had offended. Those thudding sounds echoing through the Northwest Christian hallways were classmates' jaws hitting the floor.

One girl who noticed the change was Larisa Walker. Yes, *that* Larisa Walker. As first impressions go, Jeremy hadn't exactly wowed her. But now he was different. Where before she saw pride, anger, and sarcasm, she now saw humility, kindness, and empathy.

One day, Jeremy and Larisa were walking through the school gymnasium at the same time. It was chapel day, so they were both dressed up. No one else was around.

"You look really nice today," Jeremy said.

Larisa was stunned. "Oh," she stammered, "you do, too."

Seeing daylight, Jeremy took a chance: "We should go out sometime," he said. She dismissed the suggestion with a laugh, but Jeremy was undeterred. He persisted until she said yes—despite the advice of a close friend who, like Ananias with the recently converted apostle Paul in Acts 9, was skeptical of the authenticity of Jeremy's transformation.

On their first date, Jeremy and Larisa went to a local park, sat on a blanket, and talked for hours. By the time they were seniors, the two were having great conversations, especially about religion. Jeremy's family, despite playing church hopscotch, was conservative. Larisa, meanwhile, came from a charismatic background.

"We were seventeen years old and debating theology," Larisa recalls. "I don't know if he would've asked those questions if he hadn't started dating me. It made us both grow through the years."

As Jeremy was maturing spiritually, he was dominating athletically. He enjoyed basketball, but baseball was clearly his future. He could do things on a pitching mound that opponents were powerless against. So in 1997, three days before his eighteenth birthday, the Kansas City Royals drafted him out of high school in the third round.

The Royals immediately shipped Jeremy to their Gulf Coast League rookie team in Fort Myers, Florida. He was barely old enough to vote, a relatively new believer, and marooned nearly three thousand miles from home in a very worldly environment. It was a recipe for spiritual disaster.

Yet God protected Jeremy. He found a good church, started reading a chapter of the Bible a day, and marveled at how God revealed Himself in powerful ways. In some ways, it mirrored Paul's post-conversion trip to Arabia (Galatians 1)—a time of spiritual strengthening before public ministry.

"It's amazing how God became alive to me," Jeremy said. "I chose to become a professional athlete, and He ordered my steps."

MARRIAGE AND THE MINORS

Distance—that demanding proving ground for all romantic relationships—only strengthened Jeremy and Larisa's bond. While he toiled in the minors, she completed a two-year interior design degree at two community colleges in Washington. But he missed her, and she missed him. When he came home for the offseason, the time together never felt long enough.

In February 1999, Jeremy took Larisa to a basketball game at their alma mater. The Northwest Christian gym was buzzing with fans. The fact that many of the couple's family members and closest friends were there didn't register with Larisa.

At halftime, the public address announcer encouraged the crowd to stay seated for a blindfolded three-point shooting contest. The winner, he said, would take home a big-screen TV. Four contestants were called onto the floor. Larisa was the last.

After she finished shooting, she removed her blindfold to see Jeremy on one knee, holding a ring and a big sign that said, "Larisa, will you marry me?" The brash girl who once publicly announced, "I'll never marry a guy like you!" was now shouting "Yes!" before hundreds of onlookers. Nine months later, they got married.

"He always jokes that it was a challenge, that he'd make sure I'd have to take it back," Larisa said of that day in English class.

The following spring, reality broadsided newlywed bliss. Entering his fourth pro season, Jeremy was assigned out of spring training to the Royals' Class A affiliate in Wilmington, North Carolina. It was a tough season for someone who expected to be playing in a higher league. Jeremy went 5–15 on the mound. Money was tight on a minor league salary, so Larisa got a job as the director of a children's equestrian camp. The couple shared a three-bedroom apartment with two other players.

"That was interesting," Larisa recalled.

Despite his poor stats, Jeremy was moved up to the Royals' Double-A club in Wichita, Kansas, for the 2001 season to see what he could do. This time, he and Larisa rented their own apartment, but the place was a dump. When Larisa first saw it, she cried. For furniture, they had a bed, a sofa, and some plastic furniture. They watched TV on a nine-inch screen.

To make ends meet, they both worked offseason jobs at a chain of furniture stores owned by Larisa's father in the Spokane area. It certainly wasn't the stereotypical glamour lifestyle of pro baseball, but the couple was enjoying life together. "This is fun," they would often tell each other, for reassurance. "It's just the two of us. This is an adventure."

Adventures are all well and good—for a time.

The fact is, Jeremy's faith was being tested acutely. By 2002, he was still just a middling prospect. His first five minor league seasons had been so nondescript that his 2001 season at Wichita (10–6 record, 3.90 ERA in 25 starts) qualified as his best year. He asked God hard questions and struggled for faith.

Then, like manna from heaven, success rained on him. That spring training, Jeremy had a fantastic outing during a game in Bradenton, Florida. The Royals' brass took note. So did *Kansas City Star* columnist Joe Posnanski, now a senior writer at *Sports Illustrated*.

Posnanski immediately started waving the Affeldt banner in his articles for the *Kansas City Star*. Here's how Posnanski described it years later, in a *Sports Illustrated* story on October 24, 2010, a day after Jeremy and the Giants clinched the National League pennant in Philadelphia:

> *Jeremy Affeldt.*
>
> *We go way back.*
>
> *We go back to a day in Bradenton, Fla., this had to be 2002, a boring spring training game, nothing happening, when suddenly the Kansas City Royals put in this kid, this mediocre prospect named Jeremy Affeldt.*
>
> *Nobody knew anything about him. He'd put up only decent numbers in Double A. The scouts yawned. I yawned. And then . . . he started pitching. And jaws dropped. Ninety-five mph fastball. Electric Barry Zito-like curveball. What the heck was this?*
>
> *Suddenly the scouts stood up straight. The Royals general manager at the time, Allard Baird, started leaning forward, and leaning forward more, until he was practically on the shoulder of the guy in front of him. Affeldt threw two innings. He struck out five. The other batter fouled out.*
>
> *As a scout said: The kid ain't Koufax. But for two innings in Bradenton, Koufax couldn't have been any better.*

So, I was hooked. I became the biggest Jeremy Af-
feldt fan around. Affeldt is convinced that my columns
in the Kansas City Star *got him his big-league job, and*
because of this he credits me with his career.

Said Jeremy: "In 2002, I wasn't even supposed to make the big leagues. Joe Posnanski wrote a story that sent all of Kansas City into a buzz. Every time I pitched, he wrote a great story [about me]. Even my wife said, 'I always like reading what he writes about you.' Those stories out of spring training put more and more pressure on the front office. I always tell him thanks."

Jeremy made the Royals' 2002 opening day roster and debuted on April 6. With five seasons on the farm that felt like ten, the 6-foot, 4-inch, 230-pound lefty was still only twenty-two years old.

He had finally arrived in the major leagues—out of nowhere.

MAJOR RELIEF

Jeremy's four-and-a-half years in Kansas City had all the noteworthiness of a rain delay. The Royals were mostly atrocious during that time, posting 100-loss seasons in 2002, 2004, and 2006 to mark their worst five-year stretch since the franchise debuted in 1969. In 2005 alone, the team had three managers—Tony Pena (fired after starting the season 8–25), Bob Schaefer (replaced 17 games later), and Buddy Bell.

Personally, Jeremy battled a rash of injuries and never fully established himself as a starter or closer in K.C. At the 2006 trade deadline, the Royals shipped him and his 4.77

career ERA to Colorado in a four-player swap. It was a breath of fresh, Rocky Mountain air.

"Getting traded was something I prayed for every day in Kansas City," he admitted. "I didn't hate it, but I just needed a change."

The Rockies converted Jeremy to full-time relief duty and worked with him to correct several mechanical flaws in his delivery. In 2007, he enjoyed the finest year of his career to that point, posting a 3.51 ERA, including a miniscule 1.74 ERA at hitter-friendly Coors Field. But the best was yet to come.

On September 15, during the stretch run of the 2007 season, the Rockies were 76–72 and six-and-a-half games behind National League West leader Arizona. Their postseason chances seemed to be slipping away. Then they went on one of the hottest streaks in major league history, winning 21 of their next 22 games as they snatched the NL wild card, swept Philadelphia and Arizona in the playoffs, and reached the franchise's first World Series.

Jeremy was crucial to Colorado's success. After allowing a home run to Phillies slugger Ryan Howard in Game 2 of the NL Division Series, he settled down and finished the playoffs with six scoreless appearances. Alas, mighty Boston swept Colorado in four games in the World Series. Still, it was an underdog story for the ages.

"We were a Cinderella team—one of those runs they think will never happen again," Jeremy said.

Cashing in on his success, Jeremy signed a one-year, $3 million deal with Cincinnati, where his role mostly frustrated him and he never really warmed to the city. But God continued to bless him. Jeremy threw a bunch of innings (78),

Jeremy Affeldt started his major league career in 2002 as a starter in Kansas City, but his greatest success came after he reinvented himself as a middle reliever. Since then, he has won two World Series rings with San Francisco in the last three seasons. (AP Photo/Tom DiPace)

set a new personal best with a 3.33 ERA, and caught the eye of the Giants, who handed him a sweet two-year deal in the offseason.

In 2009, Jeremy enjoyed a career year, earning MLB.com's Setup Man of the Year Award with a 1.73 ERA in 74 games. He credits much of his success to former Reds teammate David Weathers, who helped transform Jeremy from a four-seam to a two-seam pitcher by teaching him a nasty sinker.

"It gets me out of a lot of jams," Jeremy said. "If I was there in Cincinnati just to learn my pitch, that's my journey. Now I'm a ground ball pitcher, and I've been pretty effective with it since."

The 2010 season, however, was tough for him. Jeremy missed 23 games with a left oblique tear, battled a nagging hamstring injury, and disagreed with manager Bruce Bochy about his bullpen role. His ERA ballooned to 4.14, and he posted his highest WHIP (walks plus hits per innings pitched) since 2006 at 1.60.

But by November 3, when ticker tape was showering Jeremy and his teammates as they paraded through downtown San Francisco as the 2010 World Series champions, that all felt like ancient history. Thanks to a late-season collapse by San Diego, the Giants and their well-named "torture" offense had overcome a six-and-a-half-game deficit in late August to win the NL West division title.

In Game 6 of the NL Championship Series against Philadelphia, Jeremy faced the biggest outing of his career. With San Francisco leading the series three games to two, Jeremy relieved starter Jonathan Sanchez in the third inning with two men on and no outs in a 2–2 game. Antacid tablet anyone?

Not for Jeremy, thank you. He shook off a season's worth of difficulty by shutting out the Phillies for two innings in the series-clinching 3–2 win. Nine days later, the Giants claimed their first World Series championship since 1954 with a five-game win over Texas.

"It was amazing," Jeremy grinned.

The 2011 Giants missed the playoffs, but Jeremy enjoyed great personal success. He posted a 1.15 WHIP (the lowest of his career) and a 2.63 ERA (the second-lowest of his career), and he held opponents to a .207 batting average. His ERA after the All-Star break (1.21) was visible only by magnifying glass.

But the good times were cut short . . . literally. On September 8, 2011, a Thursday off-day, Jeremy was grilling in the backyard with Larisa and their two young sons when he badly lacerated his right (non-throwing) hand with a paring knife while trying to separate frozen burger patties. His pinkie suffered nerve damage that required season-ending surgery.

Jeremy could've wallowed in bitterness or self-pity. Instead, he chose to celebrate God's kindness and protection, especially the fact that the knife didn't damage any tendons and missed his throwing hand altogether.

And then there was this: The severed nerve was directly underneath a main artery. It was almost like the artery had miraculously moved out of the knife's path. Jeremy's hand surgeon said he had never seen anything like it.

"I don't know what you believe in," the doctor told Jeremy, "but keep believing in it."

In the days that followed, Jeremy purposefully pressed in spiritually to see what God wanted to teach him through the ordeal.

"God sees and He knows," Jeremy said shortly after the injury. "We choose our course, but He orders my steps. He's already seen the end of my life. He already knows. He knows how to heal my body.

"Now it's like, *What do You want from me right now? Do you want me to be more of a family man? Do You want me to spend more time with my teammates in a different scenario?* I'm constantly asking and learning and believing. When these things happen, do you have enough trust in Almighty God to believe He knows why it happens? Where do you grow? How do you increase in maturity in Christ through these things?"

"THIS IS MY PATH"

In Luke 4, we read the story of Jesus entering a synagogue on a Sabbath in His hometown of Nazareth. Before a rapt audience of devout Jews, He opened a sacred Old Testament scroll and read from the Book of Isaiah:

> *"The Spirit of the Lord is on me, because he has anointed me to proclaim good news to the poor. He has sent me to proclaim freedom for the prisoners and recovery of sight for the blind, to set the oppressed free."*
>
> LUKE 4:18

These words resonate with Jeremy—perhaps more deeply than with most folks. But why?

Why does Jeremy's heart beat so urgently for victims of sex trafficking and child slavery in remote corners of the globe where he's never been? There are a gaggle of other worthwhile charity options out there that aren't so, well, depressing. Yet here he is, diving into the cesspools of a sin-stained world with a life preserver, hoping to rescue flailing souls from the black waters of despair.

"It's really connected to his spirituality and faith in Jesus, for starters," David Batstone of Not For Sale said. "He sees that as part of Jesus' life, not an add-on to the story. That's just who Jesus was. It's not a social gospel distinct from personal faith. It's really linked in a way that's profound theologically."

Or, as Jeremy summarizes: "God has just shown me that this is my path." It's that simple.

The more Jeremy reads scripture, the more he sees how the Savior's heart broke for the lost, the downtrodden, and the helpless. Jesus dined with outcasts and befriended traitors. He touched lepers and forgave harlots. The Son of God loved the world's riffraff.

This affects Jeremy. It rattles him out of self-absorption. His compassionate pursuits are more than just feel-good philanthropy or a box to cross off on the "Public Relations Checklist of a Multi-Millionaire Athlete."

His motivation is intrinsically connected to a keen understanding of the gospel. In conversation, he uses words like *redemption* and *restoration* a lot. The doctrine of vicarious atonement propels him into action. Mercy and grace have changed his life, and he wants others to be liberated, as well.

This, of course, all comes from an extensive knowledge of scripture. He quotes the Bible like well-known movie lines. His bookshelves include titles by Tim Keller and other reformed, socially minded Christian authors.

"He's always reading a new book," Larisa marveled. "He's

not someone who's going to get stuck in life. He's always going to learn and read and put it into practice. I don't know if I've ever met someone who is so willing to improve himself."

Check out Jeremy's online presence sometime. His blog, entitled "To Stir a Movement: Christian Social Justice," includes mini-treatises on topics like modern-day abolitionism, faith-driven fatherhood, and licentiousness vs. legalism. You know, typical blog fare.

His Twitter page, too, is far from the usual tripe. You won't find any entries like "*Stuck in traffic . . . listening to Rihanna*" here. He's a serial tweeter of pithy quotes from the likes of C.S. Lewis, Aristotle, Napoleon Bonaparte, Benjamin Franklin, General George S. Patton, and Winston Churchill. He even sprinkled in a little Steve Jobs before his death.

You could describe Jeremy as a modern-day Renaissance Man, although that would probably be a slight since church theology was pretty screwed up during the Renaissance period. Oh, did we mention that Jeremy is a student of church history, too? He can easily hold his own in conversations about Luther and Calvin.

For proof, check out his left forearm. In May 2011, he got a tattoo that read *Solus Christus*, a Latin phrase that means "by Christ alone" and represents one of the Five Solas of the sixteenth-century Protestant Reformation. Shortly afterward, he wrote a four-part blog series, totaling 2,086 words, on the meaning of his first tattoo. Nothing in Jeremy's life, not even body art, is done willy-nilly.

"It's like a crest for me—in Christ, I can do the impossible," he said of his forearm ink. "That crest, I put my family under, my children under, and I compete under—everything

I do. It made so much sense."

With NFS, which is active on five continents, Jeremy found a worthy vehicle in which to pour all of his faith-fueled intellect and passions. He first heard about NFS through Mike King, the president of Youthfront, a large Christian youth ministry in the greater Kansas City area, during his time with the Royals. Alarmed to learn that human trafficking and slavery exist in the United States, Jeremy wanted to get involved. That's why he jumped at the chance to meet with Batstone when he signed with the Giants.

The two men quickly became fellow soldiers in heady spiritual warfare. In February 2011, Batstone included Jeremy in his inaugural "Montara Circle," an ambitious, two-day think tank of fifty-three business, academic, and nonprofit leaders who met in Montara, California, to address various global issues like poverty, HIV/AIDS, water scarcity, and human trafficking. The guest list was teeming with influential movers and shakers, including three billionaires. The invitation spoke volumes about Jeremy.

On day two, the attendees split into smaller focus groups and brainstormed solutions for the rampant human exploitation in a Peruvian area of the Amazon rain forest where NFS runs a children's shelter. Participants then voted on the best idea.

The winning idea was to launch an iced tea company, Smart Tea, that would harvest the drink's unique ingredients from a plant indigenous to the troubled area of Peru, thereby creating local jobs and providing residents with an alternative to selling themselves (or their children) into slavery. Profits from drink sales would then be injected back into the region to boost the economy and infrastructure.

As of the fall of 2011, Smart Tea's investment group, board of directors, and business plan were all being finalized. Guess who helped hatch the winning idea? Yep . . . Jeremy.

"He plays that card—'I'm just a dumb ballplayer here'—but he's totally engaged with world leaders," Batstone said.

Jeremy speaks with his wallet, too. In 2010, he donated more than $20,000 total to NFS. And in 2011, he upped his pledge from $100 for every strikeout to $250, including another $250 for every lead he held. He also got Cardinals slugger Matt Holliday, a former teammate in Colorado, to agree to donate $500 every time he homered in 2011.

That's not all. Thanks to Jeremy's influence, the Giants' home game against Minnesota on June 21, 2011, featured two NFS public service announcements by Jeremy on the stadium video screen at AT&T Park. He also advocates for NFS during the offseason at his home church in Spokane and local colleges. And he is the main spokesperson for NFS' Free2Play initiative, which encourages sports fans to make NFS pledges related to their favorite team.

"Even during the season, he's writing me asking what's going on in Romania," Batstone said. "He's more than just your typical baseball player. He realizes that he has financial and celebrity resources to make this [our work] more effective. The more I've interviewed with major media, the more they say, 'You realize how amazing of a guy you've got there, don't you?'"

Baseball's unofficial ambassador of social justice is certainly fighting the good fight. But he knows the next generation is infinitely more influential than one man. So he created the Jeremy Affeldt Foundation and Generation Alive. His foundation seeks to spread the gospel to youth through camps and mission trips. Generation Alive, meanwhile, is a movement he started to inspire kids and young adults to start changing the world in tangible ways.

In 2011 alone, Generation Alive teamed up several times with Youthfront's "Something to Eat" campaign to host weekend events where young volunteers packaged more than three hundred thousand meals to ship to Africa. Jeremy sees it as a great, practical way to heed the call of Matthew 25:34–40 while inspiring the next generation to action.

"I don't want a program," Jeremy says. "I don't want a youth rally. I want a movement. I want something like Martin Luther King, Jr. I want to see a movement of young people who stand up for the kingdom of Jesus Christ, but do it right."

Jeremy also sees Generation Alive as a powerful witnessing tool to socially conscious unbelievers who want to aid a charitable cause but aren't necessarily ready to sit through a church sermon. It's the Pauline principle of 1 Corinthians 9:22: "I have become all things to all people so that by all possible means I might save some."

"They've heard, 'Jesus loves you,' and they usually run from it," Jeremy said. "Jesus loved on people first. He gained a voice in their lives, and when they asked for His view, He gave it to them. He didn't soapbox it right out of the gate. That's my deal with kids. I want to empower them."

Jeremy's bold faith and winsome personality affect the entire Giants organization, too. He is the key organizer of the team's annual Fellowship Day, where church groups are encouraged to attend a game and hear Christian players' testimonies afterward.

In April 2011, when the Dodgers came to town eleven

days after the well-publicized assault on Giants' fan Bryan Stow following the teams' Opening Day game in Los Angeles, Jeremy gave a live, impassioned pregame speech to the crowd, imploring them to respect others. It was so powerful that talk radio shows in the Bay Area were talking about it for days, according to Giants chaplain Jeff Iorg.

Within the clubhouse, Jeremy is a chapel leader and a proactive gospel witness among his teammates.

"Jesus came to bring the kingdom of God to earth, because in heaven, there's nothing wrong," Jeremy said. "He came to restore things. He expects us to carry on the restoration process. We have the same spirit in us, but obviously He has a little more pop. But we are image bearers.

"So what can I do? I can help restore life. For me, it's restoration—bringing justice to where injustice is because that's the love that Jesus displayed."

2012 season update: In October 2011, Jeremy Affeldt was recovering from a freak paring knife accident that ended his season in early September. What a difference a year can make. The following October, he was enjoying a championship parade in downtown San Francisco after helping the Giants win their second World Series in three seasons. Individually, Affeldt had a season to remember, posting a 2.70 ERA in 67 appearances. He was lights-out in the playoffs, allowing no runs and striking out 10 in 10 games over three series. In the finale of San Francisco's four-game World Series sweep of Detroit, Affeldt relieved starter Matt Cain in the bottom of the eighth with the score tied 3–3. After walking Avisail Garcia, he fanned the vaunted heart of Detroit's order—Miguel Cabrera, Prince Fielder, and Delmon Young. When the historic season was over, San Francisco rewarded Affeldt with a new three-year, $18 million contract.

9

MATT CAPPS:
OPENING A ONCE-CLOSED
FIST TO GOD

The phone call came just before midnight.

Surprised, Matt Capps picked up. It was his younger brother, Chris.

That's strange, Matt thought. *Chris normally doesn't call this late.*

Chris' voice was different. The news he carried would change the brothers' lives forever.

"Dad fell."

Time stood still. The hands on the clock froze in perpetuity. At least, that's the way it felt to Matt. Like a boxer driven to the canvas by a jarring blow, he struggled to comprehend what just happened.

Matt's father, Mike, had endured plenty of health challenges before. For years, his body had run like a banged-up jalopy, sputtering along life's highway as best it could but needing frequent tune-ups.

This, however, was no tune-up situation. It was the real deal. So Matt and his wife made the nine-hour drive from their offseason home in Sarasota, Florida, to Matt's hometown of Douglasville, Georgia. In the hospital Matt found his father lying in bed, unresponsive.

None of Mike's prior health scares had fully prepared Matt for this. Everything felt surreal. And Matt felt utterly helpless.

Mike wasn't just Matt's father. He was his chief mentor, closest confidante, and best friend. Mike had once coached his son's Little League team. He had pushed his son, sometimes to tears, to achieve the levels of baseball success that Matt couldn't have envisioned. He watched all his son's games—every one—and then waited for the late-night phone call whenever Matt pitched. The two would dissect Matt's performance into the wee hours of the night. Mike was a steadying rudder for his son amidst the unpredictable swells of life as a major league reliever.

Then, suddenly, he was gone.

THE GOOD OL' DAYS

Douglasville sure has changed.

For that, the locals can thank the ever-expanding urban sprawl from Atlanta, about twenty miles to the east. Credit also goes to Arbor Place, a four-million-square-foot regional mall that opened in 1999.

But when Matt was born there—on September 3, 1983—Douglasville had a cozy, small-town feel, stemming from its roots as a nineteenth-century railroad town. During Matt's childhood, the downtown district, with its quaint, two-story brick buildings from the turn of the century, felt less touristy and more like home.

Life back then held simple pleasures, like Krispy Kreme doughnut fundraisers, which Matt's Little League All-Star team held at the local Kmart. Or Friday night family dinners either at PoFolks, the local country kitchen, or Hudson's Hickory House, where six bucks got you some mighty fine barbeque. Halcyon days never tasted so good.

Matt and Chris frolicked away their days outside with a close-knit group of neighborhood buddies. If it wasn't football in their aunt's big backyard, it was baseball in the front. There were plenty of driveway basketball and sandlot baseball games, too. On quieter afternoons, they'd head to the local fishing hole.

"It was sports all the time," Matt recalls. "I don't know about this generation. It's all video games."

In high school, Matt was a stereotypical jock. He played baseball, football, and even ran cross-country as a freshman—not what you would expect from a man now listed at 6 feet, 2 inches and 245 pounds.

But baseball was his favorite. As his skills grew in Little League, so did some gnawing spiritual concerns. Provoked by the example of a Christian coach, young Matt started asking his parents deep questions—the kind that non-church-going folks have a tough time answering.

Mike and Kathy Capps were trying hard. Their sons knew the difference between right and wrong, and the boys recited bedtime prayers each night at their parents' behest. But Matt's questions trumped Mom and Dad's theological understanding.

So the Capps family started attending First Baptist Church of Douglasville, where Matt's coach went. At age ten,

Matt prayed the Sinner's Prayer and got baptized.

In high school, though, Christianity became like a rosin bag to Matt. He'd pick it up occasionally, whenever the palms of life got sweaty, but he inevitably dropped it to the dirt again. Eventually, his church attendance stopped. By the time he reached the minor leagues, his passions were worldly, and his faith was a wreck.

STEADY RISE TO THE BIG LEAGUES

Matt was always good at baseball.

He starred at Alexander High School in Douglasville and helped Team Georgia win the 2001 Sun Belt Classic, a prestigious prep All-Star tournament in Oklahoma where he played alongside fellow future big leaguers Brian McCann and Jeff Francoeur. Matt signed a National Letter of Intent to play at Louisiana State, but he quickly chose a professional career after the Pittsburgh Pirates drafted him in the seventh round in 2002.

His first stop was Bradenton, Florida, home of Pittsburgh's Gulf Coast League (GCL) affiliate, where he blew away opposing hitters with a 0.69 ERA in 13 innings out of the bullpen. In 2003, he converted to a starter, and the good times kept rolling. Between the GCL Pirates and Class A Lynchburg (Virginia), he finished with a 5–1 record and a 2.13 ERA in 11 starts. He was looking more and more like a seventh-round steal.

Then came 2004.

In his first two months with Class A Hickory (North Carolina), he failed miserably as a starter and didn't do much better in relief—so the Pirates demoted him and his 10.07

ERA to short-season Class A Williamsport (Pennsylvania). He returned to the rotation but continued to struggle, posting a 4.85 ERA in 11 games.

It was Matt's first taste of prolonged failure in baseball. Dejection was a constant teammate. But as bad as life was professionally, it was worse spiritually.

Starting in late 2003, Matt had developed a taste for nightlife. He never did drugs, but he drank . . . a lot. And he now admits his relationships with women weren't biblical.

"It was so empty," he said of his life at the time. "It was not fulfilling."

Church was not on the radar. Neither were scripture or prayer. When his team's chapel leader would enter the room, Matt would bolt in the other direction. Everyone could see straight through his spiritual duplicity—or at least, that's the way it felt to Matt. He was ashamed of his spiraling morals but felt powerless to halt the descent.

It wasn't that Matt had renounced his beliefs or questioned scripture's claims. He just wasn't living like the "new creation" the apostle Paul wrote about in 2 Corinthians 5:17. He was running away from God, looking for a ship to take him to Tarshish. But as Jonah learned, you can't outrun the Almighty.

That offseason, the Holy Spirit started stirring in Matt's heart. By the time he arrived in Florida for 2005 spring training, the pistons of conviction were firing full-bore. The Pirates assigned the twenty-one-year-old to Hickory again to start the season. That's when Matt met David Daly.

David, a longtime minister in the area, was in his first year as the Crawdads' chaplain. David saw a spiritual hunger in Matt, and he took an immediate liking to the young man.

Matt felt comfortable around David, too. One Sunday morning early in the season, Matt confided in his new mentor.

"David," Matt said, "I've done a lot of things I shouldn't. Honestly, I've been enjoying them physically, but I know they're not right. I'm not setting a good example for others."

Matt exhaled. It felt so good to confess that to someone! Still, he braced for the hammer of condemnation from David.

Instead, David nodded. He lovingly exhorted Matt to embrace his role as an earthly ambassador of Christ. He told Matt that baseball was a platform for ministry, with nothing less than God's glory at stake.

Matt was all ears. Soon, David asked Matt to become the team's chapel representative. Matt enthusiastically said yes.

But there was much work still to be done. As spiritual warfare raged inside Matt, guilt had entrenched itself deeply in the furrows of his soul. *How,* he wondered, *could God accept a rebel like me? Look at my spiritual rap sheet. My lifestyle has been a complete affront to God's standards. Why should I expect love and forgiveness when my offenses are stacked so high?*

Matt didn't yet grasp divine mercy and grace. So David explained it. He helped Matt see that God sent his perfect Son, Jesus Christ, to cover the overwhelming debt that Matt could not pay. He showed Matt that God's forgiveness was not based on human merit, but rather on the finished work of Calvary.

Matt listened, read scripture, and asked deep questions. Slowly, his myopic view broadened into big-picture understanding. One night following the 2005 season, he was sitting in his bedroom, and—*wham!*—the liberating truth of the gospel hit him.

"That was first time, really, when I asked Jesus to

completely take over my heart," he said. "I had done it at church as a younger kid because I knew it was the right thing to do, but I wasn't sure what I was doing."

David, meanwhile, was enjoying a front-row seat in Matt's transformation.

"He began to take seriously who God had made him to be—a reflection of Christ, not a reflection of Matt," David said. "I don't think that's any small part of his meteoric rise from A ball to the majors."

WELCOME TO THE SHOW

Considering how Matt's 2004 season ended, dreaming of a big league call-up the following year would have been audacious, to say the least. In spring training, the Pirates' organization converted him into a reliever. Matt didn't particularly like the move, but something clicked.

After a virtually unhittable stint at Hickory to start the season, Matt earned an August promotion to Double-A Altoona (Pennsylvania), where he continued his mastery on the mound. In September, he joined Triple-A Indianapolis for the International League Championship Series and threw two scoreless innings in Game 1.

Three days later, barely past his twenty-second birthday, he heard the words every minor leaguer dreams of hearing: "You're going to the big leagues, son." He was headed to Pittsburgh.

The Pirates were in disarray. Ten days earlier, they had fired manager Lloyd McClendon and replaced him with bench coach Pete Mackanin as they spiraled toward a 67–95 record and their thirteenth straight losing season. But Matt didn't care. He had made The Show.

Matt Capps, a burly eight-year major league veteran, transformed himself from a seventh-round draft pick in 2002 into an All-Star closer who won the 2010 Midsummer Classic. (AP Photo/Genevieve Ross)

That day—and all its craziness—will forever be etched on Matt's mind. After learning of his promotion at 1 a.m., he boarded a plane the next morning for a 9:30 flight to Pittsburgh, where the Pirates were hosting Cincinnati in a doubleheader, starting at 5:06. But as his plane was preparing to taxi, the flight was cancelled due to engine problems.

Matt languished in the airport terminal for five hours before boarding another plane, which landed in Pittsburgh twenty minutes before the start of the first game. He arrived at PNC Park by cab in the third inning. Once there, he had to wait at the player's entrance because his credentials hadn't arrived and the security guards didn't recognize him. Finally, by the top of the sixth, a frazzled Matt reached the bullpen.

Two innings later—yikes!—he entered the game with the Pirates trailing 3–0 in an eventual 8–2 loss. On Matt's first pitch, Reds outfielder Chris Denorfia, who had made his own major league debut just nine days earlier, smacked a liner to right-center. Denorfia stole second, but Matt buckled down. He struck out a pair of Pirates, but just when he thought he was going out of the jam, a single drove Denorfia home. Welcome to the big leagues, kid. Matt got pitcher Brandon Claussen to line out to end the inning.

He made three other appearances that season and finished with a 4.50 ERA in four innings. His talent was raw, but the kid showed promise.

"That was a fun season for me," he says. "I started the season not even on the radar, and then I ended up in Pittsburgh."

The following season, Matt proved he belonged by going 9–1 with a 3.79 ERA and allowing only 12 walks in a whopping 85 innings of middle relief. The Pirates loved the way the burly right-hander pounded the strike zone with mid-nineties fastballs while keeping hitters off-balance with a wicked slider and an occasional changeup.

After starting 2007 as the Pirates' setup man, Matt replaced the struggling Salomon Torres as the closer on June 1. He responded by converting his first nine save opportunities and finished with 18 total and a 2.28 ERA.

The hard-throwing kid from Douglasville was on his way up. But even at that new elevation in life, he couldn't foresee the gathering storm clouds in the distance.

LOVE ENTERS THE GAME

"I could marry that girl tomorrow."

Brett Campbell laughed at Matt's hasty comment. This, after all, was coming from the guy who'd initially balked at the idea of meeting Jenn Martin in the first place.

"You are an idiot," Brett said.

Brett's crack didn't even register. "I don't know," Matt said dreamily. "I've just never felt this way before."

Brett started his car, and the two friends drove off. It was late 2006, shortly after Matt's rookie season with the Pirates, and the buddies had just finished a blind double date at a Texas Roadhouse in Douglasville.

Neither Matt nor Jenn entered the evening with many expectations. The whole thing was the idea of Matt's agent's daughter-in-law, who worked with Jenn. Matt wasn't a big fan of blind dates. Jenn was just coming out of another relationship and didn't want to date a baseball player.

Other than that, what could go wrong?

The evening went harmlessly enough. Matt didn't say

much. Jenn wasn't repulsed, but she wasn't exactly smitten, either. Brett had every reason for skepticism.

Matt called Jenn several times over the next two weeks, but she didn't respond. Her silence seemed awfully loud. Then, the day before he left for a vacation, she called. Matt floated the idea of another date. Jenn's tepid response didn't exactly inspire confidence, but they eventually went out again.

The ensuing courtship was slower than a Tim Wakefield knuckleball. After a couple more dates, Matt had to leave for spring training in Florida. Surviving the distance gauntlet was no guarantee.

Still, there was hope. Matt and Jenn talked on the phone almost every day, and Jenn agreed to attend the Pirates' second regular-season series in Cincinnati that April since she had family in the area.

Matt had a fairly uneventful weekend, appearing in only the Sunday finale and throwing one and a third scoreless innings. But off the field, he was falling hard for Jenn. By mid-July, he knew he wanted to marry her.

During a Pittsburgh home stand that month, Jenn flew into town to see him, and the couple went out to dinner after a day game. Had anyone had the audacity to lift up Matt's pant leg, he would have noticed a large bulge in his sock. Matt had hidden an engagement ring there.

Call it cautiousness bordering on fear. A man's mind processes a thousand thoughts when he's about to propose, and most of them explore the countless ways his romantic magnum opus can crumble into epic failure.

The site Matt had chosen to pop the question was Pittsburgh's charming Mount Washington neighborhood, which sits six hundred feet above downtown and is accessible by two historic incline railcars. At night, Mount Washington provides a stunning view of Pittsburgh's glittering skyline and the convergence of the Allegheny, Monongahela, and Ohio rivers. *USA Today Weekend Magazine*, in fact, ranked Mount Washington's nighttime view second on its list of the ten most beautiful places in America in 2003.

The moment had arrived. Matt swallowed hard. The butterflies that had been flitting about in his stomach all evening were now like fighter planes engaging in a World War II dogfight.

Then, from out of nowhere, a female voice broke the tension: "Oh my gosh, you're Matt Capps!" A local Pirates fan, enamored at her good fortune to run into the team's newly minted closer, ran up to greet Matt.

Talk about a mood-killer.

All was not lost, though. While at the lookout, Matt had noticed that the Point State Park fountain—a civic treasure in Pittsburgh for its central water plume that blasts one hundred feet high and its scenic location on the bank of the Ohio River—was finally working. It hadn't worked all season.

Coincidence? Perhaps. But Matt saw it as serendipity.

"What are we doing?" Jenn asked as they boarded a descending railcar.

"Let's go for a walk," Matt coyly responded.

At the fountain, Matt handed her a penny. "Make a wish," he said. They both threw their pennies into the water, and Matt playfully asked what she wished for.

"I can't tell you if I want it to come true," Jenn replied, smiling. By the time she asked Matt about his wish, he was down on one knee.

"Shut up! Shut up! Shut up!" Jenn screamed in raw excitement. Then, thankfully, she said yes. In November 2008, the couple got married.

"She loves the Lord and loves him," David Daly says of Jenn. "He's blessed to have her and he knows it. Her family is very kind to him."

Matt and Jenn recently bought a house on a five-acre spread in Roswell, Georgia, just north of greater Atlanta, to be close to their friends and family. In February 2012, they had their first child.

Through it all, Matt has discovered what he savors most about marriage.

"My favorite part," he said, "is knowing that every time I come home from the field, she's there waiting for me. It could be a good day, bad day or a nothing day, and I get to spend the rest of the day or night with her. It makes me a better person."

FATHER KNOWS BEST

In 2008, Matt enjoyed another solid season, posting 21 saves and a 3.02 ERA despite missing almost two months with bursitis in his right shoulder. All signs pointed to a breakout 2009. But baseball has a funny way of taking "all signs" and throwing them into a meat grinder.

Matt saved 27 games in 2009, then a career high, but otherwise it was a disastrous season. Opposing hitters batted .324 against him, almost like he was lobbing a softball underhanded. His ERA ballooned to 5.80.

"It was a pretty rough year," Matt says. "Baseball is one of those games that, as long as the season is, you've got to find a way to put the last game behind you. You can't worry about last night or the next. You have to worry about today."

After the 2009 season finale—a listless 6–0 loss to the Reds on October 4 that dropped the Pirates to 62–99, their worst record in eight years—Matt was ready for a mental break. But it never came.

Sixteen days later, Matt's father fell in his carport and hit his head on the concrete floor. When Kathy found Mike a few minutes later, he was breathing but unconscious, bleeding badly, and had significant brain damage. By the time the paramedics arrived, Mike had gone into cardiac arrest.

It was the final blow to a weary body that had endured five heart attacks, lung surgery, and more than two dozen kidney operations.

Matt and Jenn made it to the hospital to see Mike one last time. But in essence, he was gone. On October 22, 2009, two days after Mike's fall, the family took him off life support. He was sixty-one.

The loss was devastating to Matt. His father meant the world to him.

Mike was a rough-edged, no-frills kind of man. For most of Matt's life, Mike had been a real estate appraiser. But he had held other jobs, too—like working in a hospital or running a food joint called the Wiener Stand. Whatever it took to provide for his family.

The Capps family wasn't well-off, but Mike loved giving his sons opportunities. Ironically, a Little League experience was the one thing Mike initially didn't want Matt to have. He was suspicious of the local league's politics and good-ol'-boy network. But one of the Capps' neighbors, who also coached a team, persuaded Mike to let Matt join.

Mike never did anything halfway. So before you could say "Batter up!" he had purchased a baseball rulebook to learn the game's intricacies and had become the vice president of the local league's board of directors. Anytime Matt was on the field, even at practices, Mike seemed to be there, too.

In 1990, Mike made a friendly wager with Matt, only seven years old at the time, on the Cincinnati-Oakland World Series. Mike won by picking the Reds. The former Little League naysayer had transformed into a bona fide seamhead.

Father and son bonded over Atlanta Braves games at the old Atlanta-Fulton County Stadium. Young Matt would gawk in wide-eyed wonder as stars like Dale Murphy and Chipper Jones launched bombs into the bleachers.

"Man, that's got to be cool to be a major leaguer," Matt would say.

Without hesitation, Mike replied, "Someone has to be the best. Why not you?"

The words resonated in Matt like a motivational soundtrack:

Someone has to be . . .
Someone has to be . . .
Someone has to be . . .

For Mike, baseball became a teaching tool about life. He wasn't always a gentle instructor, but he was effective. He dispensed tough love, sometimes breaching his son's emotional dam. But Matt never doubted Mike's affection. *That's just the way Dad pushes me,* Matt told himself.

Even in Little League, Matt quickly learned that a bad day on the field meant a long car ride home. If he struck out or committed an error, he'd try to sneak into his mom's car. It never worked.

"C'mon, let's go," Mike would say, with a firm voice and an equally firm hand on Matt's shoulder.

In the best game of his high school career, Matt enjoyed a sublime day at the plate: three for four with a home run and two doubles. Only one problem: He didn't go four for four. The lone blemish was a strikeout.

"That's all I heard about for two weeks," Matt says. "He'd say, 'You don't know the strike zone! How are you going to go to college or play professionally?' Once I got drafted, there was more encouragement. He'd try to pick me up more than break me down. And he *did* a few times—he did break me down. But I think he knew it. I think he knew that would drive me."

Once Matt reached the majors, he started calling his father after every outing so he could scrutinize his performance, whether good or bad. Imagine: a major leaguer taking advice from a guy who hardly ever played baseball growing up! But that was Matt and his dad.

In 2008, Matt noticed a change in Mike's attitude during their late-night chats. After one game, Mike said, "I think I'm going to stop telling you things about baseball. You're smarter than me about it." Just like that, the advisor became a listener. Matt will never forget that night.

Something else peculiar: Earlier on the day he fell, Mike had called Matt to chat. The two always ended their conversations with "Love ya."

But on this day, Mike said, "I love you, son." It was a small variance, but one that stuck with Matt. Later that night, Chris called with the horrible news.

To this day, Mike's insights still reverberate in Matt. On the underside of his game hat, Matt writes: *Someone has to be*. But the most important lesson Mike taught Matt was often unspoken—and it extended far beyond baseball.

"The most important thing is impacting others," Matt said. "My dad touched a lot of lives. Every time I go home, [people] talk about the imprint that he left on their lives. It's hard for me to imagine that anything I do on a baseball field means more than what I can do off it."

MOVING ON

If Mike's death was a punch that sent Matt reeling, the next blow was a kick to the gut while he was down. Seven weeks after Mike passed away, Pittsburgh, the only team Matt had known in his first eight professional seasons, released him after a contract dispute. Matt made $2.4 million in 2009 and, despite his off year, likely would have received a raise in arbitration, a process that often favors the players. Pittsburgh decided to move on.

On January 6, 2010, Matt signed a one-year, $3.5 million deal with the Washington Nationals, who were desperately looking to shore up their bullpen after a 59–103 train wreck in 2009.

In D.C., the 2010 season could best be summed up in one word: Strasburg. The local—and national—media went gaga that summer for Stephen Strasburg, and rightfully so. The flame-throwing prodigy and No. 1 overall draft pick from 2009 captivated a slack-jawed national audience with a dazzling twelve-game rookie debut before suffering a season-ending arm injury in August.

Lost in the hullabaloo was a great career renaissance story of a quiet, down-to-earth, country music-loving Georgian whose best fastballs weren't far off Strasburgian levels. In fact, on the same night that Strasburg made his breathlessly awaited debut on June 8, 2010, Matt earned his nineteenth save with a ten-pitch ninth inning.

"The night that Strasburg pitched, which everybody seems to forget that [Capps] pitched in, he hit 97 miles per hour," Nationals pitching coach Steve McCatty recalled.

With *Someone has to be* etched onto his cap, Matt conjured up magic fireballs from his fingertips once more in 2010, earning baseball's top relief pitcher award in April and his first All-Star selection. In the All-Star Game, he struck out his only batter, Boston slugger David Ortiz, in the bottom of the sixth, then earned the win when the National League, which trailed 1–0 when he entered the game, scored three runs in the top of the seventh for an eventual 3–1 victory. Not a bad night.

The game of baseball, though, is nothing if not ironic. Matt's stock was so high that summer he became trade bait for contenders. Two weeks later, Washington dealt him to Minnesota, which eventually won the American League Central Division crown, thanks in no small part to Matt's arrival.

With Minnesota, he was even more dominant (2.00 ERA, 1.19 WHIP) than he had been with Washington (2.74 ERA, 1.30 WHIP). Matt's first trip to the playoffs ended with a first-round exit, but he finished the year with a career-best 42 saves and a 2.47 ERA.

"It was a whirlwind of a season," Matt said.

The winds of change continued in 2011. After starting the season as Minnesota closer Joe Nathan's setup man, Matt assumed ninth-inning duties in mid-April at the suggestion of Nathan, who was struggling to regain his consistency following elbow surgery. But by July 16, Matt had blown seven saves in 22 chances and struggled to a 4.76 ERA, prompting Twins manager Ron Gardenhire to switch to Nathan again. Matt finished the season with a 4–7 record and only 15 saves. He hopes to rebound with the Twins in 2012.

THE FACE OF FAITH

At the start of the 2009 season, when Matt was still a Pirate, David Daly had something he wanted to show Matt and Jenn. David recently had been named the Fellowship of Christian Athletes' national baseball director, and the ministry had published an exciting new product.

So David took the couple to dinner at Jerome Bettis' Grille 36 restaurant, wedged in between PNC Park and Heinz Field on the Three Rivers waterfront. There, over tuna, steak, and salad, he showed them a mock-up version of the new FCA Baseball New Testament. Matt was on the cover.

David expected smiles and giddiness. Instead, Jenn started crying.

The culprit wasn't sorrow, though. She was simply overwhelmed by the shocking contrast: The face of the man who once rebelled against God with an upraised fist was now on a Bible.

A smile altered the path of the tears rolling down her cheek. "I never thought God could use you like this," she said.

God loves paradoxes that bring Him glory. Matt, like all Christians, was once "dead in . . . transgressions and sins" (Ephesians 2:1). But now, he is a new creation, boldly proclaiming his life-giving faith.

When David asked Matt to join FCA Baseball's national board of directors, he jumped at the chance. Before the 2010 season, Matt shared his testimony before four hundred people at an FCA breakfast during the American Baseball Coaches Association's annual convention in Dallas. He has also spoken to hundreds of kids at offseason FCA clinics.

Still, Matt is a relatively private man. He wants to make a difference, not a headline. So he serves in ways that aren't in the camera's lens. There are financial gifts, hospital visits, and other personal interactions we know nothing about.

"I know that God loves me and there's a purpose for me being here," Matt said. "There's a reason why I struggle. There's a reason why I have success. And it's not really for me or you to understand. But there's a higher meaning behind all of it. I don't believe my sole purpose in this world is to be a professional athlete or to do anything on the baseball field.

"There's a greater reason, a better reason, for me to be on this earth. Baseball is the resource God has put in front of me to spread the gospel and make other people aware."

As Matt's father once said, someone has to be.

2012 season update: The 2012 season was a mixed bag for Capps. Statistically, the Minnesota Twins' closer was solid with a 3.68 ERA and 14 saves in 15 opportunities. But inflammation in his right shoulder sent him to the disabled list twice, and he only made three appearances after the All-Star break. On October 29, 2012, the Twins declined Capps' $6 million option, granting him free agency.

10

MARK TEIXEIRA:
HITTING ON ALL CYLINDERS

Rarely does a single set off this much celebration.

But on August 17, 2004, Mark Teixeira's leadoff single in the top of the seventh inning electrified the crowd at Ameriquest Field in Arlington, Texas.

No, Mark's hit didn't win the game. The Texas Rangers were already ahead 16–1 against the Cleveland Indians.

And no, it wasn't his three thousandth base knock, because the twenty-four-year-old had only been in the majors for a couple of seasons.

But Mark's single did make history because he'd already collected a triple, home run, and double in his previous three at-bats. So his "meaningless" single in the seventh had plenty of meaning, putting Mark in a select group of athletes who have hit for "the cycle."

Since statistics have been kept, a player has hit a single, a double, a triple, and a home run in a nine-inning game less than three hundred times in Major League Baseball's 135-year history.

On May 25, 1882, Curry Foley of the Buffalo Bisons became the first player to hit for the cycle. Since that time, nearly four hundred thousand major league games have been played ... and still fewer than three hundred players have ever hit for the cycle.

For Mark, it took him less than two full seasons to accomplish this rare feat. More impressively, he became only the seventeenth switch-hitter to do it.

Mark's evening against the Indians didn't start out in an historical manner. He struck out in his first at bat. But the second time he came to the plate, he smacked a two-run double. Then he hit a three-run home run in the fourth inning and a triple in the fifth that scored two more runs.

By the time Mark came up to bat in the seventh, he had already collected seven RBIs and just needed a single to complete the cycle.

"[My teammates] were kidding me, telling me to trip over first base if I hit one into the gap," Mark joked.

But Mark didn't have to trip or fake an injury to stay on first; he hit a line drive single up the middle. A pinch runner came in for Mark as 24,864 fans gave him a standing ovation.

That wouldn't be the last standing ovation this 6-foot, 3-inch, 220-pound power hitter would receive. Since 2003, Mark has been one of the best players in baseball.

In 2003, his first year with the Rangers, Mark hammered 26 home runs and was voted the American League Rookie of the Year. His home run total jumped to 38 the following year (to go along with 112 RBIs).

But 2005 turned out to be his breakout year. That season,

Mark crushed 41 homers and drove in a staggering 144 runs— the most for a switch-hitter in baseball history. In addition, he scored 112 runs, batted .302, and recorded his one hundredth career home run (he ended the year with 105) to become one of just five players in major league history to hit a hundred homers during his first three seasons. Joe DiMaggio, Ralph Kiner, Eddie Mathews, and Albert Pujols are the others.

Through 2010, Mark had won three Silver Slugger awards (which go to the best offensive player at each position in the American and National leagues) and five Gold Gloves (which are awarded to the best defensive player at each position in each league). In fact, in 2005 and 2009, Mark won the Silver Slugger *and* Gold Glove awards—honoring him as the best offensive *and* defensive first baseman in the American League.

How does a player get this good this young? A lot of factors combine to create an All-Star baseball player. But one word leaps to mind when studying Mark: *discipline*.

Mark shows discipline in nearly all areas of his life. From practicing his faith to practicing baseball, he has a consistent mind-set.

"I've always tried to be disciplined," Mark said. "If you're not, then it's easy to stray from the straight road. I always did my homework and took extra swings or extra ground balls."

Players around Mark have joked that his routine can sometimes border on obsessive-compulsive, but he takes his preparation and the game of baseball very seriously. From his pregame peanut butter and jelly sandwich to how he stands for the "The Star-Spangled Banner," Mark's disciplined behavior shines through.

While some players blow bubbles or look at the scoreboard

during the National Anthem, Mark has a distinct routine.

"He stands perfectly straight, head down, shirt tucked in—every single time," former teammate Torii Hunter said. "He doesn't say a word. He doesn't even have a hair out of place."

Mark's laser-like focus and awe-inspiring statistics caused people to take notice. And as his fame grew, so did his bank account. Before the start of the 2006 season, the Rangers gave him a two-year, $15.4 million contract. But Mark didn't finish out his contract in Texas. In 2007, he was traded to Atlanta. He also had a brief stint with the Los Angeles Angels of Anaheim during the 2008 season.

Before the 2009 campaign, Mark made headlines by becoming the highest-paid first baseman in baseball when he signed a $180 million, eight-year deal with the New York Yankees. His $23,125,000 salary in 2011 ranked him fourth among the highest-paid players in the sport. Only Yankee teammates Alex Rodriguez and C.C. Sabathia and Angels outfielder Vernon Wells made more.

While the awards and money are nice, they're not the reason Mark plays baseball. He knows God has given him a gift, and he wants to honor God with how he goes about his business on the diamond.

"I try to live and play baseball the way that I think the Lord would want me to," Mark said. "I try to do the right things on the field and off the field."

Some players may just say those words, but Mark lives them out with his actions and his wallet.

PUTTING HIS MONEY WHERE HIS FAITH IS

Faith has always been important to Mark Charles Teixeira,

who was born in Annapolis, Maryland, on April 11, 1980. His Portuguese surname is pronounced *Te-share-ah*.

During his early elementary school years, Mark showed tremendous athletic ability. He played baseball, soccer, and basketball, and he often participated in tournaments in which he competed in five or six games every weekend. But no matter where the family was, Mark found himself in church on Saturday nights or Sunday mornings.

"At a very young age, I learned about Jesus and how important your faith is," Mark said. "My parents were definitely the most influential people in my life . . . and they taught me the right values."

Mark dedicated his life to God as a child and has continually sought to serve Him, so as he got older and was rewarded monetarily for his athletic talents, he gave back to God.

This started in 2001 after Mark signed his first major league contract. The Rangers drafted him fifth overall and signed him to a four-year, $9.5 million package with a $4.5 million signing bonus. Once the ink was dry, Mark went back to his old high school, Mount St. Joseph, and talked with principal Barry Fitzpatrick.

During Mark's junior year, one of his best friends, Nick Liberatore, was killed in a car accident when a truck driver fell asleep at the wheel and plowed into his parked car. The loss devastated the Liberatore family . . . and Mark. Now that he had the means, Mark wanted to create a scholarship to honor his friend.

The principal told Mark that it would cost $75,000 to start the scholarship. Without hesitation, Mark wrote the check and created the Nick Liberatore scholarship program. He still funds that scholarship, helping make the college dreams of kids from his hometown a reality. In fact, President Barack Obama talked about Mark's generous spirit when the Yankees visited the White House in 2010 to celebrate their World Series victory.

"For the president to single me out, I was very honored," Mark said. "I've always thought baseball is just a tool for me to try to do work for other people. I've been very blessed in my career, and the first thing I did when I had a chance was that scholarship."

But that certainly wasn't the last thing he did. Mark gives his money and his time to a number of important causes.

After graduating from Georgia Tech, Mark established a $500,000 baseball scholarship called the Mark C. Teixeira Athletic Scholarship. Mark received a scholarship to attend the Atlanta-based university and wanted to fund the collegiate aspirations of other players.

He also gave back in a big way to Mount St. Joseph in 2008. His former high school in Baltimore was in the middle of a $10 million "Building Men Who Matter" campaign to update and expand its facilities. Mark's million-dollar donation helped make that happen.

Over the years, Mark also has created college scholarships for deserving high school seniors in the Dallas area.

Based on Mark's giving, it's obvious that education and sports are important to him.

"Ever since I started [my foundation], it has been very involved with college scholarships, education, and children's needs," Mark said. "Whether it's the Police Athletic League, or the Boys & Girls Clubs, those sort of things are really close to my heart."

So when Mark moved to the Yankees in 2009, it was no surprise that he got involved in Harlem RBI.

Started in 1991 when a handful of volunteers turned an abandoned lot in East Harlem into two baseball diamonds, Harlem RBI now serves a thousand boys and girls ages five to twenty-one. With year-round academic, sports, and enrichment programs, this organization has seen huge success in giving hope to children who come from seemingly hopeless situations.

Since 2005, 98 percent of Harlem RBI seniors have graduated high school with 94 percent of them earning acceptance into college.

In May 2010, Mark donated $100,000 and agreed to join the board of directors. But in 2011, he stepped up his commitment by giving $1 million and becoming the co-chair of a $20 million Harlem RBI capital campaign. In all, the goal was to build an $85 million, thirteen-story building that will become the home to Harlem RBI headquarters, its DREAM charter school, and ninety affordable housing units.

Groundbreaking for the Harlem RBI building is scheduled for the summer of 2012 with the project completed in 2014. Since Mark signed an eight-year deal with the Yankees in 2008, he should be able to watch the buildings go up the entire way.

"I became involved with Harlem RBI and DREAM charter because I believe the work we are doing is truly changing lives," Mark said.

Although Mark has plenty of well-paid teammates, he doesn't pressure them to give. The president may have singled out Mark, but he said a number of his Yankee teammates are involved in their own charitable endeavors. He doesn't think it'd be fair to ask them to donate when they're already doing so much in areas that are close to their hearts.

Mark enjoys being hands-on. He likes meeting kids and making a difference in their lives. But sometimes those kids have a bigger impact on him than he does on them.

That was the case when Mark visited Brian Ernst at Children's Hospital in Atlanta in 2010.

Brian loved baseball. As a star pitcher at West Hall High School in Oakwood, Georgia, he dreamed about making it to the big leagues. But shortly after his seventeenth birthday, Brian was diagnosed with Ewing's sarcoma, a rare cancer found in bone or soft tissue. Brian battled valiantly but died at nineteen.

Before Brian's death, Mark visited him through the Make-A-Wish Foundation. Originally, Brian had planned to fly to New York and play catch with Mark at Yankee Stadium. But his failing health limited travel. Instead, Mark traveled to Atlanta in February. When Mark walked into the hospital, a Make-A-Wish representative met him and said that Brian might not be feeling well enough to see him in person. But by the time the Yankee All-Star made it to Brian's room, the teen was sitting up in bed and wearing Mark's No. 25 Yankees' jersey.

Although Brian hadn't been too responsive the previous few days, he and Mark talked for several hours—not only about baseball, basketball, and football, but also about Brian's desire to help other people, especially children, fighting similar diseases.

During Brian's time at the hospital, he had kept a positive

attitude and helped cheer up younger children who had cancer.

"I've visited hospitals before and worked with the Make-A-Wish Foundation," Mark said. "You think you're giving a kid something, but after I left Brian, he gave me something. . . . Brian changed lives. He really did.

"Brian didn't lose his battle with cancer. He won the battle. It didn't break him down. He showed everybody that you can live through cancer, make a difference, and inspire people no matter what circumstance you have."

After Brian died, Mark invited his family to Yankee Stadium for the home opener on April 13, 2010. Brian's father, mother, and brother made the trip. The Ernsts sat with Mark's wife, Leigh, and his parents during the game. Mark also gave Brian's parents his game cap, which had been inscribed with "Brian, Faith, #5"—the number of Brian's high school baseball uniform. Mark wore that inscription the entire 2010 season.

"The thing that was so amazing about Brian was his faith throughout his ordeal," Mark said. "He was so upbeat, and he knew that God gave him this [trial] to teach other people about faith."

Meeting Brian strengthened Mark's faith, and he wants to have a similar effect through his actions on and off the field. At the same time, Mark doesn't want to give people the wrong idea that good actions can earn favor with God.

Mark gives his time and money to help others out of gratitude for how much God has blessed him—not to earn brownie points with his heavenly Father.

"Our deeds don't make us righteous," Mark said. "Our deeds don't make us worthy to be in God's presence or to be in His Kingdom. . . . God's righteousness is given to us, and His grace is given to us as a gift."

GIFTED ATHLETE MAKES GOOD

Mark knows his athletic abilities were also a gift. He grew up in the Baltimore suburb of New Canaan with a ball of some sort always nearby.

"My parents brought me up in a home where we worked very hard and did our best," Mark said. "But we also realized the gifts that we had were from God."

His parents didn't force him to play baseball. In fact, they wanted him to try lots of different sports. He played soccer and basketball competitively, but he always came back to America's pastime.

By the time Mark was nine, he had announced to his mom that he wanted to be a major league baseball player. That shouldn't have been too surprising. Baseball ran in his blood. His mom's brothers were good baseball players, and his dad had played for the United States Naval Academy in college. His uncle even made it into the Braves' minor league system.

Most of Mark's favorite athletes growing up were baseball players. While Mark normally bled orange and black, the team colors of his hometown Baltimore Orioles, he had a special affinity for New York first baseman Don Mattingly. The popular Yankee played from 1982 to 1995 and was known for his smooth swing, competitive drive, and defensive skills.

Mark put a poster of Mattingly in his bedroom and chose to wear No. 23 in honor of his favorite player. He even risked ridicule and injury by donning a Yankees' cap to Baltimore Orioles games when the Bronx Bombers were in town.

The preteen continued to play youth baseball, but he didn't do a whole lot to further his professional aspirations until he finished middle school. That's when the family decided to send Mark to Mount St. Joseph, an all-boys high school with a solid baseball program.

"People would think I'm crazy, but it was the greatest thing for me," Mark said about attending the private school. "I didn't have to worry about impressing girls or having distractions. . . . During those school hours, it was very important to be focused."

Mount St. Joseph did have two sister schools, so the athletic teams had cheerleaders, and the schools enjoyed dances together. But Mark was serious about his schoolwork and playing baseball.

Mark saw a little varsity action his freshman year, but when he took over third base duties as a sophomore in 1996, he never gave them up. While he sprinkled seven home runs in his first two seasons, Mark grew into a power hitter his last two. He was an All-Metro selection as a sophomore, but he gained a lot of recognition as a junior by hitting .518 with 10 home runs. During his senior year, he belted 12 homers while knocking in 36 RBIs. The slugger also batted a staggering .568.

By the time he graduated, Mark's 29 career home runs stood as a Maryland Interscholastic Athletic Association record, as did his 108 RBIs and 128 hits.

The *Baltimore Sun* named Mark its 1998 Baseball Player of the Year, which looked pretty good along with *USA Baseball* calling him Maryland's top junior the previous season.

Baseball America projected Mark as a first-round pick in the 1998 draft. But when the June draft day rolled around, the Boston Red Sox selected Mark in the ninth round.

Baseball insiders were perplexed at how someone with first-round talent, intelligence, and attitude would drop so low. Some felt it may have been because agent Scott Boras was advising Mark. Boras, one of the top agents in the game, was known as a tough, hardnosed negotiator. Others speculated that teams felt Mark (who was a member of the National Honor Society and graduated twelfth in his class) planned to go to college, so it wasn't worth wasting a pick.

Despite picking Mark so low, Boston still offered the teen first-round money—a $1.5 million signing bonus to be exact. Boras felt the offer was on the low end.

Instead of signing, Mark turned down $1.5 million and enrolled at the Georgia Institute of Technology on a baseball scholarship.

Most teens wouldn't have patience and foresight to walk away from that kind of money. But Mark wasn't a typical teenager. In addition to losing one of his best friends in a car accident, Mark had witnessed his mother fight breast cancer during high school. Seeing firsthand that life can be short made Mark serious about working toward his dreams.

Going to Georgia Tech turned out to be a great decision. Not only was Mark at a highly ranked academic school with a good baseball program, but, more importantly, he also met his future wife, Leigh, at a party during his freshman year. The couple married in December 2002.

Those were "the best three years of my life," Mark has often said. Looking at his statistics and what those years led to, it's hard to argue with him.

As a freshman, Mark batted .387 with 13 home runs

and 65 RBIs. Those numbers earned him the 1999 National Freshman of the Year and ACC Rookie of the Year honors. He followed that up with an even bigger year as a sophomore: his .427 batting average, 18 home runs, 80 RBIs, and 104 runs scored put him near the top of every batting category in his conference. His 67 walks were tops in the nation.

With Mark leading the way, the Yellow Jackets posted a 50–16 record and made it to the College World Series. The sophomore was nearly a unanimous selection as the National Player of the Year.

After playing a summer of baseball with the Maryland Battlecats in a twenty-and-under league, Mark looked forward to bolstering his professional stock with an even bigger junior year.

Seven games into the season, however, Mark broke his ankle and missed nearly the entire year.

In Mark's three years at Georgia Tech, he batted over .400 and helped the school win 129 games. (He was inducted into the Tech Hall of Fame on November 9, 2011.) He declared himself eligible for the 2001 draft and was picked fifth overall by the Texas Rangers. *USA Today* wrote that he was "at least as good a hitting prospect as past college stars Barry Bonds, Mark McGwire, J.D. Drew, and Pat Burrell."

Mark quickly lived up to the hype by collecting hits in twelve consecutive games at Class A Charlotte in the Florida State League. Before the summer of 2002 was over, Mark was playing for the Double-A Tulsa Drillers, where he drilled 24 extra-base hits in 48 games. He ended the year playing fall ball in Arizona, hitting seven home runs and knocking in 23 RBIs in just 27 games.

When Mark entered spring training in 2003, he did it

with just one goal: make the big league ball club. His spectacular play made it easy for the Texas management. After hitting a team-record eight homers in spring training, his name made the list on Opening Day.

With Hank Blalock entrenched at third base, Texas looked for ways to get Mark on the field. He played outfield, first base, and several games at third. In 146 games, he batted just .259, but his 26 home runs and 84 RBIs were tops for rookies.

By 2005, Mark had established himself as one of the best first basemen in the game. Had Texas been a perennial playoff contender, casual fans would've known his exploits. As it was, Mark was quietly making a name for himself.

During the 2007 season, with the Rangers out of the playoff picture and Mark in the middle of contract negotiations, he was traded to Atlanta. The deal came just two weeks after he had turned down an eight-year, $140 million contract extension.

Right away, Mark looked at home in his former hometown. He homered in each of his first three games as a Brave. A few weeks later, Mark put together back-to-back multiple home run games. On August 19, he hit two jacks from the left side of the plate. The next night he went yard twice from the right side.

In 54 games with Atlanta, Mark batted .317 with 17 home runs and 56 RBIs. The Braves signed their new first baseman to a one-year contract worth $12.5 million.

But Mark didn't finish the 2008 season with the Braves: he was traded to the Los Angeles Angels of Anaheim in July. Batting third for the Angels, he helped lead the team to its first-ever hundred-win season. The first round of the playoffs didn't go as well, though, as the Angels fell to Boston.

With the season and his contract over, Mark became a

Yankees infielder Mark Teixeira shows off his swing in a game against Detroit. Teixeira finished the 2011 season with 39 home runs, 111 RBIs, and a .248 batting average. Injuries, however, limited his 2012 campaign to 123 games, in which he batted .251 with 24 home runs and 84 RBIs. (Tomasso De Rosa/ Four Seam Images via AP Images)

free agent in November 2008. The Angels, Red Sox, Orioles, and Washington Nationals all bid for his services. But in the end, Mark found himself in the Big Apple.

BIGGEST STAGE ON EARTH

The move made sense for Mark. Not only was the money outstanding, but the contract also came with a full no-trade clause. Plus, it got Mark and his young family closer to their families on the East Coast.

Not that the decision didn't come without a cost. Mark had to give up his favorite number 23 because the Yankees had retired Mattingly's jersey. He chose to wear number 25. But perhaps more difficult for Mark was the fact that he was now playing in the fishbowl known as Yankee Stadium.

"No one's going to expect more out of me than me," Mark said. "I believe I have yet to tap my potential. I'm trying to get better. I haven't accomplished anything yet—I don't have a World Series ring on my finger."

After being announced as a Yankee on January 6, 2009, and going through spring training, the season started out in typical fashion for Mark—poorly. Since entering the big leagues, he's been a notoriously slow starter.

During the month of April, Mark batted .200 with just three homers and 10 RBIs. That wasn't what the New York faithful were hoping to get from their new $180 million man. The cheers that greeted Mark at the beginning of the season quickly turned to boos.

Mark started putting in extra time with Yankees hitting coach Kevin Long, who pointed out a couple of mechanical tweaks but told Mark to stay positive.

"I let him know that I was behind him all the way," Long wrote about conversations with Mark in his book *Cage Rat*. "I knew that it was just a matter of time."

In six Aprils before joining the Yankees, he amassed a total of 19 home runs and 65 RBIs. During those same six seasons in the month of September, Mark had 44 homers and 152 RBIs.

Yankee fans aren't known for their patience, and they let Mark hear their displeasure. But even in the midst of his early season slump, Mark gave them something to cheer about.

On June 12, 2009, the Yankees hosted the New York Mets in an interleague game. Mark contributed early by blasting a two-run home run in the third inning, but in the bottom of the ninth his team trailed 8–7 with two outs. The Yankees still had hope as Derek Jeter was on second and Mark stood on first with Alex Rodriguez at the plate. However, A-Rod popped the ball up in shallow right field, and Mets' Gold Glove second baseman Luis Castillo drifted over to make the final out.

Not taking anything for granted, Mark started sprinting around the bases. And then the unthinkable happened: Castillo dropped the ball!

Never slacking his pace, Mark rounded third and slid into home plate to give the Yankees a 9–8 victory.

"When you're on the bases, why not run hard?" Mark said. "There's no reason not to play the game hard. . . . It was the third month I was with the Yankees, so [the fans] were still getting to know me. So to see that play hopefully gave them a little bit of an insight into the kind of player I am and the pride that I take in playing the game."

That pride and determination eventually resulted in solid numbers at the plate. Batting third all season, Mark helped lead the Yankees into the playoffs. He even led the American League with 39 home runs and 122 RBIs—not bad considering his incredibly slow start.

New York began the American League Division Series against Minnesota. After the Yankees easily won the first game 7–2, Mark lifted his team to a 4–3 victory in Game 2 with a walk-off home run in the eleventh inning. It was Mark's first postseason homer and couldn't have come at a better time.

The Yankees swept the Twins and earned the right to face Mark's former team, the Angels, in the AL Championship Series. New York jumped out to a quick 2–0 lead in the best-of-seven series and beat the Angels four games to two.

In the World Series, New York battled Philadelphia. The Phillies won Game 1 in New York and led early in Game 2 before Mark helped jumpstart the offense. His solo homer in the fourth inning tied the game 1–1. New York added runs in the sixth and seventh to win 3–1.

New York notched victories in the next two games in Philly as Mark scored a run in each game. By the time the series returned to New York, the Yankees were leading three games to two.

The Yankees claimed their record twenty-seventh World Series title on November 5, 2009, with a 7–3 victory. Mark tallied a run and an RBI in the game.

Despite struggling in the playoffs (he batted just .136 in the World Series and .180 for the postseason), celebrating his first World Series victory was sweet for Mark.

"For us to be holding the trophy at the end of the season, it was a special year," Mark said. "We're very blessed to win the World Series in my first year here."

Mark knows he's blessed off the field as well. He and Leigh have three young children, Jack, Addison, and William, and live in Greenwich, Connecticut.

Mark enjoys getting away from baseball and spending time with his family. Hours with his kids are special, considering the amount of time he's gone during the regular season, but he says his children have also had a profound impact on his faith in Christ.

"When my first son was born in 2006, I just realized the love that God has for all of us," Mark said. "It was seeing my son born and knowing the unconditional love that I have for him."

Being a father has also increased Mark's ability to quote children's movies. One of his favorite things to do at home is pop a bag of popcorn, go into his theater room with his kids, and watch a film. His kids liked *Kung Fu Panda* so much that they wore out a couple of DVDs.

"I can probably quote the entire movie start to finish," Mark said.

Having a strong family and firm faith help Mark deal with the ups and downs of the long baseball season and with the brutal New York media.

He had his worst April ever in 2010, hitting just .136 for the month. Headlines were written that bashed Mark's abilities, including one that read: "Tex Mess." In the midst of the slump, Mark never doubted himself or God.

"Baseball is a game of failure," Mark said. "There are plenty of opportunities to be down, to feel sorry for yourself . . . but when you have God in your life and you follow Christ, you're never going to be let down. Every time you fail, He's there to pick you right back up."

And Mark's season did pick up. He rebounded to post respectable numbers by the end of the year: 33 home runs, 108 RBIs, and a .256 batting average. He even had a three-home-run game against Boston in May, making him only the second player in Yanks' history besides Lou Gehrig to accomplish the feat against the Red Sox.

The 2011 season started differently for Mark. Because he worked out less with weights and spent more time in the batting cage, his bat felt quicker. He responded by hitting home runs in his first three games. By the end of June, he already had 63 RBIs and 25 homers, including a monumental one he hit on the last day of the month.

On June 30, Mark launched the three hundredth home run of his career in a 5–0 victory over the Milwaukee Brewers. Only 130 other major league players have ever hit this benchmark. But just like hitting droughts don't get him down, this milestone didn't impress him.

"My faith keeps me grounded," Mark said. "I know no matter my success or failure on the field that there's a higher thing for me with God and with Jesus. To have that kind of faith, it makes the failures here not as important because the most important thing is my faith and my relationship with God."

2012 season update: Mark battled leg injuries throughout much of the 2012 season, causing his batting statistics to lag behind his career averages. Still, his hard-hitting Yankees won the American League East with a 95–67 record. Mark hit .353 for the Yanks as they dispatched the Baltimore Orioles four games to one in the American League Divisional Series. The New York bats, however, were silenced by Detroit in the AL Divisional Series as the Tigers swept the Yankees in four.

11

BRIAN ROBERTS:
BIG TRIALS, BIG FAITH
FOR A SMALL PLAYER

Each year, millions of tourists from around the world flock to Florida like an enormous migration of birds, enticed by the state's warm weather, natural wonders, and wide array of attractions. The famed beaches. The tropical waters. The Magic Kingdom. Universal Studios. Miami's South Beach. Fort Lauderdale. St. Augustine. The Everglades. The Keys.

Within the continental United States, you can't get much closer to paradise.

But in the summer of 2011, one man was trying desperately to escape Florida. For him, the Sunshine State felt more like a balmy prison cell with palm trees. All of Florida's allurements notwithstanding, Brian Roberts wanted to get the heck out of Dodge.

Brian, the Baltimore Orioles' longtime second baseman, spent most of the season confined to his offseason home in

210

Sarasota, thanks to a concussion he suffered during a headfirst slide into first base in Boston in the middle of May. For an ultra-competitive athlete and the face of a hapless franchise, few things are worse than being restricted by the invisible shackles of a medical clearance that never seems to come.

According to Brian, his extended time on the disabled list was the "toughest stint" of his career. "Certainly for me," he said, "it's the hardest thing that I can go through."

That's saying something. From the moment Brian was born, trials have been flying at him like fastballs from a JUGS machine gone berserk. There have been, to name a few:

- a huge health scare as a child
- a steroids scandal in 2006–2007
- multiple career-threatening injuries

And don't forget the seemingly endless epidemic of losing that has plagued the Orioles throughout Brian's career.

That's not to say there haven't been good times. Brian, a diminutive overachiever with ruffled good looks, is a two-time All-Star with a fat contract and a model for a wife. He is also a genuinely humble man who has become a poster boy for all sorts of charity work with kids.

But Brian's life has been defined by, as much as anything, a gauntlet of faith-testing ordeals. Baseball, in particular, has been like a spiritual surgeon's knife, a precise tool of sanctification that incrementally cuts away the remnants of his old self. He has grown in peace, patience, and contentment. He has learned volumes about himself and others. He has felt God's discipline and love.

Most of all, he has learned to trust the Lord.

"Proverbs 3:5–6 have really been my verses that I've lived

by as much as I can," Brian said, before quoting them: "Trust in the Lord with all your heart and lean not on your own understanding. In all your ways, acknowledge him and he will make your paths straight."

This, Brian quickly admits, is easy when things are peachy, but not so much when they're painful.

First, the pain . . .

"BUGGY-WHIPPING" TO THE BIG LEAGUES

The screams echoed off the walls of North Carolina Memorial Hospital in Chapel Hill.

Mommy! I don't want to go!

Little five-year-old Brian had a death grip on his mom's neck. He was doing everything in his half-pint power to avoid being wheeled down the long, ominous hallway to the operating room.

It wasn't supposed to be like this. He should've been in La-La Land already, but the medical orderly hadn't timed the anesthesia correctly. The kid was awake . . . and terrified.

Eventually, they peeled Brian off his mom. Mike and Nancy Roberts watched helplessly as Brian's gurney rolled through the double doors and out of sight.

Brian, the youngest of Mike and Nancy's two children, was born October 9, 1977, with an atrial septal defect, a congenital heart disorder where the wall separating the upper heart chambers does not close completely. In other words, he had a hole in his heart. The condition eventually necessitated open heart surgery. Today, he still bears a Y-shaped scar on his chest from the surgeon's incision.

Before long, little Brian—and we do mean *little*—was

back on his feet and playing baseball. No surprise there. He came from a Southern, baseball-crazy family. His grandfather, Edd Roberts, loved the game, even though he had never played much, unless you count the makeshift games in North Carolina cow pastures. (Watch your step rounding first.)

Edd grew up in the 1930s as a Cardinals and Indians fan mainly because the radio stations he could pick up were KMOX out of St. Louis and WTAM out of Cleveland. He spent many a night transfixed by the static-saturated tales of Dizzy Dean and the Gas House Gang, and Bob Feller throwing bullets off Lake Erie. During the Great Depression, Edd worked long hours hauling logs in Asheville, but he often stopped off on his way home at McCormick Field, the Asheville Tourists' home since 1924, to catch some minor league action.

Later in life, when Edd lived in Kingsport, Tennessee, he presided over the Kingsport Booster's Association and became the town's main liaison to whatever Appalachian League team called Kingsport home.

Edd transferred his passion to his son, Mike, who eventually became the head baseball coach at the University of North Carolina, holding that position from 1976 to 1998. Brian spent countless afternoons on campus, cavorting around the field with college stars like catcher B.J. Surhoff and shortstop Walt Weiss, both first-round picks in the 1985 major league draft.

Becoming a star himself, though, was going to take a lot of work. Brian was always a pipsqueak without much over-the-fence pop. So Pop decided to teach him how to drive the ball like nobody's business. By the time Brian could walk, Mike was teaching him elementary hitting drills from both sides of the plate. At age ten, Brian was hitting tennis balls from Mike, who threw them as hard as he could from thirty feet away—over and over and over.

It was all about creating quick wrists and bat speed. Mike called it "buggy-whipping" your hands through the strike zone. Back when Mike was a catcher in the Kansas City Royals' farm system, the prevailing wisdom held that good hitters needed to be strong only from the elbows down. Players were discouraged from lifting weights in favor of building Popeye forearm strength. So Mike learned to buggy-whip. It was a term taken from the arm motion Edd would use to snap a whip over a stubborn mule to make his buggy go.

"We tried to hit the ball flat—line drives," Mike said of his hitting sessions with Brian. "A ground ball wasn't right. A fly ball wasn't right."

Mike knew that a scrawny kid who could hit for average but not field worth a lick wouldn't go far. So father and son worked nonstop on defense, too. During games of catch, Mike would use neighborhood objects to incrementally increase Brian's throwing distance—mailbox to mailbox, mailbox to manhole cover, mailbox to that car way down the street, and so on. Mike made Brian throw with a ball painted half black so he could track his son's grip and spin on the ball. Every detail mattered.

Brian enjoyed a great high school career. But his size scared off most college coaches . . . except one. Want to guess who it was?

For two years, Brian made his dad look like a recruiting genius. In 1997, he won the national Freshman of the Year award by hitting a school-record .427 and setting other Tar Heel benchmarks with 102 hits, 24 doubles, and 47 stolen bases. The next season, he led the country in stolen bases with 63.

After Mike lost his job following the 1998 season, Brian transferred to South Carolina, where he earned second-team All-American status as a junior with a .353 average, 12 home runs, 36 RBIs, and a national-best 67 stolen bases.

For three years, Brian had treated college pitchers like his personal piñata and base paths like a dragster strip, but major league scouts were still wary of his size. He was passed over for the first forty-nine picks in the 1999 draft before the Orioles took a chance on him with a supplemental first-round selection.

It was a magnificent moment for Brian and his family. God had blessed all his hard work and dedication.

But pro baseball would test Brian's faith like never before.

PAIN AND PERSEVERANCE

As deep as Brian's baseball roots go, his family's spiritual roots go just as far. He remembers waking up at his grandfather's house one morning at 5:30 and shuffling downstairs, bleary-eyed, only to see the kitchen light on and Edd doing his quiet time at the table. He recalls seeing his mom studying her Bible every day, as well.

"I saw the way they lived out their faith, not only around other people, but in their own time," he said. "I had incredible examples of what it meant to really put your faith first in your life."

Mike and Nancy took Brian and his older sister, Angie, to Hope Valley Baptist Church in Durham twice a week. At age twelve, Brian placed his faith in Christ during a church revival, but he slowly drifted into worldliness. By the time he was a UNC freshman, he was trying to fit in with his teammates a little too much.

Nancy, like all good moms, could see her son was struggling, even without a word from Brian. So she gave him a copy of *Victory: The Principles of Championship Living*, a book by NBA star A.C. Green, whose bold faith included a now-famous acknowledgment that he remained a virgin until he got married. That December, during a family vacation to Hawaii, Brian devoured *Victory* and the Bible, and committed to his faith for good.

"I was trying to show my teammates that I wasn't going to run and tell Dad everything," Brian said. "I wanted to show them I was a teammate, not just Coach's son. I did a lot of things I probably shouldn't have done, but now I know that I had to go through those things to really be drawn back to the relationship with God that I needed to have."

Brian's renewed spiritual dedication came at the right time. For a select few players, the minor leagues are merely a pit stop en route to The Show. For everyone else, they are a crucible of perseverance. Count Brian among the latter group.

Despite making his major league debut on June 14, 2001, Brian spent significant time at various levels of the Orioles' farm system from 1999 to 2003, battling Jerry Hairston, Baltimore's eleventh-round draft pick in 1997, for playing time every step of the way. The constant uncertainty forced Brian to ask tough questions about his faith.

But when Hairston went on the disabled list early in 2004 spring training, the door of opportunity swung open. Brian began the season as the team's starting second baseman and leadoff hitter.

Brian's physical stature was not lost on others, certainly

not opposing fans. During a game in Seattle one year, Brian made it safely to first base, where the Mariners' Richie Sexson, a massive human being, awaited. At 6 foot, 8 inches, Sexson was a whole foot taller than Brian. Noticing the disparity, a Seattle fan yelled out, "Hey Richie, I didn't know it was Bring Your Kid to Work Day!"

Brian laughed, but the moment illustrated a question on many people's minds: Could a player the Orioles generously listed as 5 foot, 9 inches tall and 175 pounds really be an everyday impact player in the major leagues?

The answer was a resounding yes.

In 2004, Brian hit .273 with 107 runs scored and an American League–leading 50 doubles, which marked the most by a switch-hitter in AL history. That made the Orioles' choice easy. The following February, they packaged Hairston in a trade to the Cubs for slugger Sammy Sosa. At age twenty-six, Brian was the team's second baseman of the future. The little buggy-whipper with the patchwork heart had made it.

Still, few outside Baltimore took notice. After all, the Orioles finished the season 78–84 and a distant third in the AL East. The team was a blip on baseball's radar.

But if 2004 was a modest foreshadowing of the AL's newest star infielder, 2005 was a megaphone announcement. With previously unseen power, Brian took the league by storm that year, hitting .345 with 15 home runs, 49 RBIs, 18 stolen bases, and a 1.007 OPS (on-base-plus-slugging) percentage at the All-Star Break. His torrid start propelled the surprising Orioles into first place in the AL East early on, and he earned the starting nod at second base for the AL All-Star Team.

It was like someone popped a bottle of "Instant Stardom"

champagne and sprayed it all over Brian. Suddenly, his locker became a media magnet, which, of course, prompted much ribbing from his teammates.

"In batting practice, the guy couldn't even hit a home run," Jay Gibbons, an Oriole from 2001 to 2007, joked in May 2005. "I told him in spring training one day, 'Please, just hit one out for me so I can see it.' He's like, 'I don't think I can do it, man.' He finally hit one out, and I gave him a standing ovation. And a month and a half later, the guy is leading the league in homers."

Then the bubbly ran out. On September 20—less than two weeks before the season ended—Brian suffered a gruesome arm injury. A collision at first base with New York Yankees base runner Bubba Crosby dislocated his left elbow, tore his ulnar collateral ligament, and ripped his flexor mass muscles off the bone. It hurt as bad as it sounds.

Poof! Just like that, Brian's amazing season was over—and worse, his career was in jeopardy. Baseball's best second baseman was left sitting in excruciating bewilderment on the infield dirt, cradling his left arm like a mother holds an infant. Haunting questions swarmed his mind: *Why did this happen? Why now? Is my career over?*

Some players never return from such a thunderclap of physical violence. Brian did. But the recovery process was brutal.

He underwent surgeries to replace his elbow ligament (procedures also known as "Tommy John surgery") and reattach his forearm muscles to the bone. Then he had to endure six months of rehab that were both physically and psychologically taxing.

His parents spent a month with him at his off-season home in Arizona to help with his most basic needs, such as

Brian Roberts is a two-time All-Star second baseman for the Baltimore Orioles, but recently his career has been plagued by a rash of injuries. (AP Photo/Nick Wass)

cooking, cleaning, and getting dressed. He had to learn to throw again, too. Humble pie, anyone?

"I was basically like a child," Brian recalls. "I couldn't even put my clothes on."

Weak and utterly helpless, he was right where God wanted him. The truths of 2 Corinthians 12:9 hit Brian like never before. His frailty acted as a microscope that magnified God's power and love.

"It's easy to sit there and say, 'I love Jesus. This is great. God is good. He's a God that wants to bless you,' and all this when things are going great," Brian said. "But when everything comes crashing down on you, how do you handle it? Are you prepared and capable of saying, 'I still trust God. . . . I still think he's a perfect God and that He can't do anything wrong? This is right. Why not me?' "

From a numbers perspective, 2005 was still a marvelous season. Brian was named the "Most Valuable Oriole" after finishing among the AL leaders in batting average (.314), doubles (45), stolen bases (27), and on-base percentage (.387). He also set career highs to that point with 18 home runs and 73 RBIs.

But what could be expected of him in the future after such a traumatic ordeal? As it turns out, a lot.

Remarkably, Brian was ready to go by Opening Day 2006. Despite a slow start, thanks to lingering arm issues and an unrelated three-week stay on the disabled list, he managed to hit .286 with 34 doubles and 36 stolen bases. In 2007, he improved to .290 with 42 doubles, 103 runs scored, and an AL-best 50 stolen bases while earning his second All-Star nomination. That "buggy-whipping" stuff sure came in handy.

Brian had regained his status as one of the best second baseman in baseball. Off in the distance, though, storm clouds were gathering. The injury trials of 2005–2006 would feel like a quick spring downpour compared to the monsoon to come.

THE MITCHELL REPORT

The first lightning strike came on October 1, 2006, the final day of the regular season. That afternoon, Baltimore suffered a 9–0 defeat to Boston that marked a merciful end to a 92-loss season.

The Orioles were undoubtedly distracted. That morning's edition of the *Los Angeles Times* contained a story that implicated Brian and two teammates, Jay Gibbons and Miguel Tejada, as illegal performance-enhancing drug users, based on the reported testimony of former Orioles pitcher Jason Grimsley, who was under investigation for steroid use.

According to the story, Grimsley had named Brian, among others, as a steroid user in a federal affidavit. According to the article, the *Los Angeles Times* got the information from a source who viewed a copy of the document, which was filed in federal court in Arizona in May 2006, before Brian and the other players' names were redacted.

Brian flatly denied the report. A day later, he was exonerated by comments from Grimsley's attorney and the case's lead investigator in a separate story. Eventually, the *Los Angeles Times* ran a correction admitting that Grimsley had not named Brian or his teammates in the affidavit. The squall died down.

Then, on December 13, 2007, the big one hit.

Twenty-one months earlier, Major League Baseball commissioner Bud Selig had asked former U.S. senator George

Mitchell to investigate allegations of widespread steroid use in baseball. When MLB released the Mitchell Report, it sent Richter-scale-rattling shockwaves through baseball.

In all, the Mitchell Report alleged eighty-nine players as steroid users. While many names in the documents weren't surprising, one was: Brian Roberts.

Page 158 of the Mitchell Report included the following excerpt:

> *Brian Roberts is an infielder who has played for the Baltimore Orioles since 2001. He has been selected to two All-Star teams.*
>
> *Roberts and Larry Bigbie were both rookies in 2001. According to Bigbie, both he and Roberts lived in [David] Segui's house in the Baltimore area during the latter part of that season. When Bigbie and Segui used steroids in the house, Roberts did not participate.*
>
> *According to Bigbie, however, in 2004 Roberts admitted to him that he had injected himself once or twice with steroids in 2003. Until this admission, Bigbie had never suspected Roberts of using steroids.*
>
> *In order to provide Roberts with information about these allegations and to give him an opportunity to respond, I asked him to meet with me; he declined.*

After four days of silence, Roberts publicly admitted that he had tried steroids once—and only once—in 2003, a year in which he started the season at Triple-A Ottawa and was still trying to solidify his place on a major league roster.

"In a moment of weakness, I made a decision that I knew wasn't right from the beginning," he told *The Baltimore Sun*. "My size, my ability, whatever it was—none of that is any reasoning for making a decision like that."

The news shook baseball and rocked Baltimore. In the wake of Cal Ripken Jr.'s retirement in 2001, Brian had become the face of the franchise. He was a lovable, homegrown underdog with a quiet humility, a soft spot for kids, and boy-next-door looks. And now, like a twenty-first-century baseball version of *The Scarlet Letter*, he had been branded with an ignominious "S" on his chest.

Public reaction was harsh. On December 18, 2007, *The Baltimore Sun* ran a column titled "Hard to Believe Roberts." Opposing fans mocked him on the road. It was a painfully raw period of soul-searching and combating spiritual condemnation.

"It was really hard for me to forgive myself and not beat myself up over it and worry about what other people were thinking and take everything that fans yelled personally," Brian said.

In the days that followed, Brian felt God calling him to use his mistake as a teaching tool. So in 2008, he participated in a candid, seventeen-minute video with the Fellowship of Christian Athletes (FCA) and also spoke to a large group of student athletes in the Baltimore area for an anti-steroids campaign called "Playing Safe, Fair and Sober."

Slowly, the truth of 1 John 1:9 and other scriptures related to confession and forgiveness started to have their intended effect.

"We're all sinners," Brian said. "We can't look in the mirror and say we've always made the right decisions. I've been forgiven by a lot of people that I've hurt, and for that, I'll forever be grateful. Forgiving yourself and knowing that God forgives you, that's a huge part of it."

David Daly, FCA Baseball's national director, who has known Brian since 1997, believes every word of Brian's steroids confession.

"There's no reason not to believe him," Daly said. "He's not a user. He did it one time and immediately knew it was the wrong thing to do. He never did it again. Even though he made a mistake and readily acknowledged that publicly, he knew forgiveness comes from God. And his strong faith got him through that."

A HEART FOR ONE

Often, an individual's qualities are best seen through the eyes of another. And David Daly's eyes have been on Brian for a long time.

The two met when Brian was a UNC freshman and David was a local pastor. The next year, David became the Tar Heels' chaplain, and his ten-year-old son, John, became the team batboy.

John and Brian, both second basemen, immediately hit it off. Brian treated John like a little brother, instructing him (knowingly and not) in the pursuits of baseball and godliness. Brian was one of the best college players in the nation, yet he made plenty of time for his wide-eyed shadow. When John noticed that Brian wrote his favorite scripture passage, Proverbs 3:5–6, underneath the bill of his cap, the boy did the same thing.

Growing up, John never had to buy his own batting

gloves. He always had a customized Brian Roberts pair in his bag. Brian also made sure John had a wooden bat to hit with. None of that aluminum junk.

During the 2004 season, Brian found out that a friend of John's was struggling with drug abuse, and he called John. There was a lot of static on Brian's end of the line, so John asked where he was. Brian was in the middle of an exhausting West Coast road trip.

"I'm in Oakland," Brian said, "but we need to talk."

After John's high school graduation in 2007, Brian asked David if he could host John for a weekend during a Baltimore home stand.

"Sure," David said. "I'll book his hotel and make the arrangements."

"No, just put him on a plane," Brian responded. "I'll take care of him. Oh, yeah, tell him he can bring a buddy, too."

When John arrived in Baltimore, a car and driver were waiting for him at the airport. That weekend, John and his friend stayed at Brian's place, attended the Orioles series, and went out to eat with Brian after games. For John, it was the weekend of a lifetime.

"That's how Brian is," David said.

David had grown very close to Brian, too. Both men believe strongly in the mission of FCA, and Brian has been involved with the Christian sports ministry since he was a first-grader. In 2008, he accepted David's invitation to join FCA Baseball's board of directors. For years, David has supplied Brian with FCA New Testaments to give to kids he comes in contact with. David considers Brian "part of our family."

Inevitably, the Mitchell Report hit the Daly family hard.

Brian called David after the news broke. It was an emotional conversation, especially when Brian asked to speak to John. The two friends both shed tears as Brian asked for John's forgiveness.

"He felt like he had let me and John down," David said. "He hadn't let anyone down. We will always love him."

John, who now coaches baseball at Hickory Christian Academy in Hickory, North Carolina, still texts regularly with Brian. His prized possession remains an autographed, game-worn Roberts jersey with the inscription: "To John, the little brother I never had." That treasured jersey hangs framed on the wall over John's bed.

"Here's the thing about Brian," David said. "He's a better man than a baseball player, and he's an All-Star baseball player."

A HEART FOR MANY

Diana Chiafair witnessed the effect Brian has on people—his compassion and tenderness, particularly with sick and disadvantaged kids. In fact, that's what she credits for her becoming Mrs. Diana Roberts. Cue the love ballad.

Brian and Diana met on a blind date. Well, that's not exactly true—they *tried* to meet on a blind date of sorts. It was spring training 2007, and Brian was expecting to see Diana, a briefcase model on the NBC game show *Deal or No Deal*, in the stands at Fort Lauderdale Stadium, the Orioles' former spring training home. But every bottom half of the inning, he scanned the seats behind home plate. No Diana. *Ouch.* It was only a blind date, but still . . . .

Diana was oblivious to Brian's angst. Baseball was a foreign language to her. She had never been to a baseball game, and for all she knew, Baltimore Orioles were rare, winged creatures that nest in Maryland's largest city. So she arrived at the game with some girlfriends in the sixth inning, completely unaware that teams often pull their starters much earlier in spring training games. Brian was done for the day. When he called her later that night, they cleared up the confusion and laughed it off.

Three nights later, they went out to dinner. He was nervous and shy. She found his reticence cute. But it wasn't until she visited the University of Maryland Hospital for Children in Baltimore with him that she knew he was "The One."

Recalling the fears and difficulties of his own experience as a child, Brian had been visiting the hospital for years. If there's one thing he loves doing besides "buggy-whipping" a baseball, it's bringing smiles to the faces of hurting children. During the season, he usually goes to the hospital every month or two. And since 2006, he had hosted "Brian's Baseball Bash," an annual hospital fundraiser at the ESPN Zone in Baltimore that raised more than $500,000 in its first five years.

Once, when Brian found out a young friend of former Orioles chaplain Chris Adomanis had a heart condition, he sent the child a note. No fanfare. No accompanying PR campaign. He didn't even tell Adomanis. He just wanted to bless the kid.

"He's just a solid rock," Adomanis pointed out.

When Diana saw Brian's compassion firsthand, she marveled. Here was this famous athlete stooping down to play with sick kids, his face beaming as much as theirs. She had never seen someone reflect so well the heart of Christ toward children.

"I think that's the first thing I fell in love with about him because it's something we're both so passionate about," Diana said. "I was thrilled when I found out. I remember the first time we visited children at the hospital together, seeing him light up. The kids loved being around him. We were there for three hours, but it felt like five minutes. I fall in love with him all over again when we play with kids."

Brian and Diana got married in January 2009. They share a single, powerful heartbeat for broken people. In recent years, Brian has embraced Diana's passion for the Foster and Adoptive Family Connection, a ministry based in Greeneville, Tennessee. Since 2009, he has also mentored inner-city men at Baltimore's Helping Up Mission, which cares for the poor, homeless, and drug-addicted.

Whenever possible, Brian works at FCA clinics and speaks at FCA events. In 2009, he gave his testimony to about 150 baseball coaches at an FCA breakfast during the American Baseball Coaches Association annual meeting in San Diego.

In the Orioles' clubhouse, he's a trusted and well-respected spiritual voice—the guy with the Bible in his locker and a noticeable aversion to bawdy locker room banter. He has been the team's Baseball Chapel representative for many years. His faith is evident, but he's not pushy with it.

"My goal is always to learn more about why God has put me in this position and to follow the doors He opens speaking-wise, working with kids or whatever it might be," Roberts said. "I realize that I'm in a position that not many people are in, and I have a chance to reach a lot more people than I would otherwise."

MORE TRIALS, MORE FAITH

In 2008 and 2009, Brian enjoyed good health and fine seasons.

In 2009, he set the major league record for doubles by a switch-hitter with 56, joining Hall of Famers Tris Speaker, Paul Waner, and Stan Musial as the only players in MLB history with three or more seasons of at least 50 doubles. He also set career highs in runs scored (110) and RBIs (79).

But the injury bug crept back in 2010. Brian spent three months on the disabled list with a herniated disc in his back and a strained abdominal muscle. Then he missed the last six games of the season after giving himself a concussion by hitting his helmet with his bat in frustration after a ninth-inning strikeout. He battled headaches and nausea until Christmas.

Self-inflicted wounds truly hurt the most.

"Kids out there," Brian said in a moment of self-deprecating humor in an April 2011 video blog, "whatever you do, no matter how frustrated you are, no matter how down you get, *do not* hit yourself on the top of the head with a bat. Bad idea."

The disabled list, Brian's albatross, struck again in 2011. A headfirst slide in Boston in May forced him to miss the rest of the season with concussion symptoms. He even had to cancel his children's hospital fundraiser in Baltimore.

Without their star leadoff hitter, the Orioles sputtered to a 69–93 record, their fourteenth straight losing season. In various Internet chat rooms and social media platforms, long-suffering Orioles fans voiced their restlessness with Brian, an oft-injured player who signed a four-year, $40 million contract extension in February 2009.

"Mr. [Peter] Angelos [the Orioles' owner] has put a lot of investment into me and my family, the Orioles have tried to count on me for a lot and I haven't been there, and that's hard for me," Brian said in early September 2011, when he drove from his Sarasota home to St. Petersburg to visit his teammates, who were in town to face Tampa Bay. "It's hard for me to walk in there and look guys in the eye, especially knowing what they've been through the last five months. I've been there and I've done it, and it's hard."

It was another trip to life's shadow lands, where the Almighty's presence sometimes feels distant, and questions of *Why, God?* and *How long, O Lord?* hide behind every jagged rock and echo in every gulch. So Brian turned once again to Proverbs 3:5–6 and let his favorite scripture illuminate the darkness.

He also took refuge in the Psalms. He loves their realness and their rawness. Many were written by men who opened breaking hearts to God and asked tough questions. Brian especially loves reading psalms by King David, a great yet flawed man who enjoyed God's favor, endured God's discipline, and suffered through numerous life-threatening trials. David didn't approach God with canned prayers. He came with agony, tears, joy, and praise—all genuine and unfiltered. That ministers to Brian.

"Look at David," Brian said. "He was upset and angry. We can be honest with God. That's part of our relationship. That's why it's called a relationship. God isn't a lucky charm. It's a real relationship. That's why He should be your best friend, one you can talk to through the ups and downs, the good and bad. Our feelings should be relayed to Him in that same way, and I believe that He hears that and understands that."

So what are we to make of Brian's trial-riddled career so far? Perspective helps. By any standard, he has enjoyed great success. Entering 2012, he's a career .281 hitter in eleven big league seasons and ranks among the Orioles' all-time leaders in hits, doubles, extra-base hits, walks, and runs. He also plays a strong second base with a .987 career fielding percentage there.

Still, you can't help wondering how much more he could've accomplished if fully healthy. No one can blame Brian for entertaining similar thoughts. Or questioning whether he'll ever play for a winning team.

Ultimately, though, the conjecture is all moot. Life doesn't offer 70-mph, down-the-middle fastballs for long. It always mixes in the tougher stuff. What matters most, Brian has learned, is how you handle life's high heat and off-speed junk. He has come to trust in the wisdom of James 1:2–4, the mysterious paradox that life's trials are to be embraced, not cursed.

"I can rely completely on God, and it's very rewarding to know that," Brian said.

2012 season update: The hits kept on coming for beleaguered Brian Roberts in 2012—just not the ones in the batter's box. On June 12, Roberts, the Orioles' popular All-Star second baseman and leadoff man, returned from a thirteen-month layoff caused by concussions he suffered in 2010 and 2011—two seasons in which he had missed a total of 226 games. Roberts enjoyed a triumphant return with a 3-for-4 day at the plate and an RBI in an 8–6 win over Pittsburgh. But by July 1, he was batting .182 and went on the disabled list two days later with a torn labrum in his right hip. Later that month, having played in only 17 games, he opted for season-ending surgery. Roberts largely missed out on the Orioles' remarkable season in which they won 93 games and reached the playoffs for the first time since 1997.

12

JOSH WILLINGHAM:
UNDERSTANDING HOW THE LORD
GIVES AND TAKES AWAY

By any reckoning, June 13, 2009, was the worst day of Oakland Athletics outfielder Josh Willingham's life.

The previous night, Josh, who was playing for the Washington Nationals at the time, had suffered an 0-for-4, two-strikeout performance in a 4–3 loss at Tampa Bay, dropping his batting average to .252. The Nationals, at 17–43, were 18½ games back in the National League East and freefalling toward a 59–103 final record, the franchise's worst showing since the 1976 Montreal Expos lost 107 games.

Josh's head finally hit the hotel pillow after midnight. Blessed relief—but relief that was short-lived.

At 5:30 a.m., an abrupt knock startled Josh from slumber. Groggy and perplexed, he opened his hotel room door. Standing there was Rob McDonald, the National's travel director. He told Josh that he had received an urgent message from Josh's father, David Willingham.

McDonald swallowed hard. Then he delivered the terrible news: Josh's little brother Jon was dead.

What do you do when life blindsides you with a crushing roundhouse? How do you react? To whom do you turn? Where do you go?

Josh hurried home as soon as he could pack his suitcase. Home for Josh was Florence, Alabama, a modest town (population 39,319) in the state's "Shoals" area—a place that fancies itself as "Alabama's Renaissance City."

The good people of Florence like to puff out their cultural chests a bit with art shows, film festivals, renaissance fairs, and a popular annual music celebration honoring native son W.C. Handy, the "Father of the Blues." Renowned architect Frank Lloyd Wright chose Florence as the site of his only house in Alabama. The city also features the Fame Recording Studio, whose microphones have been graced by the likes of the Queen of Soul, Aretha Franklin, as well as rhythm and blues legends Etta James and Wilson Pickett.

Otherwise, life in the Shoals ambles by like a boat drifting down the Tennessee River. The Shoals, like Alabama in general, is college football country. Baseball? Not so much. Florence's main university, North Alabama, is an NCAA Division II outpost whose greatest baseball alumnus was Terry Jones, a career .242 hitter in 227 big league games from 1996 to 2001. The city certainly isn't on any major league scouts' radars.

But Josh wasn't just anyone. His prodigious power stuck out like a Handy trumpet solo from "St. Louis Blues." After the low-key slugger set plenty of records at tiny Mars Hill

Josh Willingham, a 17th-round draft pick out of Florence, Alabama in 2000, showed no signs of slowing down at age thirty-three as he enjoyed a career year with Minnesota in 2012. Willingham belted a personal best 35 home runs. (AP Photo/Tom DiPace)

Bible School—a Christian institution founded by his great-grandfather in 1946—and the University of North Alabama, the Florida Marlins drafted him almost as an afterthought in the seventeenth round in 2000. Six years later, though, he became a full-time big league starter.

At 6 feet, 2 inches and 215 pounds, Josh is a chiseled collection of fast-twitch muscles who can hit the ball a country mile. In his first six full big league seasons (2006–2011), he averaged 22 homers and 71 RBIs in only 128 games a year. He's also a career .262 hitter.

But injuries, especially a troublesome disc in his back, have long been his kryptonite. In 2006, he missed two weeks with a sprained hand. In 2008, he missed 50 games with a lower back strain. A knee injury that required surgery wiped out the last 44 games of 2010 for him. And his back and a sore Achilles' tendon nagged him in 2011.

What, one wonders, could he do in a full, healthy season? It's not a question Josh dwells on. He deals in reality, not his imagination, so he turns to scripture for reminders that trials are for his spiritual good—and to trust God no matter what.

"I just take it day by day," he said in his syrupy-sweet Southern twang. "You're not guaranteed a day in life, or in baseball, so I'm just trying to do today what I can to help us win and to do my best."

Josh's even-keeled outlook is actually a product of a strong faith that took root in a loving home. His parents, David and Denise, took him and his brother, Jon, to Cross Point Church of Christ in Florence three times a week. By 2000, when he was twenty-one years old and experiencing his first season of professional ball a thousand miles from home in Utica, New

York, with the Utica Blue Sox (Class A), Josh made his family's deep faith his own by trusting in Christ for the forgiveness of his sins.

"That's where my faith grew," he says. "I had to stand on my own."

Suddenly, on June 13, 2009, Josh felt very alone.

He and Jon, his only sibling, did everything together growing up. As kids, Josh and Jon (who was three and a half years younger) fished, biked, pelted each other in acorn fights, and created a mini chip-and-putt golf course in their yard. They loved to watch University of Alabama football together—and don't even utter the word *Auburn* nearby.

"They were very close," David Willingham said. "They kept up with Alabama football constantly. I guarantee that up to the week Jon died, they were talking football and recruiting and what was going to happen that season."

Jon's death felt surreal to Josh—both for the sudden shock and the mysterious details surrounding it. According to a June 14, 2009, article in Florence's *TimesDaily* newspaper, twenty-seven-year-old Jon was pronounced dead at a local hospital after leading police on a chase for several minutes before losing control of his 2003 Ford Explorer and slamming head-on into a tree around 1:45 a.m. A male passenger in Jon's car was placed in the intensive care unit but survived. According to the article, police were trying to pull over Jon for reckless driving and speeding.

Josh took a weeklong bereavement leave for the funeral. Death felt too familiar. Just forty-two days earlier, his paternal grandfather, a patriarch of the family faith, had passed away.

As the week's end drew near, Josh told his father, "It's going to be hard for me to go back. I don't have my heart in it." Eventually, with David's encouragement, he boarded the plane for D.C.

Sporting two wristbands and a necklace bearing Jon's name, Josh caught fire and raised his average to .309 by early August before cooling off in September for a respectable line of .260, 24 homers, and 61 RBIs in 133 games.

A left medial meniscus tear derailed another solid season in 2010 (.268 batting average, 16 home runs, and 56 RBIs in 114 games) before life rattled his comfort zone again: In December 2010, the Nationals traded Josh to the Athletics.

Florence, Alabama, and Oakland, California, are as different as the twenty-three hundred miles between them would suggest. It wasn't easy for Josh to get used to the West Coast lifestyle. Plus, with an off-season home in Florence, Josh's college-sweetheart wife, Ginger, and their two young sons couldn't fly to Oakland for extended visits as much as they had when Josh played in D.C. For all of its glamour, life in the major leagues also presents some challenging realities.

Josh's batting average dipped to .246 in 2011, but he continued to show that he's a dangerous hitter when healthy, as evidenced by his 29 home runs and 98 RBIs in 136 games. On July 15, he smashed the first home run into the Oakland Coliseum's second deck since Frank Thomas accomplished the feat in August 2006.

Josh capitalized on his power-hitting 2011 season and signed a three-year deal with the Minnesota Twins during the off-season. His career has been marked by trials and ordeals, so Josh has learned to lean more on the Rock who never moves.

"Being so far away from home and family, I have to lean on Him more," he said.

Josh thinks about his little brother every day. But life goes on, and there is much to be thankful for. He has a wonderful family, financial security, and a dream job.

Job, the Bible's archetypal sufferer, endured utter devastation and still exclaimed, "The LORD gave and the LORD has taken away; may the name of the LORD be praised" (Job 1:21). This, too, is Josh's attitude. Whether it's death, exasperating injuries, or a difficult cross-country move, he knows where to turn for hope and peace.

"I can't understand how people do it if they don't have faith, especially [regarding] eternal life," Josh said. "What kind of hope do people have? You have to really lean on God when [a trial] happens. He has basically showed me that He is the boss through difficult times."

Left fielder Josh Willingham gave the Minnesota Twins just what they were looking for—and more—when they signed him to a three-year, $21 million contract in December 2011. Willingham, a powerful right-handed slugger, anchored the heart of the Twins' batting order by leading the team with career highs in home runs (35), RBI (110), runs (85), slugging percentage (.524) and on-base-plus-slugging percentage (.890). He won his first Silver Slugger Award for being the best offensive player at his position in the American League. Despite Willingham's efforts, the Twins (66-96) suffered their second straight fifth-place finish in the American League Central Division.

13

MARIANO RIVERA:
THE CLOSER WHO GOT SAVED

Looking for a good argument? Just walk up to any die-hard base-ball fan and start talking about the greatest players of all time.

Who's the best center fielder ever to play the game? Is it Willie Mays, Joe DiMaggio, Ty Cobb, Mickey Mantle, or Ken Griffey Jr.?

How about third basemen? Good cases can be made for Mike Schmidt, George Brett, Brooks Robinson, Alex Rodriguez, and Chipper Jones.

And don't even dare to bring up first basemen, where Lou Gehrig, Jimmie Foxx, and Albert Pujols top most lists.

The truth is, baseball fans love to argue the minutia of the sport and whether the bigger, stronger players of the modern era are better than the greats from the past. No other American sport has the history and voluminous statistics that baseball affords, so the debates over the "best ever" can be never-ending.

But the position of closer is one where there's virtually no argument. When the bullpen gate swings open in the ninth inning with a game on the line, one player has dominated more than any other pitcher in history: Mariano Rivera.

In eighteen seasons since coming up with the New York Yankees in 1995, Mariano has earned 608 saves—the most in baseball history. Only he and Trevor Hoffman (601 saves) have passed the 600 mark . . . and that doesn't count Mariano's 42 postseason saves, which are also a major league record. When he's on the mound, the Yankees nearly always secure a victory. His save percentage is a hair under 90 percent—the best ever for pitchers who have had 250 or more save opportunities.

In the playoffs, where things really matter, Mariano has been nearly unhittable. And playing for the Yankees, he's had plenty of postseason experience. He has helped New York win five World Series titles and was named the Most Valuable Player of the 1999 World Series. His earned-run average in the playoffs is an unheard-of 0.70.

Only twenty-one pitchers in the history of baseball have tallied *half* the number of saves that this slender hurler known as the "Hammer of God" has earned. Mariano has won the Rolaids Relief Man Award five times for the American League and has been voted an All-Star twelve times.

Despite the accolades and accomplishments, Mariano stays humble and firmly rooted in his Christian faith. He lets his actions, instead of his words, do the talking. Not exactly the demeanor of a typical big league closer.

Almost everything about Mariano is the opposite of what most people think of when they picture a relief pitcher. This normally high-strung bunch is known for their bushy beards, waxed moustaches, big rope necklaces, nervous tics, and unpredictable behavior on the mound.

"Look at Mo's delivery, look at how he repeats it," teammate Joba Chamberlain marveled. "He does the same exact thing every time. That's a very hard thing to do—I try, but I can't do it like Mo. There's never any added stress on his arm because all the parts move the same way every time."

If Mariano could be described in one word, it would be *predictable*. He warms up the same way before every appearance. He never looks rushed or worried. His demeanor is the same, whether it's a spring training game or the World Series. Even his signature pitch—the cut fastball—is predictable. Batters know it's coming, but they still can't hit it.

Jim Thome, who has hit more than 600 home runs in his career, called Mariano's cut fastball the greatest pitch in baseball history. Longtime Minnesota Twins manager Tom Kelly once said, "He needs to pitch in a higher league, if there is one. Ban him from baseball. He should be illegal."

When asked if being called the greatest closer ever embarrasses him, Mariano answered: "Yes, it does. It does make me uncomfortable because I don't like to talk about myself. I just want to be able to contribute as much as I can for the team. And the rest is just blessings from the Lord."

In reality, he doesn't have to say anything. Teammates, opponents, and sportscasters say it for him.

"You're seeing the greatest closer of all time," Yankee catcher Jorge Posada said. "I don't care about ERAs. There's nobody better. No one can even compare. His body doesn't change. He doesn't change. He's the same Mariano as he was as a setup man, as a closer, and as a friend."

Yankee shortstop Derek Jeter has equally high praise for

the kind of person Mariano is. "He's like my brother," said Jeter, who came up in the minor leagues with Mariano. "Any time you play with someone that long, there's a connection there. . . . He's been the exact same person he was since the first day I met him."

That person is deeply committed to God, his family, and his teammates.

Mariano is the first to say that he never could've collected so many saves if his team hadn't put him in the right situation. In order to earn a save, a pitcher must record at least three outs with his team in the lead by no more than three runs. Every save opportunity brings pressure, but Mariano handles it with ease.

He appears strangely peaceful on the mound—and it's a peace that only comes from knowing the Prince of Peace.

"I don't know if we'll ever see it again," Yankee manager Joe Girardi said after Mariano notched with 600th career save. "This is a guy who I believe is the best closer that's ever been in the game, and I've had the fortune of catching him, coaching him, and managing him, and it's a treat."

Hitting against him is anything but a treat. However, Mariano has earned the respect of opposing batters, including Boston Red Sox great David Ortiz. "If you talk to him at an All-Star Game, it's like talking to somebody who just got called up," Ortiz said. "To him, everybody else is good. I don't get it. To him, everybody else is the best. It's unbelievable. And he is the greatest. . . . Good people, you want to do well."

And Mariano has done well. *Very* well, especially considering that when the Yankees first saw him, he was a *shortstop*, not a pitcher.

Since joining the New York Yankees in 1995, Mariano Rivera has gone on to become baseball's greatest closer. The all-time saves leader has recorded 608 saves through the 2012 season. (AP Photo/Rusty Kennedy)

DEVELOPING THE MIRACLE PITCH

Kansas City Royals scout Herb Raybourn first witnessed Mariano on a baseball field in 1988. He was playing for Panamá Oeste (Panama West) in the national championship game. At 6 feet, 2 inches and around 160 pounds, Mariano made an impact as a rangy shortstop with a good arm. His batting stroke, however, was less than impressive.

A year later, Panamá Oeste again qualified for the national tournament. But with his team's pitching floundering, Mariano volunteered to step onto the mound. He had thrown some growing up and, as a child, was always good at hurling rocks at a target.

Mariano wasn't overpowering as a pitcher, but he was accurate. So accurate, in fact, that he caught the eye of Chico Heron, a Yankees scout. Heron set up a tryout with Raybourn, who had since become the head of Latin American scouting for the Yankees.

Mariano traveled to Panama City for the audition. Raybourn immediately recognized him. The skinny shortstop took the ball and walked to the mound. He had thrown just nine pitches—all of which registered in the mid-80s on the speed gun—when Raybourn stopped him. Mariano thought he'd blown it. But Raybourn had seen enough.

"The radar wasn't really being lit up," Raybourn said. "But what I liked about Mariano was his looseness, a nice loose arm. And his fastball had a lot of movement. I could picture him pitching in the majors."

Raybourn figured that with some professional coaching and weight training, Mariano's fastball could gain some extra pop. He'd also have to learn a few other pitches.

The twenty-year-old signed with the Yankees on February 17, 1990, and received a $2,000 signing bonus. He had never thought about being a professional baseball player until he inked his name on the contract.

"Usually a player prepares for years," Mariano said. "Here I was signing, and I wasn't even [planning on becoming] a pitcher."

Even though Mariano didn't feel like a pitcher, he looked like one on the diamond. He was assigned to the Gulf Coast League Yankees, where he competed against other rookies. In 22 games, he pitched 52 innings and gave up one earned run while striking out 58 and walking just seven.

In 1991, he advanced to the Class A Greensboro Hornets (North Carolina). While his record (4–9) was subpar, he posted an impressive 2.75 ERA and 123-to-36 strikeouts-to-walks ratio. After the season, Mariano enjoyed a greater highlight when he flew home to Panama and married Clara Younce, whom he had known since elementary school.

Over the next several years, Mariano worked his way up to the Triple-A Columbus Clippers in Columbus, Ohio, but his 87-mile-per-hour fastball didn't impress the big league club.

Early in the 1995 season, though, injuries to several Yankees starters gave Mariano a chance to pitch in pinstripes for the first time. His major league debut turned out to be a dud when he gave up five runs and eight hits in just three innings to the California Angels. In his first four starts for the Yankees, he notched a 10.20 ERA and was quickly sent back to Columbus.

The Yankees still liked Mariano, but they wanted someone with more pop on his fastball. They considered trading him to the Detroit Tigers for David Wells. Then two weeks after Mariano shipped back to the minors, something amazing happened—he added ten miles an hour to his fastball.

On June 26, 1995, Mariano pitched a five-inning no-hitter against the Rochester Red Wings that ended early due to bad weather. But what impressed the Yankees organization most was that his fastball registered a smoking 96 miles per hour on the radar gun.

Nobody could explain where the extra speed came from, but Mariano had an answer: It was a gift from God.

The hurler had recently accepted Jesus Christ as his personal Savior. During his career in the minor leagues, Mariano had seen God show up for him time after time, often through the kindness of other people who would come forward to help at key moments. When his wife was in the hospital, a pitching coach offered to stay with the couple's first son so Mariano could be with her. Another time a lady in Panama helped out his wife while he had to play.

"Every time I was going through a hard time, somebody was there to help," Mariano said. "Even though I had nobody here, I was never alone. That made me accept Jesus as my Savior. I knew it wasn't a coincidence. It was the Lord putting someone there for me."

The extra oomph on his fastball earned Mariano a return trip to New York. This time he fared much better. On July 4, 1995, he struck out 11 in eight shutout innings against the Chicago White Sox.

In 1995, Major League Baseball's first season of expanded, four-teams-per-league playoffs, New York qualified for the playoffs as the wild card. Mariano made the postseason roster and earned a victory in Game 2 against Seattle. The Mariners won the series three games to two, but Mariano pitched well each time out—even striking out Mike Blowers in the eighth inning of Game 5 with the bases loaded.

By 1996, Joe Torre had taken over as manager of the Yankees, who were loaded with young talent, including Jorge Posada, Derek Jeter, Andy Pettitte, and Bernie Williams. With enough starting pitching, Torre knew he wanted Mariano coming out of the bullpen; he just didn't know what role Mariano would play.

The Yankees soon figured out that Mariano was the perfect setup man for closer John Wetteland. With Mariano and Wetteland coming out of the bullpen that year, the Yankees notched a 79–1 record in games in which they held a lead after seven innings.

After failing to win a World Series since 1978, the Yankees claimed the 1996 championship by defeating Atlanta four games to two. Wetteland earned Most Valuable Player honors in the Series, but everybody knew the season belonged to Mariano. He even finished third in Cy Young Award balloting, which goes to the best pitcher in each league. No setup man had ever finished that high.

A FASTBALL THAT'S A CUT ABOVE

If God had given Mariano a gift by adding extra zip to his fastball, He was about to perform a miracle that has kept Mariano at the top of the game for years.

The Yankees let the high-priced Wetteland go in the offseason and moved Mariano to closer. The decision seemed like a no-brainer. But after the 1997 season started, Mariano blew four of his first six save opportunities.

The slow start resulted in a meeting with Torre and Yankees pitching coach Mel Stottlemyre. Mariano felt terrible. He hated letting down the team.

"The harder I tried, the tougher it got," Mariano said. "It was like moving in quicksand. I kept sinking. Joe told me that, 'As long as you are here, you'll be the closer.' That's exactly what I needed to hear."

Shortly after the meeting, something remarkable happened. Mariano had made it into the majors with a four-seam fastball that sometimes had good movement. He got batters out with velocity and accuracy. But as he warmed up before a game with pitcher Ramiro Mendoza, Mariano tried holding the ball a bit differently as they played catch. Mariano noticed that his throws dipped and darted when he gripped the ball a certain way, moving so much that Mendoza had a tough time even catching them.

Mariano had always liked fiddling with how he held the baseball. His long fingers and flexible wrist were perfect for a pitcher. But now he had a problem . . . or did he?

At first, Stottlemyre tried working with Mariano to remove the cutting action and make the ball go straighter. But after discovering his new pitch, Mariano recorded the save that day. He converted his next three save opportunities, as well.

Suddenly, Mariano possessed a pitch that looked like a fastball but acted like a slider when it got close to the plate. And it wasn't long before Mariano developed perfect precision with his signature cut fastball. He controlled its location by putting different pressure on the ball with his fingers. Greater pressure with his middle finger made it move one way. Using the index finger a little more caused it to move another.

From a hitter's perspective, Mariano's delivery looked effortless. But in an instant, the ball exploded past the plate at more than 95 miles per hour.

Scientists have studied thousands of Mariano's pitches. What makes him so devastating is that he throws the cut fastball and four-seam fastball with the exact same motion. Contrary to popular belief, big league batters don't possess supernatural reflexes and reaction speeds. What allows a batter to hit a ball are visual cues and tons of practice. If a pitcher drops down in his delivery or flicks his wrist, a batter can anticipate where the ball is going to be.

"You can't see the spin on it," six-time All-Star Lance Berkman said about Mariano's cutter. "A four-seam fastball rotates a certain way. A slider or a cutter is going to spin a certain way—you see a red dot on the ball as it's coming at you from the seams as it spins. And once you see the rotation on it, you react a certain way. The good cutters, like Rivera's, rotate like a four-seamer—you don't see the red dot, you don't know it's going to come in on you until it's too late."

Batters often think they're seeing a hittable pitch over the plate, but by the time they make contact, the ball has moved several inches and is either in on their hands or hit off the end of the bat. Mariano has unofficially led the major leagues in broken bats every year since he developed his cut fastball. Some sportscasters have joked that bat-maker Louisville Slugger should pay Mariano a bonus because of all the business he's brought its way.

But this pitch is no joke to Mariano—it's a blessing.

"That is my miracle pitch," Mariano said. "That's what I call it, because it's God's gifting. I didn't have that pitch before and nobody taught me that. It came as a miracle."

Since mastering the pitch, Mariano throws his cutter more than 90 percent of the time. He might mix in an occasional two-seam fastball. And about four times a year, he'll throw a changeup just to keep batters honest.

Once Posada became the Yankees' everyday catcher, it got to the point that he didn't flash signs to tell Mariano what pitch to throw. Posada would simply signal to throw the pitch over the inside or outside *corner* of the plate. Mariano rarely throws one down the middle. With pinpoint accuracy and a determination to win, Mariano goes after the black edges of the plate.

Unlike a lot of closers, Mariano doesn't resort to intimidation. He doesn't believe in throwing brushback pitches. One, because he isn't out there to show up hitters. And two, because that would waste a pitch. All Mariano wants to do is throw strikes.

"My mental approach is simple: Get three outs as quick as possible," he said. "If I can throw three, four pitches, the better it is. I don't care how I get you out, as long as I get you out."

HIS OLD MAN AND THE SEA

Mariano developed his workmanlike attitude as a child, thanks largely to his father.

Mariano was born on November 29, 1969, the son of a fisherman in the little town of Puerto Caimito, located about thirty miles north of Panama's capital, Panama City. His house sat about a hundred feet from the Pacific Ocean and consisted of concrete blocks and a corrugated tin roof.

Mariano's sport of choice as a child was soccer, but he also played baseball . . . if using a stick to hit a ball made of electrical tape wrapped around fish netting counts as a baseball.

During his early elementary years, Mariano and his friends would make a ball, cut a few straight tree branches for a bat, and form gloves and chest protectors out of cardboard. Games were played on a stretch of beach at low tide or in the streets.

When Mariano was twelve, his father bought him a real leather glove. The youngster was so excited that he slept with the glove and took it everywhere with him, even to school.

Mariano's father worked hard as a fisherman, earning around $50 a week, to provide for his four children. He was also a strict disciplinarian. Mariano remembers receiving a lot of spankings, but he knew his father punished him for his own good.

"My childhood was wonderful," Mariano said. "Basically, I didn't have anything. But what we had, I was happy."

As Mariano entered Pablo Sanchez High School, he dreamed of becoming a professional soccer player. He had quick feet and a smooth athleticism. What he didn't have was the ability to stay healthy. Numerous ankle injuries caused him to give up on his *fútbol* aspirations.

Instead of bending it like Beckham, Mariano was going to try to fish 'em like Roland Martin. Following his graduation from high school at sixteen, Mariano tried his hand at the family business. He wasn't afraid of hard work, but he soon realized that fishing wasn't for him. The boats would go out for six days a week. Everybody slept onboard, and sometimes it got dangerous when the seas were up. Once, his boat full of fish capsized and sent the crew into the ocean. Fortunately, everyone made it to the safety of a nearby vessel.

"It's hard. Extremely hard," Mariano said of being a fisherman. "I wanted to study to be a mechanic. Obviously, I didn't do it because the Lord had different plans for me."

While Mariano didn't follow his father's footsteps into fishing, he did pick up a lot from Mariano Sr.—including his strong character and generous spirit. If his father can help someone, he will, Mariano says—even if that means giving a person his last ten dollars. (Panama uses the American dollar as its currency.)

Mariano's generosity shows through in numerous ways. After making it with the Yankees, he always made sure to give back to his home country. Mariano purchased baseball equipment for local children. He donated medical equipment and supplies to a hospital. He sent Christmas presents. He honored area mothers by holding a party on Mother's Day (which is celebrated on December 8 in Panama) and giving away furniture and appliances. He even built a church in his hometown.

Mariano is also helping rebuild a church in his new home city. During the summer of 2011, Mariano and his fellow Spanish-speaking congregants at *Refugio de Esperanza*—Refuge of Hope—announced they were buying and restoring the historic North Avenue Church in New Rochelle, New York. Built in 1907, the church had been under public ownership for decades and fallen into disrepair. Renovation costs were estimated at $3 million.

Mariano fell in love with the building from the moment he saw it and has big plans for the church.

"We have a lot of goals to work with the youth," Mariano said. "That is my passion. We are working hard to make it open as soon as possible."

Mariano added that he plans to devote himself to the church full time once he retires from baseball. Yankees fans, of course, hope that's years down the road, but it isn't the first time they've heard that kind of talk from their closer.

In July 1999, Mariano stood on the mound in Yankee Stadium as the Bronx Bombers hosted the Atlanta Braves. Between pitches, he heard something that he'd never heard before—a joyous, yet powerful sound. He described it as the voice of God telling him, *I am the One who has you here.*

When the season ended and the Yankees had won their second straight World Series, Mariano went back home to Panama and spoke to a church, saying that he planned to play baseball four more years before retiring to become a minister.

Obviously, Mariano didn't end up walking away from baseball in 2003. But his desire to serve God hasn't changed.

"This was something special, and God wants me to concentrate on bringing Him to other people," Mariano said of the encounter. "That meant the only reason I'm here is because He's my strength. He put me here. Without Him, I'm nothing. I think it means that He has other plans for me, to deliver His Word."

Mariano is an extremely private man who's protective of his wife and three sons: Mariano Jr., Jafet, and Jaziel. But when it comes to his faith, he will boldly step out. He often reads his Bible in the Yankees locker room and is a regular at team chapel services.

Mariano also stays involved with a number of charities and was honored for his charity work with the 2003 Thurman Munson Award, named for the great Yankee catcher.

BIG MO

When it comes to great Yankees pitchers, Mariano already tops most lists—above other legends such as Lefty Gomez, Whitey Ford, Ron Guidry, Red Ruffing, and Goose Gossage.

At the end of the 2011 season, Mo—as his teammates

call him—held twenty-nine MLB pitching records and eight career Yankee records, including a couple he set during an incredible streak from 1998 to 2000.

During those years, the Yankees won three consecutive World Series—and Mariano was nearly unhittable. In 1999, Mariano actually recorded more saves (45) than hits he allowed (43) all season. That was also the year he won the World Series Most Valuable Player award. A week later, Panamanian president Mireya Moscoso gave him the Order of Manuel Amador Guerrero, one of the country's highest honors.

The following year, when Mariano notched the final out against the New York Mets in the World Series, it marked the first time in MLB history that the same pitcher had nailed down the last out in three straight Series.

Following their 2000 championship, the Yankees had to wait nine years before getting back on top. At times, Mariano carried some of the blame, like when he committed a throwing error on a bunt in the bottom of the ninth inning in Game 7 of the 2001 World Series against the Arizona Diamondbacks. Arizona capitalized by scoring two runs off broken-bat hits and winning the game 3–2, claiming the Series four games to three.

But even after the disappointment, Mariano saw God's hand at work. Had the Yankees won the game, a ticker tape parade was planned for the whole team. Without a championship, Yankees' teammate Enrique Wilson changed his plane flight and went home to the Dominican Republic early. He had originally planned to be on American Airlines Flight 587 on November 12, 2001. That plane crashed in Queens, New York, killing all 260 passengers on board.

"I'm glad we lost the World Series," Mariano said, "because it means that I still have a friend."

The Florida Marlins defeated the Yankees in the 2003 World Series, but New York earned its record twenty-seventh world championship on November 5, 2009. And who was on the mound when the Yankees recorded the decisive out against the Philadelphia Phillies? Mariano, of course. By his side were Jeter, Pettitte, and Posada—four players with five world championship rings apiece.

"That comes from God, having the ability to perform," Mariano said. "I always thank God that He has given me the chance to be part of a team like the New York Yankees and to be able to do my job every time I get there."

Mariano's consistency and dominance are truly amazing. Sportswriters have predicted his decline for years. After several blown saves early in one season, the *Albany Times Union* published the headline, "Rivera No Longer Mr. Automatic." That was in 2002. Since then, he's had some of his best years and has been every bit as automatic as he was in the late nineties.

In 2004, he earned a career-high 53 saves.

In 2011, at age forty-one, Mariano had one of his best seasons by amassing 44 saves, including two record-breaking performances.

On May 28, 2011, Mariano appeared in his 1,000th game as a Yankee. Fourteen pitchers before him had appeared in a thousand games, but he was the first one to do it with one team. His stats that night: four batters, three outs, and twelve pitches—ten of which were strikes.

On September 19, Mariano became baseball's all-time saves leader when he closed out a game against the Minnesota

Yankees closer Mariano Rivera holds the World Series trophy after New York defeated Philadelphia 7–3 on November 4, 2009. It was the fifth time that Rivera and his Yankee teammates had celebrated a world championship together. (AP Photo/David J. Phillip)

Twins. With a 6–4 lead in the ninth, Mariano took the mound, retired three batters, and preserved the win. The final out came in typical Mariano fashion. He started Minnesota's Chris Parmelee with a belt-high strike on the outside edge of the plate. Mariano followed with an inside strike that Parmelee fouled off, breaking his bat in the process. With new lumber in his hands, Parmelee could only watch as Mariano's signature cutter caught the outside corner for strike three.

Three pitches. Three strikes. One historic out.

Yankees fans and players jumped around with emotion as Mariano calmly took the game ball from catcher Russell Martin and smiled. After Mariano hugged his fellow Yankees, Posada nudged him back onto the mound to accept the adulation of the fans. He blew a kiss to the faithful at Yankee Stadium and took off his hat to thank the fans who had cheered for him for seventeen years. He looked almost embarrassed by the applause as he smiled and threw up his arms.

Immediately following the game, Mariano deflected attention away from himself and to his teammates and God.

"The whole organization, my whole teammates have been a pillar for me," Mariano said. "I always have to talk about God, because that's the most important thing in my life. Yes, there have been bumps in the road, but God gave me the strength."

Mariano credits his longevity to God's blessing and to living a clean lifestyle. After most games, he hurries home or to his hotel, where he's in bed about an hour after throwing the last pitch.

The fact that Mariano takes care of himself and has avoided major arm problems, following his elbow surgery in 1992, makes people believe that the closer may have a number of years ahead of him.

When asked about his future, Mariano joked that he could pitch until he's fifty. But more seriously, he said he's under contract for the 2013 season, and he'll evaluate how he feels and how much he can contribute after the season is over.

No matter what the future holds for Mariano on the mound, one thing is certain in the minds of many fans: they'll never see a pitcher like Mo again.

"When you talk about the greatest relievers of all time, there's only one guy," Yankees teammate Mark Teixeira said. "That conversation begins and ends with Mo."

Posada agreed. "There will never be anybody like Mariano Rivera."

Mariano, on the other hand, honestly doesn't care where he'll be remembered in baseball history. He does hope, however, to be remembered for the impact he made on people.

"I don't pay too much attention to that," Mariano said when asked if he cared about being called the greatest relief pitcher who ever lived. "I just want to be the greatest person you've ever met. If I am, then I'm comfortable with that."

2012 season update: Mariano's 2012 season can be summed up in one word: rehabilitation. After tearing the anterior cruciate ligament (ACL) in his right knee on May 3, his season was over as quickly as it had begun. Mariano did presurgery physical therapy before being operated on June 12. "I'm coming back," Mariano told reporters the day after tearing his ACL. "I'm not going out like this." When Mariano signed a one year, $10 million contract on November 29, 2012, it ensured that he'd return to the field in 2013, making him the last player born in the 1960s on a major league roster.

ABOUT THE AUTHORS

Mike Yorkey, a former *Focus on the Family* magazine editor and author, co-author or editor of more than seventy-five books, has written about sports all his life for a variety of publications, including *Breakaway, Brio, Focus on the Family Clubhouse, Tennis, Skiing*, and *City Sports* magazines.

Mike's a lifelong baseball fan, thanks to his parents, who are San Diego Padres season ticket holders. He has collaborated with former San Francisco Giants pitcher Dave Dravecky (*Called Up* and *Play Ball*) and is also the co-author of *Every Man's Battle* with Steve Arterburn and Fred Stoeker and ten other books in the *Every Man's Battle* series. He is also a novelist who, with Tricia Goyer, co-authored the World War II thriller *Chasing Mona Lisa*, which was released in early 2012.

Mike and his wife, Nicole, are the parents of two adult children, Andrea and Patrick. They make their home in Encinitas, California.

Mike's website is www.mikeyorkey.com.

Jesse Florea has worked at Focus on the Family for more than eighteen years. He is currently the editorial director for youth magazines. He oversees *Focus on the Family Clubhouse* (for kids eight to twelve) and *Clubhouse Jr.* (for three- to seven-year-olds). He also co-hosts the biweekly "Official Adventures in Odyssey Podcast," which often exceeds 100,000 listeners.

Jesse is an avid sports fan who has written thousands of high school sports stories and more than a hundred magazine articles on sports personalities, and he was the co-author of two devotional books for sports-minded children: *The One-Year Devos for Sports Fans* and *The One-Year Sports Devotions for Kids*. He's co-written or edited more than a dozen other books as well.

Jesse's greatest baseball memory is taking batting practice in Coors Field in the mid-1990s with the Colorado Rockies and alongside the "Blake Street Bombers": Andrés Galarraga, Dante Bichette, and Larry Walker. He lives in Colorado Springs, Colorado, with his wife, Stephanie, and two teenagers, Nate and Amber.

Joshua Cooley, a former full-time sports editor/writer at *The Baltimore Examiner* and *The Gazette* newspapers in Maryland, has worked in the sportswriting industry since 1996. His first book—*The One-Year Sports Devotions for Kids* (Tyndale), a collaboration with Jesse Florea and Jeremy Jones—was published in October 2011.

Joshua currently works full time at his church, Covenant Life, in Gaithersburg, Maryland, and freelances for a variety of publications. His freelance credits include *Sports Illustrated*, the *Atlanta Journal-Constitution*, the *Baltimore Sun*, the *Orlando Sentinel*, the *Pittsburgh Tribune-Review*, *Bethesda Magazine*, *Orioles Magazine*, and *Nationals Magazine*. He has also written for Christian publications such as *Sports Spectrum*, *Sharing the Victory*, *Breakaway*, *Brio*, *Focus on the Family Clubhouse*, and *Susie*. In 2006, he contributed to the International Bible Society's *"Path to Victory" Sports New Testament*.

Joshua bleeds Baltimore Orioles' black and orange, for better or worse. He and his wife, Kelly, are the parents of four children. The Cooleys make their home in Germantown, Maryland.

SOURCE MATERIAL

1. Clayton Kershaw: Standing on the Precipice of Greatness
All quotations used are from personal interviews between co-author Joshua Cooley and Clayton Kershaw, except the following:

"Probably the best in the world . . ." from "Clayton Kershaw's Great Expectations" by Jeff Passan, *Yahoo! Sports*, May 14, 2008, and available at http://sports.yahoo.com/mlb/news?slug=jp-kershaw051408

"Might as well go by Zeus . . ." and "These guys don't come along often . . ." from "Kershaw Takes the Stage" by Jeff Passan, *Yahoo! Sports*, May 26, 2008, and available at http://sports.yahoo.com/mlb/news?slug=jp-kershaw052608

"Ceiling? There is no ceiling . . ." from "Kershaw Looking Ahead to Life Without Limits" by Ken Gurnick, *MLB.com*, February 23, 2010, and available at http://losangeles.dodgers.mlb.com/news/article.jsp?ymd=20100223&content_id=8120062&vkey=news_la&fext=.jsp&c_id=la

"There's no reason to really set limits . . ." from "Dodgers' Clayton Kershaw Continues to Shine" by Ben Bolch, *The Los Angeles Times*, August 13, 2011, and available at http://www.latimes.com/sports/la-sp-0814-dodgers-astros-20110814,0,6852499.story

2. Ben Zobrist: The PK Who's a Zorilla on the Field
All quotations used are from personal interviews between co-author Mike Yorkey and Ben Zobrist and his father, Tom Zobrist, except for the following:

"Ben first attracted notice for playing his wife's . . ." from Julianna's page on the Zobrists' website at www.thezobrists.com and available at http://goo.gl/hrl5g

"Dad, this is more important to others than it is to me . . ." from "Former AIA Player Makes It to the Big League" by Elaine Piniat, published June 25, 2009 on the Athletes in Action website and available at http://goo.gl/S5uqY

"She was just this awesome, godly woman . . ." from "Ray of Light: Tampa Bay All-Star Ben Zobrist" by Jill Ewert, published in *Sharing the Victory* magazine and available online at http://goo.gl/DRquR

3. Albert Pujols: A Home Run Hitter with a Heart for Others
"That was me twenty-five years ago . . ." from the *60 Minutes* segment "The Incredible Mr. Pujols," which aired on April 10, 2011, on CBS, and available at http://www.cbsnews.com/video/watch/?id=7362328n

"Believe it or not, baseball is not the chief ambition of my life . . ." from "A Message of Faith from Albert Pujols" by the Pujols Family Foundation and available at http://www.pujolsfamilyfoundation.org/faith/

"Growing up in the Dominican, that's pretty much all I did is play baseball . . ." from "Albert and Dee Pujols: Giving Honor to God," *Focus on the Family*, Daily Radio Digest, August 15–16, 2006.

"It's the farthest and hardest I've seen a baseball hit . . ." from "Albert Pujols: Revisiting the Early Years" by Arne Christensen, *The Hardball Times*, June 15, 2010, and available at http://www.hardballtimes.com/main/article/albert-pujols-revisiting-the-early-years/

"Have power even if he used a toothpick . . ." from "Albert Pujols: Revisiting the Early Years" by Arne Christensen, *The Hardball Times*, June 15, 2010, and available at http://www.hardballtimes.com/main/article/albert-pujols-revisiting-the-early-years/

"He's the best hitter I've coached or seen . . ." from "Albert Pujols: Revisiting the Early Years" by Arne Christensen, *The Hardball Times*, June 15, 2010, and available at http://www.hardballtimes.com/main/article/albert-pujols-revisiting-the-early-years/

"I'll never, never get over it . . ." from the *60 Minutes* segment "The Incredible Mr. Pujols," which aired on April 10, 2011, on CBS, and available at http://www.cbsnews.com/video/watch/?id=7362328n

"I went to church every once in awhile growing up . . ." from "Albert Pujols Testimony," Baseball Chapel video, July 20, 2011, and available at http://www.youtube.com/watch?v=n9yz9inU5XY&feature=youtube_gdata_player

"I wouldn't say it was easy and that the Lord starting turning things around [right away] . . ." from "Albert Pujols Testimony," Baseball Chapel video, July 20, 2011, and available at http://www.youtube.com/watch?v=n9yz9inU5XY&feature=youtube_gdata_player

"I had been praying for God to be able to use Albert to share Jesus and wanted it to be bigger . . ." from "Albert and Dee Pujols: Giving Honor to God," *Focus on the Family*, Daily Radio Digest, August 15–16, 2006.

"It must've been the highlight of the year for them . . ." from the *60 Minutes* segment "The Incredible Mr. Pujols," which aired on April 10, 2011, on CBS, and available at http://www.cbsnews.com/video/watch/?id=7362328n

"One thing I have learned is that it's not about me; it's about serving the Lord Jesus Christ . . ." from "Albert Pujols Testimony," Baseball Chapel video, July 20, 2011, and available at http://www.youtube.com/watch?v=n9yz9inU5XY&feature=youtube_gdata_player

"He's like the best baseball player in baseball now . . ." from "My Wish: Albert Pujols," *ESPN Sports Center: My Wish*, July 19, 2010, and available at http://espn.go.com/video/clip?id=5392781

"Albert is such a great player . . ." from "My Wish Q&A: Debbie Trammel," by Scott Miller, *ESPN.com*, July 21, 2010 and available at http://sports.espn.go.com/espn/features/mywish/news/story?id=5367335

"I'm glad it was him . . ." from "For Pujols, a Game for the Age", by Tyler Kepner, *The New York Times*, October 23, 2011, and available at http://www.nytimes.com/2011/10/24/sports/baseball/for-albert-pujols-of-st-louis-3-home-runs-for-a-record-night.html

"I think the last month of the season . . ." from "Cards Win World Series, Beat Texas 6–2 in Game 7," Associated Press, October 28, 2011, and available at http://sportsillustrated.cnn.com/baseball/mlb/gameflash/2011/10/28/40004_recap.html

"Enjoy it. Respect it. Appreciate it . . ." from "Pujols Is a Faith-Based Mystery" by Jeff Passan, *Yahoo! Sports,* July 14, 2009, and available at http://sports.yahoo.com/mlb/news?slug=jp-pujols071409

"Albert has no glaring weaknesses, and he doesn't chase many bad pitches . . ." from "Albert Pujols Quotes," *Baseball Almanac,* and available at http://www.baseball-almanac.com/quotes/albert_pujols_quotes.shtml

"I'd rather walk in a run than give up four . . ." from the *60 Minutes* segment "The Incredible Mr. Pujols," which aired on April 10, 2011, on CBS, and available at http://www.cbsnews.com/video/watch/?id=7362328n

"He's the face of baseball . . ." from the *60 Minutes* segment "The Incredible Mr. Pujols," which aired on April 10, 2011, on CBS, and available at http://www.cbsnews.com/video/watch/?id=7362328n

"I would never do any of that . . ." from "Cardinals Slugger Albert Pujols Is Batting Cleanup for Baseball" by Bob Nightengale, *USA Today,* July 13, 2009, and available at http://www.usatoday.com/sports/baseball/nl/cardinals/2009-07-12-pujols-cover_N.htm

"I don't believe in all that science stuff . . ." from "Pujols Is a Faith-Based Mystery" by Jeff Passan, *Yahoo! Sports,* July 14, 2009, and available at http://sports.yahoo.com/mlb/news?slug=jp-pujols071409

4. Carlos Beltran: Praying All the Way to the Ballpark
All quotations used are from personal interviews between co-author Joshua Cooley and Carlos Beltran.

5. Adrian Gonzalez: Gonzo for God
All quotations used are from personal interviews between co-author Joshua Cooley and Adrian Gonzalez, except for the following:

"I still have my reports on him . . ." from "On Baseball: Gonzalez Recalls Time in Portland" by Kevin Thomas, *Portland Press Herald,* April 20, 2011, and available at http://www.pressherald.com/sports/say-goodbye-to-winter_2011-04-01.html

"Everybody is just going crazy over him . . ." from "The Secret Is Out on Gonzalez" by Bob Nightengale, *USA Today,* July 12, 2011, and available at http://www.usatoday.com/SPORTS/usaedition/2011-07-12-Cover-Adrian-Gonzalez_CV_U.htm

6. Josh Hamilton: Baseball's Bat Man Comes Back from the Brink

"But that wasn't the amazing thing . . ." from "180 Degrees of Separation" by Jeff Pearlman, *Sports Illustrated,* April 12, 2004, and available at http://sportsillustrated.cnn.com/vault/article/magazine/MAG1031772/index.htm

"I've gotten a lot of trophies over the years, but the Ashley Pittman Memorial Award is special to me . . ." from *Beyond Belief: Finding the Strength to Come Back* by Josh Hamilton with Tim Keown (New York: Hachette Book Group, 2008), page 33.

"We've watched him for a long time . . ." from "Rays Feel Hamilton Has Makings of a Star," CNNSI.com, June 2, 1999, and available at http://sportsillustrated.cnn.com/baseball/mlb/1999/draft/news/1999/06/02/hamilton_lamar/

"I'm thinking three years in the minors, then fifteen years in the big leagues . . ." from *Beyond Belief: Finding the Strength to Come Back* by Josh Hamilton with Tim Keown (New York: Hachette Book Group, 2008), page 37.

"Their fears became real in our first game . . ." from *Beyond Belief: Finding the Strength to Come Back* by Josh Hamilton with Tim Keown (New York: Hachette Book Group, 2008), pages 7–8.

"I didn't expect you'd be out here tonight . . ." from *Beyond Belief: Finding the Strength to Come Back* by Josh Hamilton with Tim Keown (New York: Hachette Book Group, 2008), page 38.

"I got saved when I was eighteen years old . . ." from the *Larry King Live* show on CNN, October 28, 2008, and available at http://www.youtube.com/watch?v=rJ2xN_xHT0g

"He plunged the needle into my spine till it felt like it was grinding on bone . . ." from *Beyond Belief: Finding the Strength to Come Back* by Josh Hamilton with Tim Keown (New York: Hachette Book Group, 2008), page 76.

"I had a lot of 'firsts' that night . . ." from the *Larry King Live* show on CNN, October 28, 2008, and available at http://www.youtube.com/watch?v=rJ2xN_xHT0g

"The display still hadn't been fixed and was covered by a banner that promoted the team's website . . ." from "If You Build it, They Will Come, or Will They?" by Matt Martz, Bakersfield.com, October 17, 2008, and available at http://people.bakersfield.com/home/ViewPost/78184

"Everybody knew who Josh was in high school . . ." from "Josh and Kate Hamilton, Parts 1–3 Live Interview, February 14, 2010," West Lonsdale Baptist Church, February 14, 2010, and available at http://www.youtube.com/watch?v=dM_M8JTjkvM&feature=related

"I was a shell of a human, a soulless being . . ." from *Beyond Belief: Finding the Strength to Come Back* by Josh Hamilton with Tim Keown (New York: Hachette Book Group, 2008), page 150.

"I was a wreck—dirty, twitchy, barely coherent . . ." from *Beyond Belief: Finding the Strength to Come Back* by Josh Hamilton with Tim Keown (New York: Hachette Book Group, 2008), page 154.

"I went back in the room where I'd just been using drugs, grabbed a Bible, and the first verse I read James 4:7 . . ." from "Josh and Kate Hamilton, Parts 1–3 Live Interview, February 14, 2010," West Lonsdale Baptist Church, February 14, 2010, and available at http://www.youtube.com/watch?v=dM_M8JTjkvM&feature=related

"Baseball is third in my life right now, behind my relationship with God and my family . . ." from "I'm Proof That Hope Is Never Lost," an excerpt from *Beyond Belief* by Josh Hamilton with Tim Keown, *ESPN, The Magazine,* July 5, 2007, and available at http://sports.espn.go.com/mlb/news/story?id=2926447

"God has given me such a platform to share what He's done in my life . . ." from "Hamilton's Drug Comeback 'Beyond Belief,'" Associated Press, October 19, 2008, and available at http://www.youtube.com/watch?v=942OxgJT0ec&feature=relmfu

"I was out there for three weeks and stopped praying, stopped doing my devotions, stopped reading the Word . . ." from "Josh and Kate Hamilton, Parts 1–3 Live Interview, February 14, 2010," West Lonsdale Baptist Church, February 14, 2010, and available at http://www.youtube.com/watch?v=dM_M8JTjkvM&feature=related

"I'm embarrassed about it for my wife, Katie, for my kids, and for the organization . . ." from "Hamilton Admits to Relapse with Alcohol" by Joe Resnick of the Associated Press, August 8, 2009, and available at http://www.breitbart.com/article.php?id=D99UTUGG1&show_article=1

"When he walked in the door, and I [saw] how broken and repentant and remorseful he was . . ." from "Josh and Kate Hamilton, Parts 1–3 Live Interview, February 14, 2010," West Lonsdale Baptist Church, February 14, 2010, and available at http://www.youtube.com/watch?v=dM_M8JTjkvM&feature=related

"Rooted in his Christian beliefs and his rigorous daily devotions . . ." from "Josh Hamilton Finds Strength after Misstep in Recovery from Addiction" by S.C. Gywnne, *Dallas Morning News,* October 4, 2010, and available at http://www.dallasnews.com/incoming/20101003-Josh-Hamilton-finds-strength-after-misstep-1474.ece

"Just another night in the life of the best player in baseball went something like this . . ." from "Hamilton Leaving No Doubt He Is the Best Player in Baseball" by Tom Verducci, SI.com, August 17, 2010, and available at http://sportsillustrated.cnn.com/vault/article/web/COM1173399/index.htm

"Everybody yelled 'Ginger ale!' and I just jumped in the middle of the pile and they doused me with it . . ." from "Josh Hamilton Included in Celebration" by Richard Durrett, ESPNDallas.com, October 12, 2010, and available at http://sports.espn.go.com/dallas/mlb/news/story?id=5679952

"Could I have reached people being that clean-cut kid coming out of high school?" from "Hamilton's Drug Comeback 'Beyond Belief,'" Associated Press, October 19, 2008, and available at http://www.youtube.com/watch?v=942OxgJT0ec&feature=relmfu

"One thing I can't live without is obviously Jesus . . ." from "Josh and Kate Hamilton, Parts 1–3 Live Interview, February 14, 2010," West Lonsdale Baptist Church, February 14, 2010, and available at http://www.youtube.com/watch?v=dM_M8JTjkvM&feature=related

7. Stephen Drew: Good Things Come in Threes

All quotations used are from personal interviews between co-author Joshua Cooley and Stephen Drew.

8. Jeremy Affeldt: *Solus Christus*—By Christ Alone

All quotations used are from personal interviews between co-author Joshua Cooley and Jeremy Affeldt, except the following:

"Jeremy Affeldt. We go way back . . ." from "Giants' Biggest Hero in Game 6 Fits Team's 'Improbable' Bill" by Joe Posnanski, *Sports Illustrated*, October 24, 2010, and available at http://sportsillustrated.cnn.com/2010/writers/joe_posnanski/10/24/nlcs.game6/index.html

9. Matt Capps: Opening a Once-Closed Fist to God

All quotations used are from personal interviews between co-author Joshua Cooley and Matt Capps.

10. Mark Teixeira: Hitting on All Cylinders

"[My teammates] were kidding me, telling me to trip over first base if I hit one into the gap . . ." from "Teixeira Hits for Cycle in Rangers' Win," August 18, 2004, and available at http://www.redorbit.com/news/general/79812/teixeira_hits_for_cycle_in_rangers_win/index.html

"I've always tried to be disciplined . . ." from "Mark Teixeira Works on His Form" by Lee Warren, *Breakaway* magazine, September 2007, page 19.

"He stands perfectly straight, head down, shirt tucked in . . ." from "Straight-up Talent" by Lee Jenkins, *Sports Illustrated*, November 11, 2009, and available at http://sportsillustrated.cnn.com/vault/article/magazine/MAG1162901/2/index.htm

"I try to live and play baseball the way that I think the Lord would want me to . . ." from "Mark Teixeira Works on His Form" by Lee Warren, *Breakaway* magazine, September 2007, page 20.

"At a very young age, I learned about Jesus and how important your faith is . . ." from "Mark Teixeira Works on His Form" by Lee Warren, *Breakaway* magazine, September 2007, page 19.

"For the President to single me out, I was very honored . . ." from "President Barack Obama Singles Out New York Yankees First Baseman Mark Teixeira for Charitable Works" by Mark Feinsand, *New York Daily News*, April 27, 2010, and available at http://articles.nydailynews.com/2010-04-27/sports/27062767_1_college-scholarship-mark-teixeira-white-house

"Ever since I started [my foundation], it has been very involved with college scholarships, education, children's needs . . ." from "Yankees' Teixeira Goes to Bat for Kids" by Jim Wilkie, ESPN.com: The Life, May 4, 2010, and available at http://sports.espn.go.com/espn/thelife/news/story?id=5161392

"I became involved with Harlem RBI and DREAM charter because I believe the work we are doing is truly changing lives . . ." from Eric NYC Department of Housing Preservation & Development press release by Eric Bederman, June 13, 2011, and available at http://www.nyc.gov/html/hpd/html/pr2011/pr-06-13-11.shtml

"I've visited hospitals before and worked with the Make-A-Wish foundation . . ." from "Inspired by Young Cancer Patient, Yankees' Mark Teixeira Shares Life Lesson" by Jason Rovou, Larry King Live Blogs, April 13, 2010, and available at http://larrykinglive.blogs.cnn.com/2010/04/13/inspired-by-young-cancer-patient-yankees%E2%80%99-mark-teixeira-shares-life-lesson/

"The thing that was so amazing about Brian was his faith throughout his ordeal . . ." from Teixeira's Mission: Raise Awareness for Cancer to Honor Ernst's Memory" by Ashley Bates, *Gainesville Times,* April 28, 2010, and available at http://www.gainesvilletimes.com/archives/32589/

"Our deeds don't make us righteous . . ." from "Bright Light in the Big City" by Chad Bonham, *Sharing the Victory,* October 2009, and available at http://www.sharingthevictory.com/vsItemDisplay.lsp?method=display&objectid=EDA179A5-C29A-EE7A-E8E85C89FA8CE71A

"My parents brought me up in a home where we worked very hard and did our best . . ." from "Program 246," *Personally Speaking with Jim Lisante* podcast, Jim Lisante, Catholic Communication Campaign, January 16, 2011, and available at http://old.usccb.org/audio/psradio.shtml

"People would think I'm crazy, but it was the greatest thing for me . . ." from "Program 246," *Personally Speaking with Jim Lisante* podcast, Jim Lisante, Catholic Communication Campaign, January 16, 2011, and available at http://old.usccb.org/audio/psradio.shtml

"No one's going to expect more out of me than me . . ." from "Mark Teixeira's Wife Leigh Nudged Hubby toward Yankees" by Anthony McCarron, *New York Daily News,* January 6, 2009, and available at http://articles.nydailynews.com/2009-01-06/sports/17913844_1_mark-teixeira-yankees-offer

"I let him know that I was behind him all the way . . ." from *Cage Rat: Lessons from a Life in Baseball by the Yankees' Hitting Coach* by Kevin Long with Glen Waggoner (New York: Ecco, 2011).

"When you're on the bases, why not run hard?" from "Mark of Excellence" by Bob Bellone, *Sports Spectrum,* Summer 2010, page 38, and available at http://mydigimag.rrd.com/display_article.php?id=426780

"For us to be holding the trophy at the end of the season, it was a special year . . ." from "Mark Teixeira Interview Post 2009 World Series," Steinersports, November 10, 2009, and available at http://www.youtube.com/watch?v=Uewfl9vfUJw

"When my first son was born in 2006 . . ." from "Bright Light in the Big City" by Chad Bonham, *Sharing the Victory,* October 2009, and available at http://www.sharingthevictory. com/vsItemDisplay.lsp?method=display&objectid=EDA179A5-C29A-EE7A-E8E85C89FA8CE71A

"I can probably quote the entire movie start to finish . . ." from "Yankees' Teixeira Goes to Bat for Kids" by Jim Wilkie, ESPN.com: The Life, May 4, 2010, and available at http://sports.espn. go.com/espn/thelife/news/story?id=5161392

"Baseball is a game of failure . . ." from "Bright Light in the Big City" by Chad Bonham, *Sharing the Victory,* October 2009, and available at http://www.sharingthevictory.com/vsItemDisplay. lsp?method=display&objectid=EDA179A5-C29A-EE7A-E8E85C89FA8CE71A

"That's not a major milestone . . ." from "Derek Jeter to Play in Trenton This Weekend Before Returning to Yankees" by Zach Berman and Conor Orr, *The Star-Ledger,* June 30, 2011, and available at http://www.nj.com/yankees/index.ssf/2011/06/derek_jeter_will_play_in_trent.html

"My faith keeps me grounded . . ." from "Mark Teixeira Texas Rangers—Today's Christian Videos," Trinity Broadcasting Network, and available at http://www.godtube.com/ watch/?v=JCC291NU

11. Brian Roberts: Big Trials, Big Faith for a Small Player

All quotations used are from personal interviews between co-author Joshua Cooley and Brian Roberts, except the following:

"Toughest stint . . ." and "Certainly for me . . ." from "Roberts Plans to Be Part of Orioles' Future" by Jeff Zrebiec, *Baltimore Sun,* August 16, 2011, and available at http://www.baltimoresun. com/sports/orioles/bs-sp-orioles-roberts-0817-20110816,0,5149721.story

"Brian Roberts is an infielder . . ." from "The Mitchell Report," which was released December 13, 2007, and is available at http://mlb.mlb.com/mlb/news/mitchell/index.jsp

"In a moment of weakness . . ." from "Roberts Admits He Used Steroids" by Jeff Zrebiec, *Baltimore Sun,* December 18, 2007, and available at http://www.baltimoresun.com/sports/bal-te.sp.roberts18dec18,0,769248.story

"Kids out there . . ." from Brian's video blog entry entitled "Improved Team Chemistry Could Result in Improved Record," April 22, 2011, and available at http://www.masnsports.com/brian_roberts/2011/04/improved-team-chemistry-could-result-in-improved-record.html

"Mr. Angelos has put a lot of investment . . ." from "Emotional Roberts Admits that 2011 Return Not Looking Good" by Jeff Zrebiec, *Baltimore Sun,* September 2, 2011, and available at http://weblogs.baltimoresun.com/sports/orioles/blog/2011/09/emotional_roberts_admits_that.html

12. Josh Willingham: Understanding How the Lord Gives and Takes Away
All quotations used are from personal interviews between co-author Joshua Cooley and Josh Willingham.

13. Mariano Rivera: The Closer Who Got Saved
"He needs to pitch in a higher league, if there is one . . ." from "Mariano River's a True Yankee, Almost Mythical in His Dominance" by Joe Posnanski, SI.com, July 2, 2009, and available at http://sportsillustrated.cnn.com/2009/writers/joe_posnanski/07/01/rivera/index.html

"Yes, it does. It does make me uncomfortable, because I don't like to talk about myself . . ." from "The Michael Kay Show," ESPN New York (1050 AM) podcast, September 16, 2011, and available at http://espn.go.com/new-york/radio/archive?id=2693958

"You're seeing the greatest closer of all time . . ." from "Mariano Saves" by Tom Verducci, *Sports Illustrated*, October 5, 2009, and available at http://sportsillustrated.cnn.com/vault/article/magazine/MAG1160757/index.htm

"He's like my brother . . ." from "Modern Yankee Heroes: From Humble Beginnings, Mariano Rivera Becomes Greatest Closer in MLB History" by Christian Red, *New York Daily News*, March 13, 2010, and available at http://articles.nydailynews.com/2010-03-13/sports/27058930_1_puerto-caimito-cardboard-cousin

"I don't know if we'll ever see it again . . ." from "Mariano Rivera Gets 600th Save" by Andrew Marchand, ESPNNewYork.com, September 14, 2011, and available at http://m.espn.go.com/mlb/story?w=1b0rl&storyId=6968238&i=TOP&wjb=

"If you talk to him at an All-Star Game, it's like talking to somebody who just got called up . . ." from "Mariano Saves" by Tom Verducci, *Sports Illustrated*, October 5, 2009, and available at http://sportsillustrated.cnn.com/vault/article/magazine/MAG1160757/index.htm

"The radar wasn't really being lit up . . ." from "Modern Yankee Heroes: From Humble Beginnings, Mariano Rivera Becomes Greatest Closer in MLB History" by Christian Red, *New York Daily News*, March 13, 2010, and available at http://articles.nydailynews.com/2010-03-13/sports/27058930_1_puerto-caimito-cardboard-cousin

"Usually a player prepares for years . . ." from *Mariano Rivera* by Judith Levin (New York: Checkmark Books, 2008), page 18.

"Every time I was going through a hard time, somebody was there to help . . ." from "The Secret of Mariano Rivera's Success" by Peter Schiller, baseballreflections.com, November 7, 2009, and available at http://baseballreflections.com/2009/11/07/the-secret-of-mariano-riveras-success/

"The harder I tried, the tougher it got . . ." from "Yanks' Rivera Continues to Learn" by Mel Antonen, *USA Today*, October 9, 2006, and available at http://www.usatoday.com/sports/soac/2006-10-09-rivera_x.htm

"You can't see the spin on it . . ." from "This Is the Game Changer," by Albert Chen, *Sports Illustrated*, June 13, 2011, and available at http://sportsillustrated.cnn.com/vault/article/magazine/MAG1187105/index.htm

"That is my miracle pitch . . ." from "Mariano River's Cutter 'The Miracle Pitch,'" interview with Pastor Dewey Friedel, courtesy the Trinity Broadcasting Network, and available at http://www.youtube.com/watch?v=L0tTLssCKZU

"My mental approach is simple: Get three outs as quick as possible . . ." from "Mariano Saves" by Tom Verducci, *Sports Illustrated*, October 5, 2009, and available at http://sportsillustrated.cnn.com/vault/article/magazine/MAG1160757/index.htm

"My childhood was wonderful . . ." from "Modern Yankee Heroes: From Humble Beginnings, Mariano Rivera Becomes Greatest Closer in MLB History" by Christian Red, *New York Daily News*, March 13, 2010, and available at http://articles.nydailynews.com/2010-03-13/sports/27058930_1_puerto-caimito-cardboard-cousin

"It's hard. Extremely hard . . ." from "Modern Yankee Heroes: From Humble Beginnings, Mariano Rivera Becomes Greatest Closer in MLB History" by Christian Red, *New York Daily News*, March 13, 2010, and available at http://articles.nydailynews.com/2010-03-13/sports/27058930_1_puerto-caimito-cardboard-cousin

"We have a lot of goals to work with the youth . . ." from "Yankees Pitcher to Open Church" by Danielle De Souza, *New Rochelle Patch*, June 28, 2011, and available at http://newrochelle.patch.com/articles/yankees-pitcher-to-open-church

"This was something special, and God wants me to concentrate on bringing Him to other people . . ." from "Baseball; Love of God Outweighs Love of the Game" by Jack Curry, *New York Times*, December 10, 1999, and available at http://www.nytimes.com/1999/12/10/sports/baseball-love-of-god-outweighs-love-of-the-game.html

"I'm glad we lost the World Series . . ." from "The Confidence Man" by Buster Olney, *New York Magazine*, May 21, 2005, and available at http://nymag.com/nymetro/news/sports/features/9375/index2.html

"That comes from God, having the ability to perform . . ." from "World Baseball Classic Pool D: San Juan," an interview with Mariano Rivera by ASAP Sports, March 7, 2009, and available at http://www.asapsports.com/show_interview.php?id=54723

"Look at Mo's delivery, look at how he repeats it . . ." from "Mariano Rivera Pitches in 1,000th Game for Yanks and Has a Lot of Mo" by Bob Klapisch, *The Record*, May 28, 2011, and available at http://www.post-gazette.com/pg/11148/1150003-63-0.stm?cmpid=sports.xml

"The whole organization, my whole teammates have been a pillar for me . . ." from "Mariano Rivera Gets 602 to Become All-Time Saves Leader" by Bryan Llenas, *Fox New Latino*, September 19, 2011, and available at http://latino.foxnews.com/latino/sports/2011/09/19/mariano-rivera-gets-number-602-to-become-all-time-saves-leader/

"When you talk about the greatest relievers of all time, there's only one guy . . ." from "Mariano Rivera: Saving with Grace" by Kevin Baxter, *Los Angeles Times*, September 17, 2011, and available at http://articles.latimes.com/2011/sep/17/sports/la-sp-0918-down-the-line-20110918

"Amazing that he's been able to do it with one pitch over and over again . . ." from "Modern Yankee Heroes: From Humble Beginnings, Mariano Rivera Becomes Greatest Closer in MLB History" by Christian Red, *New York Daily News*, March 13, 2010, and available at http://articles.nydailynews.com/2010-03-13/sports/27058930_1_puerto-caimito-cardboard-cousin

"I don't pay too much attention to that . . ." from "The Michael Kay Show," ESPN New York (1050 AM) podcast, September 16, 2011, and available at http://espn.go.com/new-york/radio/archive?id=2693958

MORE EXCITING STORIES OF SPORTS
AND FAITH FROM MIKE YORKEY

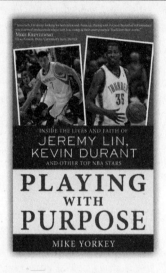

Meet the "dream team" of talented NBA players with fascinating faith stories in *Playing with Purpose: Basketball*. This book chronicles the lives of several players who stand strong for their Christian faith.

Veteran CBA author Mike Yorkey, whose *Playing with Purpose* biography of NFL rookies Sam Bradford, Tim Tebow, and Colt McCoy was a bestseller, now profiles NBA stars both established and up-and-coming— such as Jeremy Lin, Kyle Korver, Anthony Parker, Luke Ridnour, and Chris Kaman.

With a foreword by Ernie Johnson, host of TNT's NBA coverage, *Playing with Purpose: Basketball* is perfect for any hoops fan.

Available in bookstores everywhere

ISBN 978-1-62029-813-8 / 5.375" x 8" / 272 pages / Includes 16 photographs / $12.99